PAINTED BY [illegible] ENGRAVED BY [illegible]

KOSSUTH.

HUNGARY

AND

KOSSUTH:

OR, AN

American Exposition of the late Hungarian Revolution.

BY REV. B. F. TEFFT, D. D.

PHILADELPHIA:
J. W. BRADLEY, No. 48 NORTH FOURTH STREET.
NEW ORLEANS, JOHN BALL, NO. 56 GRAVIER ST.
1852.

PRINTED BY SMITH & PETERS,
Franklin Buildings, Sixth Street below Arch, Philadelphia.

TO

The National Assembly of Hungary,

AND TO

The Patriots of the late Hungarian Revolution

IN PARTICULAR,

THE FOLLOWING WORK

IS RESPECTFULLY DEDICATED

BY THE AUTHOR.

PREFACE.

THE following work is not intended to be either a history of Hungary, or a biography of Kossuth; and I indulge the hope, that the critical reader will not look down upon it from too high a stand-point. Perhaps a frank statement of the circumstances, by which I was led to its composition, will be the best justification I can offer for its imperfections, as well as the most satisfactory exposition of its design.

In the autumn of 1842, while a resident of Boston, I enjoyed frequent opportunities of conversing with the well-known Signor Alvanola, the Italian revolutionist and refugee, who, on several occasions, directed my attention to the Protestant Hungarians as the stanch and powerful friends of popular liberty, and the political hope of Southern Europe. He represented them as the unbending opponents of Austrian despotism, living in the heart of the Austrian Empire, to whom Italy, as well as several other of the Southern nations, would owe its ultimate liberation, if it was ever to be delivered from its bondage. The Hungarians, he said, were not only to give political freedom to those countries, but they were destined, he thought, to become the champions of the Protestant religion, and to bring about the downfall of papal Rome.

Such remarks, respecting a people but little known out of Europe, and unappreciated even there, at once arrested my attention, and caused me to look somewhat into their former history. From such works as were then accessible to me, several of which are frequently quoted in the following pages, I have obtained the fullest conviction, that the words of the Italian patriot were undeniably true. From that day forward, I looked upon Hungary as the most interesting country of Southern Europe; and when the recent revolutions broke out, what Hungary would do, and what she did do, now her expected day had come, were the questions that interested me more than any others of the kind. I watched her carefully, and with indescribable interest, through her long and bloody conflict. I regularly searched the leading newspapers of this country, and of Great Britain, to see what signs might possibly appear, that she would now fulfill the expectations of her friends. I saw the cloud that rose up in the Banat, then spread over Croatia and Sclavonia, and burst with fury on the Magyar land. With every American, I rejoiced to see the invasion of the Croats broken, and the infamous but talented Jellachich hunted from Hungarian soil. With every American, I rejoiced also to behold the armies of the Austrians, sent into Hungary to crush the first hopes of independence there, met, routed, and driven with indignation over the Hungarian frontier. With the civilized world, so far as that world is free, I suffered more than I can tell, when I saw the soldiers of two tyrants, Austrian and Russian, marching down upon three sides of the ill-fated country, instructed never to leave the land until Hungarian liberty should be no more. When the final struggle came, in common with the friends of human freedom everywhere, I became almost absorbed in the progress of the war, seeing, as all men saw, that republican principles and the Protestant religion, in the whole south of Europe, would rise or fall with these brave defenders of the truth; and when, after a hundred battles, the electric telegraph and the foreign journals brought to us the mournful intelligence, that the Magyars had been betrayed, that the army was disbanded, that Hungary was fallen and Kossuth a refugee, I felt, as did every American, what no language can describe.

The cause of Hungary being thus lost, for that time at least, my whole interest began to center in that glorious man, who, with a patriotism almost unparalleled, and with efforts nearly superhuman, had given himself up to the work of liberating and restoring his native land. No sooner, however, were the battles over, and Austrian despotism had again laid its fetters on the press, than the hireling papers of Vienna began to circulate all sorts of falsehoods, not only respecting the late disturbances, but particularly respecting the part acted by the immortal Kossuth. They represented him, not as a patriot, but as an artful and ambitious demagogue, who, from the beginning, had wished to take advantage of the troubles of Europe to put himself at the head of Hungary, and to extend his hand of tyranny over the provinces connected with the Magyar realm. In this way, they expected to blunt the sympathies of the free nations of the world, and thus pave the way for his extradition by the Porte, and for that ignominious death to which he had been unanimously and barbarously doomed.

The falsehoods thus put into circulation were copied into the government organs of Great Britain, because it was found necessary, in order to appease the anger of the people, to justify the ministry for pledging the good will of the nation to the Austrian despot, and for turning a deaf ear to the supplications of the Magyar patriots. From England, the shameful slanders of Hungary and her champion were imported into this country; and very soon, there were certain writers astir, who, for the notoriety of being singular, or for some other cause, began to adopt the falsehoods, and cast a shade upon the patriotic object and glorious deeds of the revolution.

At this point, being called upon to deliver a lecture before the New England Society of the city of Cincinnati, I took occasion, with a special object in view, to devote the entire address to the life, labors, and character of Kossuth. I wished, within my limited circle of influence, to do what I could in making the motives and conduct of that great and true man more perfectly understood. I wished, also, to direct the attention of my friends to his condition as a prisoner, that something might be done for his release. I had no further object in view; but this object, very far beyond my most sanguine expectations, was welcomed by a large and enlightened audience. The lecture was repeated, by request of many citizens of Cincinnati, before the same society and in the same place; and, in addition to a series of stirring resolutions, a memorial to Congress was passed by the Society and assembly in the following words: "To the Senate and House of Representatives of the United States, in Congress assembled— We, your memorialists, citizens of Cincinnati, Ohio, and others of the United States, would most respectfully ask your aid in procuring the liberation and freedom of General Kossuth, by appointing one or more persons as an Embassy of Peace, to be dispatched in one of our best ships of war to the Court of Turkey, to request of said government the liberation of Kossuth, and to tender him the hospitalities of our country." This is the course of procedure that had been laid down, as the duty of this country, in the body of the lecture.

A few evenings afterwards, by request of the citizens of Springfield, Ohio, the address was read before the Springfield Lyceum, whereupon another memorial, of the same character with the one just presented, was adopted by a very large meeting, and at once put into circulation among the people. The inhabitants of Springfield were exceedingly ardent in their efforts to further the great purpose.

On returning from Springfield, I found a letter from the Hon. William Dennison, in relation to the same subject; and, that the honorable position of Ohio may be hereafter understood, respecting this matter, I subjoin the correspondence that at this time occurred, together with parts of the subsequent proceedings of the Legislature:

COLUMBUS, January 19, 1850.

REV. B. F. TEFFT, D.D.:

DEAR SIR,—The undersigned, members of the General Assembly of this State, having heard of the high consideration entertained in regard to your lecture on Kossuth, by those who have had the good fortune to hear it read, will esteem it as a distinguished favor if you will consent to visit this Capital, at your earliest convenience, and read before us, and such others as may be disposed to form a part of your auditory, the same lecture.

If your engagements will permit of your acceptance, we will be pleased to have you, by return of mail, designate the time when we may anticipate your presence among us.

With great respect,
We are truly yours,
W. DENNISON,
And the Members of both Houses.

The following is the reply to this communication:

CINCINNATI, January 21, 1850.

HON. WILLIAM DENNISON,
And the Members of the General Assembly of Ohio:

GENTLEMEN,—In reply to your note of invitation, to read my lecture on Kossuth before the Legislature of Ohio, and such other citizens as may be inclined to listen to it, I have only to say, that I do not feel at liberty to decline; and my anxiety to see something done, in behalf of the great Hungarian hero, by the General Assembly of Ohio, and by the Congress of the United States, would lead me to perform almost any labor, and undergo almost any sacrifices. My compliance, in fact, with your kindly expressed wishes, is only from the strong and fervent hope, that the Legislature of the State will take the matter under immediate consideration, and *do* something, according to its wisdom, which shall rouse the nation to its duty. Providence permitting, I will be ready to lecture at Columbus, according to such arrangements as you may make, on the 29th instant.

With sincere regard,
I am yours,
B. F. TEFFT.

The citizens of Columbus, and the General Assembly, *did* do something, and something worthy of them. The former, on motion of Mr. Lawrence, among many others, passed the following resolution: "Resolved, That this meeting earnestly urge upon the President of the United States, and upon Congress, to exercise their utmost power to procure the liberation of Kossuth, his associates and family, at the earliest practicable period: *also*, to intercede with the Powers of Europe for the liberation of all Hungarians in captivity, in such manner as may be most efficient and speedy, and to provide them an asylum in the United States." On motion of Mr. Burns, the following resolution passed unanimously: "Resolved, That a copy of the proceedings of this meeting be communicated to the President of the United States, and to each of our Senators and Representatives in Congress, with the request that the same be presented to each branch of Con gress."

The General Assembly, on the other hand, after a brilliant discussion of the subject, passed the following resolutions, which were preceded by a lengthy and able preamble, setting forth the causes and occasion of their action:

"*Resolved, by the General Assembly of the State of Ohio,* That in our deliberate judgment, the present critical condition of General LOUIS KOSSUTH, and of his family, loudly call for the friendly and peaceful interposition of the American people.

Resolved, That we believe it to be the duty and privilege of the Congress of the United States, to send immediately an embassy of peace to the Sultan of Turkey, in one of our national ships, who shall be instructed respectfully and urgently to solicit of the Sublime Porte, the liberation of Kossuth and his fellow captives, in the name of the American people, and to take such other steps as shall be best calculated to secure the removal of the great Hungarian, and of his afflicted family, to this country.

Resolved, That our Representatives in Congress be requested, and that our Senators be instructed, to bring this subject, as soon as possible, before Congress, and to pursue such other measures as shall most certainly and speedily carry out, if possible, the objects set forth in the foregoing resolutions.

And be it further resolved, That the Governor be requested to forward a copy of the foregoing to the President, and to each of our Senators and Representatives in Congress."

Another step was taken, at the time now mentioned, which, though it did not lead to the end proposed by it, was the immediate occasion of the composition of the work, here offered to the public: "On motion of Mr. Perry"—the quotation is from the published proceedings—"a committee of five, consisting of Messrs. Perry, Chase, Thrall, Randall, and Pugh, was appointed to confer with Dr. Tefft for the purpose of inducing that gentleman to proceed to Washington, and there deliver, in the presence of Congress, the lecture read by him on the liberation of Kossuth." To comply with such a request, however, was not only impracticable, but, as I felt, very unbecoming a private citizen having no connection with public business. The honor was therefore declined; but, feeling that I might do something in another way, not only toward the accomplishment of the object, but in preparing the citizens of this country generally to understand the true character of the Hungarians, and the nature and extent of their own duty, should Hungary ever make another effort for her independence, I undertook, at the request of many persons, to expand the lecture to a small volume. In the mean time, as was expected, the President of the United States promptly adopted the suggestion of the General Assembly of Ohio, and of the citizens of Springfield and Cincinnati, and made the overtures to Turkey that had been thus recommended.

No sooner, however, had the labor of composition been fairly begun, than it was cut short by a sudden and nearly fatal sickness; and when, after a suspension of nearly six months, a part of which period was spent in the libraries of New York and Boston, the work of writing was again undertaken, it was plain enough, that there was a demand for a very different book than what had been at first intended. Numerous false statements, very unjust to Hungary, chiefly from the source already indicated, had been put into circulation in this country. The former history of the Magyars, their character as a people, and nearly every thing connected with them, that had any relation to their late revolution, had been strangely misrepresented by certain writers. Therefore, though still adhering to the humble plan of merely giving an exposition of the Hungarian war of independence, I concluded to do so by so enlarging the compass of my work, as to admit of brief discussions of all those topics, which needed to be understood in order to a clear comprehension of the general subject. Not only the character and condition of the country, the origin and condition of the people, their religions, their language and literature, their constitution and government, but the relations of the country to other countries, the numerous attempts of the Austrians to overthrow its independence, and the many memorable efforts of the Hungarians in defending the liberties of their father-land, seemed to be essential, as the matter now stood, to the attainment of correct ideas respecting the origin and character of the revolution. When once engaged upon these several subjects, it seemed also admissible to allow the pen to run along with them a little farther, in each case, than was strictly demanded by the main object of the work; for it was supposed, that, if the unity of the subject was maintained, the American reader would be willing, while making a special examination of the great question, to extend his acquaintance with so novel and deeply interesting a people as the Magyars. Nearly every reader, however, will doubtless meet with some pages, and perhaps some chapters, that he will think it unnecessary for him to read very closely; but, in general, it will be found, I think, that a due comprehension of the question of the work will require a perusal of what is written in the text, while the more abstruse and less popular portion of the matter has been thrown into the margin in the form of notes.

Finally, after the following pages were in type, conscious of my want of due preparation for such a labor, I laid the proof-sheets into the hands of two well-educated Hungarians of my acquaintance, requesting them to correct whatever errors they might detect; and though I received them back again with their approval, and without marks of correction, I am still conscious that the critical reader will find many things over which he will have to lay the mantle of his charity. The truth is, during all the time while the composition was in progress, I was pressed with the onerous duties of an editorial office; and, during the greater part of it, in addition to this burden, I have had the general oversight of a literary institution, which demanded much of my attention.

With this frank avowal, therefore, of all the facts and circumstances connected with the preparation of this volume, I commit it to the public with the hope, that it may contribute something to a more perfect understanding of the Hungarian revolution, as well as awaken a more lively interest in the welfare of the most interesting people of modern Europe.

B. F. T.

CINCINNATI, August 15, 1851.

TABLE OF CONTENTS.

CHAPTER I.

CHAPTER II.

CHAPTER III.

CHAPTER IV.

CHAPTER V.

CHAPTER VI.

CHAPTER VII.

CHAPTER VIII.

CHAPTER IX.

CHAPTER X.

CHAPTER XI.

CHAPTER XII.

HUNGARY AND KOSSUTH.

CHAPTER I.

CHARACTER AND CONDITION OF THE COUNTRY.

NOT very far from the centre of continental Europe, and north of the Danube and the Save, lies one of the most fertile and fortunate countries in the world. It consists of two immense plains, northern and southern, lying at different elevations, and both presenting their broad areas to the sun, by gently inclining toward the south. The great plains are cut, in all directions, by ranges of wooded hills, sometimes approaching almost to mountains, by which countless valleys are formed, each, it would seem, as beautiful as the Tempean vale.[1]

The soil of this country, though various in its character, is everywhere very deep and rich. Many of its hills are arable; its numerous prairies are composed of a black, brown, or reddish mold; and its vast bottom-lands, lying on the lower

---

[1] Paget, in his Hungary and Transylvania, vol. ii. p. 98, Am. ed., as in other parts of his work, is in raptures with the scenery of the country. After climbing a lofty and steep hill, while going from Várhley to Hátszeg, he exclaims—"Fortunately, we were not without cause for consolation; for, on getting out of the carriage to walk, and looking back, our eyes fell on such a scene as I do not think the world can equal in loveliness." Miss Pardoe, who travelled in Hungary four years after Paget, while she corrects some of his statements respecting other subjects, confirms his eulogies on the beauty of its rural landscapes. City of the Magyar, *passim*.

Danube, and bordering its smaller rivers, find their parallels only in the American valleys of our own great West.[2]

In a land of such beauty and fertility, husbandry is a recreation, rather than a toil. Fruits and flowers grow spontaneously, and in great luxuriance, upon the uncultivated hills and plains. Every vegetable production indigenous to Europe, from Iceland moss to the rice and cotton plants, from the fir of the mountains to the olive of the vales, from the fruit-bearing brambles of the natural hedges to the loaded vineyards cultivated by the hand of man, springs up to bear, or to bloom.

The intersecting hills, abounding in the most precious gifts, iron, coal, cobalt, zinc, alum, salt, antimony, litharge, lead, copper, silver, gold, carry into every section mineral resources scarcely rivalled in any quarter of the world. The coast of India, it is true, is lined by banks of the oriental pearl; Brazil can boast of whole provinces sparkling with the gem of gems; the mountains of California pour down streams of gold; but the land here referred to, filled with such a variety of treasures, constitutes a kind of cabinet of nature, where vast quantities of nearly all the precious and useful metals have been stored.[3]

---

[2] "The same crops," says Paget, vol. ii. p. 52, "are here repeated year after year, on the same spots; the ground is only once turned up to receive the seed; a fallow is unknown; manure is never used, but is thrown away as injurious; and yet, with the greatest care and labor in other places, I never saw such abundant produce, as ill-treated, unaided Nature here bestows upon her children." The traveller is describing the Banat.

[3] The country furnishes, also, unknown quantities of precious stones, such as amethysts, opals, chalcedonies, together with many varieties of crystals and petrifactions, to all the cabinets of Europe. The royal cabinet of Vienna, the wonder and glory of modern naturalists, received nine-tenths of its specimens from this source. City of the Magyar, vol. i. p. 206. The Pesth Museum is more recent. City of the Magyar, vol. ii. p. 209.

Though a region of innumerable plains, and prairies, and other open lands, more than one third of it, when its hills and mountains are included, is covered with heavily timbered forests, which add greatly to its beauty and its wealth. In these forests flourish the oak, the beech, the pine, and many other trees important in house-architecture, in ship-building, and in all the useful as well as ornamental arts. The poorest inhabitant, who may not be able to supply himself with coal, is every where surrounded by thrifty woods, and, through the long evenings of winter, can enjoy the luxury of a warm and a high-blazing hearth.

Hundreds of streams, great and small, rising in the northern districts, run southwardly to join the Danube, leaping over the rough and rocky edge of the upper plateau, and rushing along through many a steep mountain gorge, thus creating a vast number of the best seats for factories and mills. The distribution of these natural powers, so certain to secure the full developement of the resources of a country, has been the object of universal admiration to all who have visited this favored land. Not only where the tastes and tempers of the people most loudly call for them, but where the raw materials of manufacturing industry and wealth more especially abound, and where that industry would most necessarily lead to wealth, are these ready-made, costless, and available forces most uniformly found.

The four largest rivers, one of them the largest and longest west of the Euphrates, pass directly through the country, connecting it commercially with the Euxine on the east, with the Mediterranean on the south, and, through the straits of Gibraltar, with all the waters of the globe. The great river, in particular, broad and deep enough to bear a navy upon its breast, seems not to be contented with even a diagonal passage through the land, but wanders and winds about, as if bent on visiting and uniting the most promising localities, and thus doubling its value with its increase of length. Its tributaries, dashing down from the adjacent Carpathians of the north and east, or flowing more serenely from the distant Alps on the south and west, are not more ready to answer the behests of mechanism and of art, than through the great central thoroughfare into which they enter, to exchange exports and imports, at the very doors of the people in every district, with the richest and remotest portions of the earth.

A generally level country, with its mountain ranges so frequently cut through by streams, is a country where the modern railroad, that iron and ever navigable river, speedier and safer than its predecessor, is sure to undertake its wonders. The metal of that country's mines, the wood on its thousand hills, as well as the vast stores of coal deposited in its subterranean beds, furnish, so abundantly, materials for the construction and employment of these artificial ways, that they can not fail to run from valley to valley, to cross and recross innumerable plains, and to weave the whole region together into a mighty web of business and of profit, scarcely to be paralleled in any clime or age.

The dominant population of this chosen land is of mixed Caucasian extraction, partly descending from the best race of men. By a very salutary law, which fixes the age of manhood at twenty-four, they have been more successful than any other people in maintaining the original vigor of their line. Their pride of birth has prevented them from mixing, so far as any intermarriage with other nations has been practiced, excepting with the most perfect specimens of mankind. Thus, while preserving the general purity of their stock, they have not failed to improve it, to a very considerable extent, by crossing it with the best of other stocks, and in this way acquiring that peculiar versatility of powers, which comes from such a union of blood with blood. Their dark hair, their black piercing eyes, their thin and firmly compressed lips, their high bearing, their perfect symmetry and manliness of form, their quick and nervous action, contrast them strangely with the sallow and slow

Sarmatian, as well as with the clumsy and flaxen-headed German, by whom they are surrounded, and over whom they bear such a legitimate and natural sway. From the beginning of their history, they have been celebrated for their physical hardihood, for their intellectual sprightliness, and for nearly every moral virtue, which strengthens and adorns the character of a man. While the female is extremely beautiful, the male is generally healthy and robust—naturally industrious in peace, and next to invincible in war. A race remarkable for such endowments, called to action by such a promising position, could scarcely do less than cover the land of their inheritance with every manifestation of wealth, intelligence, virtue, and universal prosperity and joy.

This national inheritance, filled with so many blessings, is surrounded on all sides by lofty mountains, excepting a short distance on its southern border, where it is protected by the weakness of a neighboring government. It is thus completely shut out from other nations to the quiet and safe enjoyment of its own happiness. Lying entirely between the forty-fourth and fiftieth parallels of latitude, which in Europe are the geographical limits of the most delightful climate within its bounds, it enjoys all the advantages which the seasons can confer, through all the changes of the rolling year. In its northern sections, during the winter months, it is blessed with that peculiarly healthful, elastic, bracing atmosphere, so common to the higher latitudes, which gives such a buoyancy and vigor to the mind. Along its southern boundary, on the contrary, which, if extended westward, would leave the best part of Italy above it, the flowery and fruitful country is warmed and lighted by an Italian sun, fanned by Italian breezes, and canopied by the pure cerulean of an Italian sky.[4]

[4] Paget, vol. ii., p. 53, says expressly: "The climate of the Banat, in summer, approaches nearly to that of Italy." Virgil, it is true, Georg. lib. iii., vv. 349—356, who had never seen the country, gives a very different description of the Hungarian climate:

Such a country, it will be at once acknowledged, of such fertility, abounding with such a variety of resources, peopled by such inhabitants, characterized by such a climate, walled in by impassable mountain barriers from all foreign trouble, and left to the undisturbed and grateful task of developing and multiplying its own means of individual and social happiness, would seem to have been marked out by the hand of God for a second paradise. Here, we naturally infer, a new social miracle is to be performed. Here, a pure people is to have its theatre, a pure civilization is to be set in motion, a pure, a new, a more glorious era is to be begun. Here, agriculture, so long baffled by the stubbornness of other soils and climes, is to reach perfection, scatter flowers upon every valley, wind every hill with vines, pour its cereal treasures around the hearth-stones of every home, and over all the land. Here, manufacturing industry, so expensive and difficult in most countries, so natural and cheap in this, is to outdo itself, call forth the resources of every productive power, put into requisition every hardy and needy hand, and sit as a presiding and propitious genius on the skirt of every forest, and by the bank of every stream. Here, commerce, that higher genius, by

"At non, qua Scythiæ gentes, Mæotiaque unda,
Turbidus et torquens flaventes Ister arenas,
Quaque redit medium Rhodope porrecta sub axem;
Illic clausa tenent stabulis armenta; neque ullæ
Aut herbæ campo apparent aut arbore frondes.
Sed jacet aggeribus niveis informis et alto
Terra gelu late, septemque assurgit in ulnas;
Semper hiems, semper spirantes frigora Cauri!"

Ovid, also, who *had* seen the country, having spent nine years of exile near the mouth of the Ister, or Danube, tells us even a worse tale about the cold of that barbarous region; but it would be almost too much to expect an exile from the Flaminian gardens, in a land so utterly uncultivated, to speak the truth of the place of his banishment. The curious scholar will find a touching lamentation in the poet's Tristium lib. iii. El. 10, but will not trust it.

which the basest products are so magically transformed to gold, is to lade her trains and ships, send forth to foreign lands her best works and wares, bring back the choicest commodities of other countries, and thus crown the physical triumph of this teeming land.

More than this, however, is to be expected of such a country. History shows, that when a high-minded people have acquired the means of an agreeable and easy life, they naturally turn their attention to intellectual pursuits. It was so in ancient Egypt and Chaldea. It was so both in Rome and Greece. In such pursuits only can a thoughtful and reflecting man satisfactorily employ the leisure thus secured. Here, then, science is to be stimulated to a more than common life. The pure, blue sky, by which it is overhung, will invite the eye of the curious and aspiring to leave the sordid things of earth, and, like the wise men of Babylon before them, to make the first beginnings of their national learning, by studying and resolving the complicated but orderly motions of the stars. Astronomy, the prolific parent of the sciences, will call into existence and demand the intricacies of mathematics. Mathematics, as applied to celestial bodies, based on terrestial observations and measurements, will give being to geography. Geography, though purely mathematical at first, afterwards becomes descriptive, deals in lines and limits, sketches continents and oceans, describes lakes and landscapes, discovers and classifies the earth's inhabitants, and closes with a historical and political exhibit of the nations. Nations, the moment they are studied, are seen to be dependent upon the hidden treasures as well as the superficial resources of the earth, and demand the best endeavors and largest contributions of every science. All the sciences are thus linked together; all, in every age and country, have followed each other in this natural succession; and in the fair land now before us, they are all so liberally provided for, that each must flourish beyond all precedent.

The arts, moreover, are founded directly upon the sciences—living upon their life, and advancing with their success. Science, indeed, is mostly intellective, and can flourish in countries of physical barrenness, if not oppressed by poverty. Art, on the other hand, is not only in itself creative, but demands a great wealth of material to supply it with the motives and the means of growth. Here the materials have been poured out by a lavish hand. Here, then, among a people of wealth and knowledge, the arts of social life will be found revelling and rejoicing in their most happy state. Nowhere will the returns of agricultural labor so bountifully repay every outlay of genius in perfecting the implements by which that labor is performed. Nowhere can the spindles of the factory, or the hammers of the forge, or the trowel of the mason, or the mallet of the carpenter, or any of the most tiny or gigantic of the engines and the tools of art, find such incentives to action—such means to work with, or such rewards. Nowhere can a model of a ship, or a paragon of a steamer, or a miracle of a locomotive, be more welcome, more profitable, or more at home. Everywhere, throughout this wonderful country, you will behold the demonstrations, everywhere you will listen to the busy hum, of art. In no region of the world, will you say, do the sons of toil construct such vessels, such railroads, such machines to multiply productions, such engines to lighten labor. In no region do the mill, the foundry, the manufacturing establishment rumble, and blaze, and thunder with such enormous efforts, or with such infinite results. It *is* because it *must* be so. A people so proud and perfect, a land so fertile and fortunate, will have it so. The soil of every valley, the growth of every forest, the metal of every hill, the rush of every water-fall, the broad and placid bosom of every rolling stream, calls out for art.

Literature, it will be added, will flourish among a people of such physical perfection, of such intellectual sprightliness, under circumstances so uncommonly propitious. The land they live in lies almost at the commercial as well as geographical centre of the earth as depicted on the classic map. Their country is traversed, as we have seen, from corner to corner, by the great natural thoroughfare between Asia and Europe, and thus constitutes a necessary portion of the route to be taken by commerce, civilization, and human progress in their illustrious circuit about the globe. Asiatic in their origin, but European in their growth and education, like the river on whose banks they dwell, they form the connecting link between the ancient and modern condition of mankind. They are the natural carriers of human knowledge between the prior and the present world. Their language, ancient and oriental in its original structure, modern and western in its subsequent developement, embraces all times and places in its mighty scope, fitting them to read and appreciate, with the least amount of study, the literary productions of the Semitic, the Scandinavian, and the Teutonic tongues. The works thus laid open to them, from the hymns of Orpheus to the tragedies of Shakspeare, from the reveries of Pythagoras to the revelations of Bacon, and from Shakspeare and Bacon to the passing hour, contain every thing worthy of the attention of an inquiring or ingenious mind. Such a people, allied by nature and prejudice to that mighty family of Caucasians, whose history is the history of both Asia and Africa for more than four thousand years, and connected by residence and interest with the mightiest branches of that family, whose glory has spread over the whole of Europe, and is now spreading over our own vast hemisphere, from the Atlantic to the Pacific shore, must feel such impulses to intellectual action, must be bound by such chords of consanguinity and affection to the entire brotherhood of man, that nothing can deny them the possession of the widest, deepest, richest literature ever enjoyed by man.

But splendor is the legitimate offspring of educated wealth. The glory of such a people will be visible in every thing on which the eye can rest. Gorgeous cities, filled with luxury,

3

will here rise on every plain, on the margin of every lake, and at the confluence of all the rivers. Broad and beautiful highways, lined by ornamental trees and hedgerows, and skirted by rural mansions, will wind through the blooming country in all directions. Architecture will crown every hill with beauty. Horticulture will strew roses over every landscape. Painting will perform wonders with the pencil. Sculpture will do her best in marble. Eloquence will make every hall and temple vocal. Music will burthen every breeze with melody. Over all the land will throng out the joyous populace—the children of ease and plenty—rejoicing in the work of their hands, and thankful for the blessings of the Almighty. Justly did the Italian poet, living in the happy days of this favored country, and filled with the vision of its future, rapturously exclaim:

"Beata Ungheria!"

for never, in all respects, since the world dropped in beauty from the plastic touch of its Creator, has there been seen by mortals such a land of promise.

Alas! a land of promise only! Such as has been described, considering what nature and circumstances have done for it, is what it ought to be. It is, therefore, only the more mournful to contemplate what it is. Let us dispel the vision, and look for a moment on the sad reality, painful as will be the task.[5]

Not one-third of the available soil of Hungary, rich and easy of tillage as it is, is at present under cultivation. The northern portions of it, as well as all its hills, are yet covered by primeval forests, or rendered forbidding to the farmer by the miserable scantiness of their crops. The southern sections, including one of its largest provinces, are only partially recovered from the state of nature, which, in that latitude, is characterized by woods, and fens, and swamps. The middle parts are

[5] Dante himself, as if prescient of coming evil, couples his exclamation with a doubt:

"Beata Ungheria! Se non si lascia
Più malmenare."

cultivated in the most primitive and unproductive manner. The ground is allowed to fallow every alternate year. The idea of a rotation of crops, and the practice of manuring and restoring lands, are almost entirely unknown. Barns and granaries are seldom seen. The implements of agriculture are of the rudest form, scarcely surpassing the rough instruments of barbarous nations, and not equalling those used by the old Romans according to the descriptions of their georgic and bucolic bard.[6] The plough is a one-handled instrument, heavy, and totally incapable of fitly turning up a soil. The fork is a small sapling, or the branch of a young tree, to which nature has given the proper bifurcation. The grain, when cut, is seldom garnered, or even stacked, but is beaten out under the hoofs of oxen in the centre of the field; the wooden flail is sometimes used; and machines for threshing are just barely known. Notwithstanding the capabilities of the soil, which is adapted to the most unexampled variety of crops, wheat and corn are almost the only grains sown. Barley, which agricultural England has found so profitable, is rarely seen. Green vegetables, and garden esculents, and the savory herbs so important in modern cookery, are generally neglected. The tables of the people are served by a rude and short list of dishes to which they are confined through every season of the year. The vehicles of the farm, so correct an index of the agricultural condition of a country, instead of having followed the most ordinary improvements of modern times, rather remind the reader of the classics of those *barbara plaustra* so despised by Ovid.[7] From a land more fertile than Sicily,

[6] Virgil's Georg., lib. i., v. 160.

[7] If the reader will compare vol. ii., chap. iii. of Paget with the tenth elegy of the poet, and see how little improvement has been made in this particular during the last nineteen centuries, his philosophy may be a little puzzled. He may now see, in any part of Hungary, the original of the picture:

"Ducunt Sarmatici barbara plaustra boves?"

more healthy than Holland, more favored than England, more densely populated than the great valley of the Mississippi, scarcely a box of corn, or a bushel of wheat, or a barrel of fruit, or the smallest quantity of any other agricultural product, is exported to any distant country. Though producing the best wines in the world, which might be multiplied in amount to almost any limit, they are so dear at the very places where they are produced, that the laboring people think no more of using them than of drinking nectar. So miserable is the yield of this rich country, when the season is the least unpropitious, that, every few years, a general famine spreads death and desolation among the laboring classes, unless their wants are gratuitously supplied by the hand of charity. While all other parts of the world are vieing with each other in the career of improvement, especially in the profession of husbandry, no improvement, no amelioration ever reaches the populace of this land of poverty. So far as all popular wealth, and ease, and the luxuries of domestic life are concerned, in their relations to the masses of the people, the most beautiful as well as bountiful region of the earth might as well be a desert.[9]

If we turn our eyes toward the rivers of the land, and seek after the mills and manufacturing establishments so amply provided for and so urgently demanded, we shall suffer an equal disappointment. The mines, it is true, are here and there worked by machinery; but beyond a scythe and a soap factory, all Hungary has nothing, in this respect, more important than two or three large structures for the production of German pipe-bowls.

Commerce is equally low in this miracle of a country. Be-

for not only the clumsy cart of the field, but in Transylvania and the Banat, the carriages of the highway are yet drawn by these Sarmatian oxen.

[9] Madame Pulszky, in her Memoirs, vol. i., p. 64, gives a lively description of a Hungarian famine.

tween town and town, or plantation and city, it is often next to impossible to convey a load. The roads are narrow, unworked, and, in the rainy season, extremely muddy. In some parts they are but little better than mere cattle paths. There are but two or three short and unfinished railroads; and, until the year 1830, in a land of about twelve hundred miles of navigable rivers, not one steamer, great or small, was anywhere to be discovered. There was not even a Hungarian sail vessel to be seen passing up the Danube; for the practice still obtained, for which the *via Trajana* was probably constructed by the Romans, of tugging the awkwardest of all tow-boats up the current, by the means of ropes passing from boat to bank, on which two or three scores of peasants were sometimes tackled. In 1835, there were thirteen steamboats on the Danube and its several tributaries; and, though their elegance and speed have been liberally eulogized by an English traveler, an American gentleman, whose experience of the world is ample, and whose word is the limit of controversy on a matter of personal observation, describes them as flat-bottomed boats, propelled with feeble engines, at an average rate, perhaps, of three miles an hour.[10] Hungary, indeed, has really no commerce. The fact is wonderful. Lying, for seven or eight hundred miles, on the banks of the greatest of European rivers, and almost within view of that inland sea, on whose bosom the first voyage recorded in history was undertaken and completed, she has no intercourse whatever with foreign nations![11]

So far from wealthy, the whole country is impoverished, the very nobles themselves being often bankrupt. The people,

[10] Paget calls the Zrini, one of these vessels, a "remarkably fine ship," but steamboats in England are not models. Dr. Olin, the other traveler referred to, made the whole voyage of the Danube, in one of the thirteen steamers built by count Szhechenyi, from the mouth of the river to Vienna. Paget, it must be added, was going down stream.

[11] The city of Tomi, situated just south of the Danube, where Me-

generally, are crushed in hopeless poverty. All modes of industry are at a stand. All enterprise is laughed at as vain. The largest city contains less than ninety thousand inhabitants, though a portion of it, Buda, was built by the Romans in the time of Trajan. The towns are miserably sustained; while the villages, after all the apparent comfort of their long white cottages with neatly thatched roofs, are badly built, and as destitute of business as the places of human habitation can conveniently be made.

All over this land of promise extreme ignorance prevails. The dominant people, it is true, are intellectual, sprightly, full of genius and of action; but all the other races are heavy, slow of thought, caring nothing for education, showing nothing, of course, of its influences, and possessing as little of its power. The best race itself is only beginning to have a science. If we look for the useful arts, we shall find the oriental gypsy, here called Zigeuner, who carries his blacksmithing kit and forge upon his back, a very fit representative of them all. The fine arts are almost entirely unknown. Architecture, beyond the walls of the three larger cities, builds but rude dwellings for the rural gentry, and nothing but the long and narrow Hungarian cabin for those who cultivate the soil. Two or three painters, of no great abilities, are mentioned by the Hungarian writers. In poetry and belles-lettres, the names of Horvath and Döbrentei stand almost alone. In history, the count John Mailath is the only author who has acquired any universal fame. In philosophy, or rather in political economy, the count Szechenyi is the only person known. Ferenczy is the only sculptor of any note; and Francis Liszt, who, it is true, is acknowledged to be the greatest pianist of his age, is the only genius ever raised up by Hun-

dea cut up the body of her brother, when she returned with the Argonauts from Colchis, is still called by its inhabitants, *Tomisvar*—an evidence that the region of Hungary is not a land of change.

gary, who could not be repeatedly overmatched by many of the smallest countries of modern times.[12]

With resources sufficient for one hundred and fifty millions of well-fed, well-educated and happy people, a fraction less than fifteen millions draw out an uncertain existence on Hungarian soil. Each sub-division of its seven provinces, every one of its fifty-two counties, is capable of rearing up for Hungary a larger population than now occupy the most favored republic of our own flourishing New England; and yet there is a spot in that same New England, not much more than ten miles square, rocky and barren as it is, that contains a tenth part as many people, and ten times as many successful and prospering people, as all the counties, divisions and provinces of Hungary combined. Indeed, the smallest of the New England states, so small that nearly every part of it can be seen from the highest steeple of its first capital, within fifty years has exported more products, manufactured more fabrics, employed more ships, accumulated more wealth, printed more books, educated more minds, done more in every way for the well-being and progress of mankind, than the whole of this modern Eden for the last three centuries of time. For three hundred years, which are the years of modern history—the years at the beginning of which the new era of the world began—a dense cloud has rested on this unhappy country; and, at this moment, that cloud is denser, darker, drearier than it has ever been before.

So strange a problem would, under any circumstances, arrest the attention of a philosopher or a statesman; but the masses of mankind become interested in it only when it has formed some practical connection with the general welfare of man. Such a connection has really been formed. The cause of Hungary has become the cause of the human race. Seated,

[12] The works relied on for these statements are the City of the Magyar, Memoirs of a Hungarian Lady, Paget's Hungary and Transylvania, and the Historical Introduction by Francis Pulszky.

as she is, upon the social centre of the world, with all her unemployed abilities and opportunities, she would spring with joy to the work of self-regeneration, then to the larger work of redeeming and blessing continental Europe, and finally to a glorious co-operation with universal civilization in the work of spreading light and liberty over all the globe, were she not bound, hand and foot, by some mighty and mysterious spell. Let her become what America now is, and a new age would spring from her and shed its splendors, not only upon Europe, but upon Africa, upon Asia, and upon the nations of the seas. That spell, however, is upon her. Exertions have been made to break it; but the exertions did not prevail. Sufferings almost superhuman have been borne and braved to dispel it; but it binds its victim not less securely than before. Battles have been fought, victories have followed after victories, yet this land of the Huns, this natural paradise, this country chosen for some wonderful destiny and duty by the providence of God, is now covered with a wretchedness scarcely to be paralleled in the annals of mankind. The victim, after a thousand heroic struggles, has just now fallen to the dust. Amidst the stillness of its sepulchral rites, while the nations of Europe are keeping quiet about the grave of their buried hope, not only the philosopher and the statesman, but the citizen of every enlightened country, will contemplate its untimely fate with pitying, if not tearful, eyes. The same tears, also, that bewail the nation's calamity, will embalm the memory of the man, who, at the hazard of all things, struggled to save it from this ruin, and who failed to accomplish his object only by the treachery of his friends.

CHAPTER. II.

ORIGIN AND CONDITION OF THE PEOPLE.

THE original inhabitants of the two tracts of country, Dacia and Pannonia, now known under the double appellation of Hungary and Transylvania, were, probably, the old Cimmerians, so often mentioned in Greek and Latin fables, who, amidst the mountains and the fogs of their native or adopted land, lived a life of barbaric independence. Their dark valleys, on which the sun seldom shone, and where the people dwelt in perpetual darkness, supplied the poets of the earliest times, from Orpheus to Homer, with their most marvellous and captivating fictions. The soil of their country was so fertile, as to produce all the necessaries of existence without human labor; and they are said to have passed their time in idleness and in sleep. Like the citizens of the Italian Sybaris, they declared war upon cocks, not wishing to be disturbed, in early morning, by the cackling and crowing of the fowl; and every article of convenience, or of luxury, was prized by them in proportion to its power of contributing to their repose.[1]

[1] An example of the classic stories may be taken from the pages of the bard of Scio:

"We reached old ocean's utmost bounds,
Where rocks control his waves with ever-during mounds;
There in a lonely land and gloomy cells,
The dusky nation of Cimmeria dwells,
The sun ne'er views th' uncomfortable seats,
When radiant he advances or retreats.
Unhappy race! whom endless night invades,
Clouds the dull air, and wraps them round in shades!'

This fairy-land would furnish materials for a most amusing boo

Such a race could not long maintain themselves in a region as desirable as the one they held. About six hundred and forty years before Christ, a Scythian tribe, driven from their homes near the Caucasian mountains by the Massagetae, fled westward and entered the territory of the Cimmerians. From fugitives they soon became conquerors. The aboriginal people were expelled; and their rich vales were occupied by the invaders.

These Scythians were, probably, not of that royal race, whose exploits fill so large a place in ancient history. While in their original country, they were undoubtedly the conquered subjects of that higher family; and it is equally supposable that their expulsion was the result of a servile insurrection. On taking possession of their conquest, they remained a long time the same barbarians, that they had been before. They had no towers or fortified cities. They resided, not in houses, but in covered wagons drawn by oxen. They were particularly fond of horses, which ranged in immense herds along the rich intervals, ready for the demands of war. Bordering, however, upon the territories of ancient Thrace, which the lyre of Orpheus had rendered a civilized country, they subsequently borrowed from it many of the arts of social life, and settled down to cultivate and enjoy the exuberant fertility of their adopted land.[a]

About the middle of the first century of the Christian era, the Scythians were conquered by the Sarmatians, whom He-

---

of Greek and Latin legends. Ovid makes it the dwelling-place of the god of sleep. Homer's Odyssey, Lib. xi. "There are still to be found in Scythia," says Herodotus, Lib. iv. c. 12, "walls and bridges which are termed Cimmerian."

[a] We are told by Herodotus, Lib. iv. c. 76, *et supra*, that the Scythians were, nevertheless, opposed to the introduction of foreign customs. He divides them into two classes—those who ploughed, and those who did not plough. Though resembling our Indians in many particulars, they were, apparently, a little more civilized.

rodotus makes the natural descendants of the Amazons and royal Scythians, who dwelt on the northern border of the Caucasian mountains. In the geographical works of Ptolemy, these Sarmatians are styled the Metanastae, as if they did not occupy their native country, but had "wandered" to a foreign place. By the Roman writers, they are generally called Jazyges, of whom there were three distinct families. The first family, surnamed Maeotae, remained in their native seat, between the Borysthenes and the Tanais, north of the present sea of Azof, where the Cossacks now reside. The second, called Basilii, occupied the greater part of European Sarmatia, of which the modern Russian empire is principally composed. The third, roused by the desire of conquest, rushed down upon the plains and into the valleys of their Scythian neighbors, who, after a long and bloody opposition, submitted to their conquerors.

The territory thus acquired extended westward no farther than the river Tibiscus, now called by the German name of Theiss, beyond which was Pannonia, inhabited by a tribe of Celts. Scythia was first styled Dacia by Ptolemy, who wished to distinguish it from the Asiatic Scythia, with which it was connected on the east. Pannonia, at the period of this Sarmatian conquest, was a Roman province, it having been subdued by Tiberius in the reign of the emperor Augustus. The Sarmatians, flushed with their recent victories, pushed toward the Roman camps, but were repulsed with great slaughter. They made also several hostile incursions into the provinces lying south of the Danube. Here, again, they were met by the Roman legions and driven homeward. Though beaten, at every such attempt, by the superior discipline of the imperial soldiers, they were not discouraged, but kept up their predatory practices till the days of Trajan. They compelled Domitian, the cruel persecutor of the Christians, to pay them an annual tribute as a reward for their promised quiet.

Trajan, whose abilities as a warrior have been immortalized

by the matchless style of Pliny, could not brook such an insult to the throne he occupied. In a five years' war, in which he employed all the resources of the military art, he prosecuted his great design of making a final subjugation of the barbarous Dacians. By the help of his architect, Apollodorus, he threw a mighty bridge over the broad waters of the Danube, and marched an invincible army against Decebalus, at that time king of these wild Sarmatians. A most violent engagement followed. Such was the spirit of the barbarians, that, in the Roman camp, there was not linen enough to bind up the cuts and gashes of the wounded, nor men enough unemployed to attend to this humane duty. Decebalus, however, at last yielded. His palace, and his chief city, were destroyed. His army was cut to pieces. Glad to save himself and his former subjects from utter annihilation, he consented to resign the purple, whereupon Dacia became, at the beginning of the second century, a Roman province.

During a period of one century and a half, the emperors of Rome spent large sums of money on this new possession, in order to make it a safe bulwark against other barbarians farther north and east. Colonies were sent into it. Towers and cities were built. Roads were made, and bridges were erected, in so substantial a manner, that the ruins of them are frequently met with by modern travellers.[3]

At the middle of the third century, a new race of barbarians arose in north-eastern Europe, who looked with a lustful eye upon this beautiful country, where nature had been lavish of her bounties, and which Roman civilization had carried to a yet higher pitch of splendor. This new race were the Gotones, or Goths, who inhabited the vast plains lying east

[3] Paget's Hungary and Transylvania, vol. ii. 35, and many other places. Some Roman inscriptions, on Roman tablets, have been deciphered. The one at Drenkova, I believe, is the most perfect. The ruins of the colonial towns of Romula and Castra Nova are in Wallachia, fifteen miles above the junction of the Olt and Danube. At this place, also, are patches of a Roman road.

of the Vistula and along the shores of the Baltic. For a whole century prior to the period of their irruptions, they had looked with longing appetites on the wide savannas and grassy valleys of the south. Led away and onward by this attraction, they had even left their snowy fatherland, and gradually hovered along the frontiers of Dacia and Pannonia, and fixed their temporary habitations on the northern slope of the Carpathians. Not venturing to attack the Roman garrisons, which had been scattered all over these important provinces, they had found means of crossing the Euxine, and pouring down upon the less protected regions of Thrace and Macedonia. They had even penetrated the east as far as Asia Minor, where, in spite of the imperial armies, they had plundered the wealthiest cities, and burnt to the ground the celebrated temple of Diana at Ephesus. Sweeping backward, they entered Dacia with a resistless daring, drove the Roman legions from their strongholds, reduced the garrison at Ulpia Trajani, the provincial capital, and held the country against all opposition. The emperor Aurelian concluded a treaty with the victors, by which he relinquished to them the whole of Dacia, but broke down the famous bridge erected by his predecessor, that the barbarians might be the more easily restrained within their acknowledged borders.[4]

The reign of the Goths was of brief duration. After spending a century and a quarter upon the soil of Dacia, where they had been gradually enervated by the easy blessings they enjoyed, another nation of barbarians, whose name was as strange as their persons were hideous, swarmed in the north-eastern valleys of the Carpathians, ready for the first favorable opportunity to make their descent. Born on the barren steppes of northern Asia, between the snows of Siberia and the silk-growing groves of China, their history could be traced backwards for about four-

[4] The exact date of the Gothic conquest is A. D. 250. Anthon's An. & Med. Geog. 233.

teen centuries. Within this space of time, they had established an independent empire on their native plains, spread the terror of their arms from the shores of the Yellow Sea to the confines of Europe, frequently attacked and once humbled the emperors of China, and erected the largest dominion then known to man. At length, however, the policy of the Chinese monarchs was too much for them. Their empire fell by the undermining influence of bribery and civil wars. A portion remained as dutiful subjects of China in their northern homes. A portion emigrated southward to the neighbourhood of Canton and Sintechou. The more resolute, however, disdaining to be accounted slaves, seized their weapons, and undertook a perilous emigration towards the west. Before reaching a place of settlement, this horde of adventurers divided into two parts, one of which reached the eastern banks of the upper Volga, while the other found a more agreeable resting-place on the productive prairies of Sogdiana, between the Aral and the Caspian. The first division becoming wearied with the savage condition of their country, soon took up their line of march again, and sought for a milder and more generous climate. Having conquered the Alani in their course, and swelled their own numbers by the deed, they stood, at the moment above mentioned, a vast band of hungry robbers, on the extreme border of their last conquest, and looked greedily through the mountain passes of the Carpathians upon the fertility and beauty of the Dacian valleys. The sight was the signal of attack. They rushed through the defiles. The Gothic population were taken by surprise. The victors, under the conduct of the brave Rugilas, and afterwards under the still braver and more formidable Attila, put the inhabitants to flight, took possession of the homes thus bereft, and settled the name of Hungary, which they had before fixed upon the regions of the upper Volga, on the Dacian and Pannonian plains.[5]

[5] After a long and laborious examination of the opinions of Gibbon,

Toward the close of the ninth century, when the Huns had held undisputed possession of their conquest for more than five hundred years, their kindred of the Caspian, who, during their long residence in their new country, had taken upon themselves the name of Magyars, sent a powerful colony to the west in search of a wider and better theatre for the nation. Under the influence of a more temperate climate, and by a politic mixture of their blood with that of the Caucasian tribes about them, they had changed their swarthy complexions to a delicate brunette, become taller and more regular in their features, put off the barbarous customs and habits of the Tartar, and assumed the appearance and manners of the European. Ignorant of the fate of their lost companions, nor knowing even the route they had taken in their emigration, it is singular that they should themselves have followed in nearly the same path, and come at last to precisely the same termination. They came to the country of their brethren; but their brethren were scarcely to be discovered. During their long occupation of Dacia and Pannonia, they had undergone many misfortunes, by which their power had been completely broken. In the first place, they had been distracted and weakened by civil wars, excited by chieftain against chieftain in the struggles of personal ambition. In the next place, they had been overrun by the Abares in the sixth century, and almost conquered by several new northern hordes. The Goths, too, who had been expelled their country, had met with unlimited success in the eastern and western provinces of the Roman empire, after which many of them had returned in triumph to the homes they had once abandoned. The want of genius in the Huns themselves, however, after the death of their great commander, had been the principal cause of their disasters. They had cut

Milman, Des Guines, Schlözer, Klaproth, and Malte-Brun, respecting the genealogy of the Huns, I have been forced to the conclusions stated in the text.

their way to empire by the superior sharpness of their swords; but those swords could neither make just laws, nor raise up a civilization, by which the power of the conquerors could be consolidated and confirmed. Their decay had been almost as rapid as their success. When the Magyars crossed the Carpathians, they found a mixed race of people, made up of numerous unknown tribes, who came out to dispute the progress of the invading hosts. The contest was of short duration. After the first few battles, in which the title of Magyar had been rendered synonymous with every martial virtue, the business of fighting nearly ceased. Huns, Goths, Sarmatians, the entire population of the country, now mixed together under the general appellation of Sclaves, fled in wild disorder before the foot-steps of this new race of Huns. Some of them, who had the means of emigration at command, left their native land altogether, and escaped into the north of Italy, or into Germany and France. The greater part of the inhabitants, however, who had dwelt in ease upon their fertile prairies, flew to the circumjacent mountains, while the invaders settled down upon the deserted plains.

The Magyars, however, were not contented with these easy spoils. Leaving a sufficient number in their new home, to guard their recently-acquired possessions, they dispatched large bodies of soldiers to the west, to the north, and to the south, that the circle of their victories might be complete. Everywhere they were crowned with the most wonderful success. At their approach, armies sent against them would throw down their weapons and basely fly; villages, towns and cities would either take up their moveable effects, and abandon their fire-sides and homes, or secure their personal safety by a submission without reserve; and the people of whole provinces, struck with sudden fear, would hastily assemble their cattle from the fields and forests, and move in immense masses to less exposed positions, leaving their lands and houses to their foes. With a daring never surpassed and seldom equaled, they penetrated to the most densely-populated regions, crossed the confines of Germany into Italy and France, reveled in blood amidst the snow-fields of the farther north, and stayed their progress only at the base of some absolutely impassable mountain range, or on the shore of some unknown sea. In this manner, with their central camp on the fertile prairies, where their brave descendants yet remain, they overran all of eastern and southern Europe, from the Adriatic to the Baltic, in an incredibly short space of time.[6]

But, with their rude forms of government, it was impossible for them to keep such vast possessions against original owners almost as warlike, and quite as savage, as themselves. So soon as their various marauding bands returned to the central encampment, their distant subjects, conquered only for the moment, were as free, as independent, as hostile as before; and, though they were often reconquered, and as frequently punished for their rebellions, the conquerors at length became weary of their victories, and gradually gave up those remote regions, which they found it so difficult to hold.

Though, on the first arrival of the Magyars, the Sclaves were dispersed to the mountains, which nearly surround this land, it could not be supposed that they would always find it necessary to dwell in those rugged fastnesses, unless their new masters should prove infinitely more merciless and short-sighted than most conquerors have been. So soon as the first heat of passion had found time to cool, the terrified mountaineers gradually descended from their barren strong-holds; and their children, taking still farther advantage of the clemency of the invaders, have ventured to occupy most of the valleys in the

[6] The curious reader will find in Sismondi's Literature of the South of Europe, vol. i. 35, a Latin poem composed about the year 924, "which was sung," says the elegant historian, "by the Modenese soldiers as they guarded their walls against the Hungarians." If the music was not better than the poetry, the song must have been as formidable to the Magyars as the weapons of the Italians.

immediate vicinity of this panoramic mountain range. It could not be presumed, however, on the other hand, either that the victorious Magyars would utterly relinquish the rich and central plains to the original inhabitants, or that those inhabitants would ever cease to look upon their victors with an eye of jealousy secretly seeking for revenge. Such is the general position, and such are the feelings, of the two principal races of Hungarians at this day.[7]

The Magyar, though Tartar in his extraction, had crossed his blood so often with the best blood of other nations, that, on his arrival in Hungary, he constituted a race by himself, quite superior to most other races. In the day of his Asiatic glory, when he could stand against the power of imperial China, he not only drew from it vast tributes of money and silk, but an annual contribution of the fairest of the Chinese damsels. These maidens were given in marriage to those officers, who, by their high qualities and daring conduct as commanders, had merited the favor of the nation. In this way, without appreciating the natural result of such a practice, the Tartars gradually raised up a new rank altogether above the highest classes of the people. When the nation finally submitted to the Chinese, it was that portion of the army, in all probability, which had not been conquered, that refused to yield, but grasped their trusty weapons and traveled westward. The army, however, was made up of this superior race and the common soldiers; and the two grades, when they ceased to be held together by the necessities of the military

[7] It is a common error to confound the name of Sclaves with that of Sclavonians. The mistake should be corrected. Sclave is the generic title for the great race of which the Sclavonians, who dwell in the provinces of Sclavonia and Croatia, are only one of its several subdivisions. Paget, vol. i. p. 58, has called the attention of his readers to this distinction. The Sclavonians are Sclaves; but the Sclaves are not necessarily Sclavonians. For other subdivisions, see Pulszky's Memoirs of a Hungarian Lady, vol. ii. p. 50.

service, would very naturally seek their fortunes in distinct companies. If this were so, that portion of the adventurers, who first conquered Hungary, were certainly the lower soldiery. The higher, being more particular in their tastes, found fit companions in the tribes dwelling in the neighborhood of the Caucasus, and consequently settled down among them. As their settlement with the Caucasians, however, could not be effected without conquering a territory on which to settle, they were compelled to assert and prove their superiority over the resident inhabitants by force of arms, before any associations could be formed between the two races. When this superiority had been asserted and maintained, the friendship offered by the victorious Tartar would be extended as a condescension; and if the Tartar youth, as was most natural, should begin to be smitten with Caucasian beauty, which the world has never rivaled, their hand would be granted only to the highest specimens of female attraction. And if this cause of national improvement were in itself sufficient, the time given to it for action was certainly ample enough, to work the most radical changes. Thus, after intermarrying for several centuries with the best families of China, and the mingling and mixing for five centuries more with the Caucasians, and in the peculiarly fortunate manner here mentioned, the high-minded and independent Tartar had become the higher-minded and more independent Magyar, whose physical, intellectual and moral traits rendered him almost a paragon of his species.

The present aspect of the Magyar is a living confirmation of his origin. In support of his Caucasian genealogy, he is tall and manly in his bearing, symmetrical in shape, easy, elastic, and yet dignified in movement. In the somewhat irregular form of his head, and in the lively brunette of his speaking face, you behold the traces of his Tartar relationship. His hair, too, is generally very dark, his eye piercing and black, his countenance grave and full of thought, his speech, when not excited, slow, impressive, oriental, grand. When roused, there is a spirit, a power, an impetuosity, in his entire person and action, that declare the brilliancy and fervor of his mind. He is naturally a genius. With his quickness of perception, his rapidity of thought, his resistless power of will, his lofty and aspiring disposition, he could be nothing less. His moral sentiments are of the highest order. He is too proud to be dishonest, low, or mean. He is governed, at all times, by a high sense of what is right and just. As a master, he is careful, kind and generous. As a subject, he is fixed, resolute, unyielding to what is wrong. If rich, he is profuse in his expenses, elevated in his tastes, liberal in his charities. If poor, his pride will not suffer him to complain, while his general demeanor cannot be distinguished from that of the wealthiest baron in the land. In all the relations of domestic life, as a husband, father, brother, son, he is unimpeachable in his conduct, or follows every aberration with dignified regret. His hospitality is unbounded. Whether rich or poor, he receives his visitors with joy, and dismisses them with unwillingness. In religion, he is sincere, devout, but never contentious or fanatical. The liberty which, in all things, he demands for himself, he freely acknowledges in all others. Freedom, indeed, is the word which concentrates in itself the whole life and being of a Magyar. His physical structure, his walk, his speech, his modes of thinking, his style of living, all his ways and habits, proclaim him a man whose soul cannot be fettered. His very clothing, the style of his apparel, shows him to be a natural freeman. Dwelling in a climate, where a rather close dress is absolutely needed, he disdains, nevertheless, to bind up his free limbs in the contemptibly tight fits of other Europeans. The lower part of his person he condescends to dress somewhat in the usual French fashion; but his chest, his arms, his head, he grants a more ample liberty. His Attila, a loose frock coat, with a light military collar, ornamented in front with a rich embroidery of gold lace, he wears over his shirt of genuine linen. On his feet are high shoes, or gaiter boots, armed with a silver spur. Over all, when the weather calls for it, he throws a more ample coat, or robe, resembling a modern cloak, but decidedly more convenient as well as ornamental, which is lined with fur and fastened in front by a chain of gold. On his head, at all seasons of the year, he lays his beautiful *kalpag*, or national cap, made of the richest fur, from which the white heron's plume, or aigrette, fixed to it by a costly brooch, nods gaily to every breeze that blows. Such a being, dressed in his cherished uniform, which is never complete without a rich sword and belt, and moving in the majesty imparted to his action by his mind, may very justly claim, as he always has claimed, the particular admiration of mankind.

The peasant, it is true, cannot maintain all this magnificence of apparel; but, in every other respect, he is equal to the proudest magnate of his race. The material of his dress may be plain or coarse; his hair may hang in loose braids, or long flowing locks, upon his shoulders; his broad-brimmed hat may throw a shade over a face of rather rustic mold; but, after all, the marks of a true Magyar are always visible. Somewhere about his person, there will be seen some token of his relationship, if he be the poorest countryman in the land. Either his trowsers will be embroidered, or his vest will be trimmed with lace, or his cap will have some peculiar finish, which will distinguish him from every other race of men. If, as in the northern districts of his country, he mixes too freely with the lower population, he may, as it is certain he does, lose a portion of his neatness, of his taste; yet, even there, he can be easily singled out from his associates, by the expressiveness of his features and the dignity of his form.

The shepherd, in Hungary, is below the peasant; but he, also, if a genuine Magyar, will not fail to justify his origin by his bearing, his spirit, and his dress. While standing upon the margin of his prairie-pasture, or in the bottom of some grassy vale, with his white and shaggy-coated watch-dogs around him, every attitude and turn of his person indicates that he cannot be a slave. There is a dignity in his manners, an air of independence in his action, that can never be mistaken, or overlooked. He wears a loose linen shirt, black instead of the ordinary white, which descends but a little below his breast. His trowsers are of the same color, and generally of the same material, unless the weather is severe. Over the shirt he has an embroidered waist-coat, or jacket, of variegated colors, which covers but does not confine his chest. On his feet is a curious kind of boot, made of wool, but soled with leather, with the sides cut down and laced in the style of gaiters. His head is protected from the hot sun by a hat of very ample brim; and from his neck is suspended a sort of bag, in which he carries the dry morsel that constitutes his frugal meal. Over all he throws a plain but patriotic imitation of the national coat, which he calls a *bunda,* around which he wears a belt, or sash. This bunda, coarse as it may be, not only serves to keep up the nationality of its owner, but furnishes him an opportunity of displaying his magnificence, or his taste. If made of nothing better than a sheepskin, with the wool in its natural state, the seams show great art and beauty of execution, while characteristic scenes of the pastoral life, surrounded by a wreath of indigenous flowers, are skilfully painted or embroidered upon the arms and back. He lives almost a soldier's life. His flock he looks upon as his people, whom he is bound not only to feed, but also to protect. To do so, he is ready to meet a wolf, or a bear, or any other beast, armed, or unarmed, as he may happen to be at the moment of attack. Sometimes he is called upon to defend his woolly tribe against more formidable antagonists; but the wandering robber, who attempts depredations, will learn, before he completes his theft, that a Magyar, though in the lowest phase in which a Magyar is ever seen, is a warrior, and generally a victor, by virtue of his blood.[s]

[s] Paget's Hungary and Transylvania, vol. i. 291.

The real soldier, however, among this remarkable people, is the beau-ideal of their life. It is so not because they are irascible, or quarrelsome, or covetous, as a nation. They are not even quick to resent an injury. They will suffer any amount of oppression, so far as it relates to business, without manifesting much concern upon the subject. Their honor, however, their nationality, their ancestral rights and customs, they watch with jealous determination. Touch the person, or the reputation, or the sacred liberties of a Magyar, and you rouse him. Then he is seen to best advantage. His proud horse is always ready to be mounted. His rich uniform hangs always in his hall equally submissive to the moment. Buckling upon himself the one, and throwing himself astride the other, he is at once the handsomest and the bravest trooper of all countries.[9]

The highest physical perfection of a race, so far at least as symmetry and beauty are concerned, is always exhibited, however, in the female sex. Woman is ever more beautiful than man; but, in no country, where the male is himself so superior, is there so great a pre-eminence of feminine grace and loveliness, as in the country of the Huns. Southern Europe has been celebrated, by many grave philosophers, and by all the poets, for the unrivaled charms of its fair inhabitants. In Spain, the wandering Troubadour; in France, the passionate Trouvère; in Germany, the profound but susceptible Minnesinger, have risen up in successive schools to assert the claim of superiority for their respective lands. Modern writers have generally given to the Georgian and Circassian beauties

[9] The reader is of course aware, that the hussar, the most splendid of all the military companies of modern nations, is only the imitation of the regular Hungarian cavalry. His uniform consists of breeches with stockings buttoned to them, a doublet, a pair of red or yellow boots, and a high cap with a plume of different colors. His arms are a sabre, a carbine, and pistols. He is the most perfect horseman in the world.

the contested palm. Hungary, however, has been a sealed country, almost from the beginning of its history, to the judges of female beauty throughout the world. It is now revealed; and the elegant debate is closed. Neither the dark-eyed daughters of Castile and Arragon, nor the blue-eyed beauties of Languedoc, nor the auburn-haired belles of the Suabian or Bavarian line, can vie with the maidens of the Magyar land. The country of the Caucasus itself, where the most perfect of the human races was produced, and where the Turk still finds the fairest of his concubines and slaves, must yield. The Magyar *beauty*, with as fine a complexion as any Georgian or Circassian, tinged though it slightly is with the lively brown of her oriental birth, has an expression not easily to be matched. Hers is not the face of a mere physical beauty destitute of thought. There is a soul beaming through every feature. Her eyes and hair are dark. Her head is of the most finished mold. Her lips are thin and delicately formed. Her chin is light, or moderate in size, indicative of the acknowledged elegance of her mind. Her cheeks are round and full, but not massive, with that native dimple which always adds such a peculiar sweetness to the fair. Her figure is symmetry itself. Tall and slender, her movement is exceedingly easy and dignified, though, in a moment of excitement, her action becomes at once expressive of the quick and powerful emotion of her heart. In conversation, she is rather grave, her words are well chosen, her reach of thought is elevated, her feelings are earnest and sincere. She is not inclined to laugh. Her soul is too deep for laughter; but there is a remarkable power and significance in her smile. Her national dress, though not worn in every-day life, but reserved for suitable occasions, is tasteful, elegant, and rich. Her bust is exhibited in a tight bodice, laced in front by pearl-covered bands, from the lower fringe of which falls an ample skirt of velvet or brocade, terminating in a flowing train. The head is bare, with its dark locks, braided and set off with pearls, while the neck, arms and waist are radiant with jewels, as if sparkling with so many stars. If the Magyar maidens seldom realize, either in form or style, the full perfection of this *ideal* of their race, there is a decided tendency toward it in them all.[10]

The Sclave is a very inferior character to the genuine Magyar. How far we are to regard him as the representative of all the peoples, who have inhabited Hungary from the earliest times, having the mingled blood of the Cimmerian, the Scythian, the Goth and the Tartar in his veins, it is not easy precisely to determine. It is extremely probable, however, that, in the successive expulsions undergone by these various tribes, the country was never entirely cleared of any one of them; and, consequently, the one now known as the Sclavic, which certainly differs to some extent from the same tribe as seen in Russia and other parts of Europe, may have received as many modifications as there have been immigrations to the country where they dwell. One thing, nevertheless, is certain. To whatever extent this mixture of bloods may have been carried in their case, they have not derived the physical and mental advantages from it, which the science of physiology would lead us to expect. However indolent may have been the slumbering Cimmerian, we should presume, from what experience has taught the world, that, by the time the spirit and fierceness of the other barbaric nations had been thus infused into his natural temperament, he would have risen above the slow, heavy, stupid Sclave, who now inhabits the mountain border of this country. No race of people were ever so entirely mean. Their very name has been adopted in all languages, as the word of the greatest possible contempt, since there is no worse reproach than to call a man a *slave*.

The Sclave, however, cannot be fully described by any general epithets, however just the epithets may be, as he

[10] The costume of the Hungarian lady is given by Paget, vol. ii. p. 265. Her beauty is celebrated by all travelers.

differs, not only in his personal traits, but also in his provincial title, in the different sections where he makes his residence. The largest division of this great family are denominated Sclavacks, who are found in the barren mountains lying in the north and west of Hungary. They are a poor, illiterate, filthy, degraded race, without sense enough to appreciate their position, or spirit enough to attempt any self-improvement, could they realize their want. Their persons are of middling size and hight, with very broad shoulders, coarse features, and ill-shaped heads, which are rendered still more ugly by a covering of long, shaggy, flaxen hair. Their clothing is as unclean, as irregular, as uncomely as their persons. Their houses are constructed of unhewn logs, laid up in quadrangular piles, with the interstices closed with mud. One end of their cabin, not always separated from the remainder by a partition, is devoted to the larger cattle; while the smaller ones, such as pigs and goats, are allowed to hold a more particular intimacy, in every part, with its human occupants. Drunkenness is a prevailing vice; and, as in other countries, it brings with it nearly all the other vices.

The Sclavonians, another branch of the great family of Sclaves, occupy a couple of provinces of their own, which, however, have been, since the eleventh century, an integral part of Hungary. Sclavonia and Croatia, the provinces referred to, are always spoken of together, because their population is homogeneous, and their fortunes have been united. The people are not only very small in stature, but miserable in aspect, wearing apparel still coarser than that of their Sclavack brethren, and presenting every indication of poverty and misery.

The Serbs, though slightly more elevated than the two preceding branches of the great Sclavic race, are still Serbs, or Serfs, which, from the natural history of the word, can be nothing else than slaves. The term, a corruption of the Latin *servus*, or servant, has been justly applied to them, ever since they have been known to Europe, as a mark of their servility and meanness. It is the Italian synonym for the German *sclave;* and never was a general appellation more characteristically affixed. They are the last remnant of a horde of Sarmatians, who, like the conquered Britons, retired in a body from the scene of conquest, and settled in that fertile but uncultivated tract of country around the confluence of the four great rivers of the land. A large accession was made to them, so late as the second half of the seventeenth century, from a larger body of their tribe in Turkey. Though now quite numerous, they are extremely low, poor, and wretched, but little more refined than the best of our own savage tribes. Under the various sub-cognomens of Servi, Illyri, and Rasciani, or Raczes, they are always the same ignorant, indolent, degraded beings so graphically described by the name of Serbs. Both Servia, and the Serbian portions of the Banat, are sufficient demonstrations of the character of the generations which successively vegetate and rot upon their soil.

The Wallack, who is fastened to the fiefs of Transylvania, boasts of a descent from the Romans of the imperial times. He claims to have remained in the country after the Goths had taken possession of it and the larger portion of the Roman colonies had retired. His claim, however, can be only partially admitted, as his physical and mental traits indicate as much of Sarmatian as of Roman blood. Whatever be his genealogy, indeed, his abject condition can not be misunderstood. Not only in appearance, or in title, but in fact, he has always been a slave. While the Sclavonian himself, insignificant as he is, has received an acknowledgement of his freedom, and talks loudly about a nationality, the Wallack, until very recently, has never aspired to a personal recognition by the government, or dreamed of being free. Bound to the soil on which he lives, as much as the rude hut in which he dwells, he seems to have confessed his inferiority with a stupid willingness, which nothing but an actual and essential servility and barrenness of spirit could have brought about.

In Transylvania, also, are found the Szeklers, a singular race of people, who profess to be the descendants of the Attilan Huns. They were found in the country by the Magyars, living where they now live, and, from their physical aspect, language, customs and style of dress, were recognised, or at least acknowledged, as kindred of the conquering tribe. They were at once adopted as free citizens, and in return for this distinction, they bound themselves and their posterity for ever to guard and defend the eastern section of the Hungarian frontier. Darker in countenance than their Magyar brethren, as well as smaller in stature and less symmetrical in shape, they are evidently below them in a physical point of view; and their intellectual character, though decidedly more elevated than that of the Sclavic tribes, and possessing many interesting features, shows just brilliancy and power enough to justify their relationship to the dominant people of the land. Their moral character, however, entitles them to great respect. Like the Magyars themselves, they have a high sense of honor, which would carry one of them to the dungeon, or to death, rather than to break his word. In all the troubles of Hungary, since the final conquest of it, they have been generally true to their plighted faith; and, when any lack of zeal on their part has occurred toward their kinsmen and benefactors, it has arisen more from some misunderstanding of their duty, than from ungenerous design. It would seem, indeed, that, though their bodies and minds have not been improved by any mixture with more gifted nations, as their brethren have been, the common and inalienable characteristic of both races is a great honesty of purpose, which, without other qualities, will always secure the good opinion of mankind.

The Magyars, Sclavacks, Sclavonians, Serbs, Wallacks and Szeklers are to be considered as the native tribes of Hungary. There are others, however, whose presence in the country has been brought about by various causes, and whose character and condition must be described.

Bordered on the west and north-west by Germany, and having been connected with it politically for more than three hundred years, Hungary has received from it many accessions to her population at different times. In the north of Hungary, but particularly in Transylvania, are the settlements of the Saxons, who were first invited into the land in the twelfth century, while Bela the Blind was king. His widow, the princess Helena, extended the invitation the second time, when large immigrations took place. Those settling in Transylvania were erected into a distinct municipality by Andreas the Second, who permitted them to elect their own magistrates, to make their own private laws, to choose and support their own clergymen, to trade throughout the country without the payment of any tax, and to cut their wood and pasture their cattle on lands belonging to other tribes. Such privileges could not fail to give them prosperity in business. They have consequently thrived. They are the best farmers in Hungary; but, in every other respect, they are immeasurably inferior to the Magyars. In physical appearance, they are coarse, clumsy, ill-made beings, with gray and greedy-looking eyes, with large but irregular and heavy heads covered with flaxen hair, and with every other mark of stupidity common to such a race. They have not the first indication of delicacy about them. They aspire to nothing better than the animal, or brutish, life. Their women, even, have not the slightest token of refinement in their habits, or in their dress. Like the men, they live and labor in the field, spending their whole time in the coarsest employments of the farm. If found in the Hungarian cities, as these Saxons and other Germans often are, their aspect and style of life is equally disgusting. The males go about with their dirty pipe-bowls hanging a foot below their mouths. The females walk the streets with large burdens upon their heads. Their dwellings are uncouth, filthy, devoid of every degree of taste, while their occupants pass an existence more like cattle than like men.

Among the alien population, in spite of their long residence in the country, must be ranked the sons of Abraham according to the flesh. As is their custom everywhere, they make their residence almost wholly in the towns, and gain their livelihood by their ordinary methods of taking usury and selling jewelry and clothes; and many a Shylock among them has amassed his millions, though living among his enemies, and in spite of oppressions scarcely to be paralleled even in the bloody annals of his race. Their fortunes have been extremely checkered in this unhappy land. They were settled in the country, in large numbers, when it was first conquered by the Huns. At one time they have prospered to such a degree that they held the Magyars themselves in a state of financial bondage, governed all the monetary interests of the nation, and claimed to have mortgages upon many of the crown-lands as security for large sums of lent money, which the impoverished or needy monarchs found it impossible or inconvenient to restore. At another time they have been expelled by public edict from their possessions, stripped of their natural and civil rights, and banished from their firesides and homes. Still, after every calamity, here they are at the present day, plying their two trades with unflinching avarice, with sordid energy, and with that insanity of submission, under every vicissitude, which has always marked them out as the devoted, if not self-conscious, children of the second curse. Their condition has ever been, and is now, precarious. Their character need not be described. It is enough to say, that, in Hungary as elsewhere, they never fail to follow the richest promises, or yield to the heaviest bribes.[11]

[11] Miss Pardoe, who traveled in Hungary in 1839, gives a lively description of the past oppressions and present condition of the Jews. City of the Magyar, vol. iii. p. 297. She also states, that, at a recent period, Baron Sina was the creditor of all the nobles of the land. Vol. ii. p. 289.

Next to the Magyars in interest, but decidedly the lowest and most wretched of all the people, are the Zigeuners, or Hungarian gipsies, whose origin is entirely unknown. They have been the subject of a great deal of ingenious speculation; but neither their physical structure, their color, their customs, or their language, has been enough to unravel the mystery in which their genealogy is involved. Nothing can exceed the wretchedness in which they live. The men are slightly covered by a single garment of the coarsest kind of cloth. The women are vailed, rather than clothed, in rags. Their children are not clothed at all. They have no fixed habitations, but wander over all the country, begging where they are allowed to beg, and stealing where they can. Their stature is low, their size is small; and the color of their skin, which is nearly black, separates them entirely from every branch of the Caucasian race. They have dark glossy hair, very black and brilliant eyes, and teeth as white as ivory itself. In form they are rather graceful, particularly their young women, who walk with a quick, tripping, elastic step, and show their spirit by the restlessness of their feet, hands and eyes. They live in communities, following the instincts of nature, rather than the dictates of reason, or the regulations of the land. No woman knows her husband. No husband knows his wife. The children are regarded as the common property of the tribe. The relation of father, as well as that of brother and sister, excepting on the mother's side, are utterly unknown. They have no dwellings, or lands, or property of any kind, excepting their instruments of music, a few tools of their tinkering craft, and the rude vessels in which they cook their food. Sometimes a colony of them will fix their abode on the confines of a town, or village, where they will remain for months, rarely for a whole year, after which they will suddenly decamp without giving the slightest notice of their intentions to the inhabitants among whom they dwell. Their occupation is restricted to a little black-smithing, to the manufacture of certain trinkets, and to the use of musical instruments. In music they decidedly excel. Their ear is acute, their taste is very fair; and they are consequently employed as musicians at every festal occasion throughout the land. No political meeting can be held, no young man can marry, scarcely can a child be born, without the help of the Zigeuner bands. When young, the Hungarian gipsies are often comely, if not beautiful; but, such is the filth in which they dwell, they become exceeding ugly and disgusting toward the close of life. They are not all as degraded, however, as they are here described. There is a wide difference of social character and position among them. Young men of enviable parts, particularly in their favorite profession of music, have been discovered by travelers in their most miserable colonies; while the maidens are occasionally not only pretty, but intellectual, considerably refined in their manners, and really good, virtuous and benevolent at heart. Such a one, if she sees a wayfarer in difficulty, will become almost a heroine in his behalf. She will leave her menial occupation, in whatever place she may be employed, leap over a fence to the public road, salute her protegé with kindness, mount to the top of his carriage by a single bound, and never leave him till he is wholly extricated from his embarrassment, or distress. In all respects, in their traits of character, not less than in their genealogy, the Zigeuners of Hungary are a mystery, which it would be interesting to investigate and useful to resolve.[12]

The total population of the country of the Magyars amounts

[12] The example here presented is not an imaginary one. Precisely such a case of heroism occurred to Paget. Hung. and Trans. vol. ii. p. 99. The beautiful and beneficent Lila! The traveler discusses the gipsy question more at large in another place, vol. ii. p. 150. See also City of the Magyar, vol. i. p. 167, and Pulszky's Mem. Hung. Lady, vol. i. p. 48. Madame Pulszky thinks the Zigeuners are outcasts from India, who were expelled by Tamerlane in his celebrated wars; but they were in Hungary many centuries before that period.

to little less than fifteen millions. This sum has never been distributed, with any degree of accuracy, to the different races. The Magyars may have about five millions; the Sclavacks, two millions; the Sclavonians, including the Croatians, two millions; the Serbs, one million and a half; the Wallacks, one million; the Szeklers, one million; the Saxons, and other Germans, including Moravian and Bavarian Sclavacks, one million and a half; the Jews, half a million; and the gipsies, one hundred thousand.[13]

It will be seen, therefore, that the Magyars, though not so numerous as all the other races, are more than twice the number of any one of them. The superiority, which they have always maintained, and ever must maintain, is based entirely upon their character; for, if we except the Szeklers, their distant kindred, together with certain portions of the Germans, one genuine Magyar has more of the manly and ruling elements of humanity, than ten of the remaining people. In one of the Southern States of our own great Union, the black *Sclaves* of America are to the dominant population as four to one. In Hungary, the ratio between the ruled and the ruling is only two to one; while there is nearly as great a difference, in every thing but color, between the Magyar and the majority of his countrymen, with the exception above stated, as between the American and the negro. The African as often rises above the general level of his race, in this country, as does the Sclavack, the Sclavonian, or the Serb in the country of the Magyar.

---

[13] McCulloch, who follows Paget, makes a lower estimate, setting down the whole population at about ten millions; but Kossuth, in the Declaration of Independence and other official documents, declares it to be full fifteen millions. With his statement I have compared many authorities, mostly written, but some verbal; and I have come to the conclusions above stated. We shall never know the truth exactly till Austria shall dare to take a correct census of her people.

CHAPTER III.

THE RELIGIONS OF HUNGARY.

Religion, after making every allowance for the hard-heartedness and infidelity of mankind, is the most powerful and the most universal element of the social state. Though the greatest number of individuals appear to live by sight, rather than by faith, yet, in all nations and ages, the majority have had their various ways of closing their eyes upon this state of being, and of opening them, with more or less clearness, upon another. They have been willing, too, not only to undergo a considerable degree of self-denial in the practice of their faith, but absolute losses, deprivations, and sufferings in the defence of it.

The wars of the earliest nations, so far as we can now judge from their scanty annals, were chiefly religious wars, in which the gods of the conflicting nations were understood to have acted a conspicuous part, and to have taken a profound interest. It was not only the object but the fortune of the Babylonians, Persians and Greeks, in their successive and successful struggles after universal empire, to spread their several systems of theology over the length and breadth of their world-wide conquests. The hostilities waged by the Egyptians against the Hebrews, and by the Hebrews against the nations of Canaan, were also entirely theological in their character. The breaking up of the oriental countries, first by Confucius, and afterwards by Genghis and Tamerlane, was occasioned by the same species of contention. Mahomet, in his sweeping and devastating marches over a third part of the globe, professed to be only the herald of a new religion, the prophet of his God. The establishment of the Roman empire is almost a solitary exception, in the history of ancient countries, to the rule now alluded to; and even this universal government, though founded from secular and civil motives by the use of merely military instrumentalities, was at last subverted by religious partizans and parties.

Nothing, indeed, is considered by a man so vital to his present and future welfare as his system of divine worship; there is nothing which a man takes a greater interest in extending; and there is certainly nothing for which he will make greater sacrifices, while in successful practice, or for which he will brave more dangers, when it happens to be threatened with disasters. To defend his faith, Socrates will die in prison; and, with an increased ardor in proportion to the superior value of his profession, the Christian martyr will defy the dungeon and the rack, and even embrace death with the smile of triumph.

These things being so, it is not strange, that, in Hungary as everywhere, the religions successively professed by its inhabitants have been, almost from the beginning, numbered among the causes of its revolutions; that, in all ages of its existence, they have formed important constituents of the national politics; and that, at this moment, it is absolutely impossible to present, or to understand, the theory of its recent effort to regain its liberties and independence, without some exposition, however brief, of its religious history and condition.

Since the first general apostacy of mankind from the revealed but originally unwritten will of God, paganism, under a great variety of phases, has been the primary religion of every land. It is probable, from the little that is told of the first inhabitants of Hungary, by Herodotus and two or three other classic authors, that the Cimmerians, like their neighbors of Thrace, adhered to that original and simple form of pantheism, so beautiful and yet so fanciful, which, from the foundation of the eastern nations to the days of Thales and Pythagoras, reigned over the greater part of the oriental world.

The visible universe was their God. The one was all; and all was one. They had no idea of a supreme Being, or all-pervading and omnipresent Spirit, distinct from matter and its attributes. Nature, according to this system of religion, was a living animal, vast, almighty, uncreated and eternal. The entire sum of existence was its body; the east and west points of the horizon were its horns; its eyes, which alternated the duties of universal inspection, were the sun and the moon; the winds were its wings; and on its head sat the canopy, like a glorious crown, ribboned with rain-bows and inlaid with stars. This was the religion, if it may be so called, of the slumbering Cimmerians, who passed a dreamy and speculative life amidst the mountain-shadows of their beautiful, fertile, and quiet land.[1]

Polytheism, the child of this early pantheism, more and more puzzled with the immensity, variety and intricacy of material nature, gradually dropped the idea of a unity in this vast and manifold totality, and began to pay divine honors to the sun, moon, and stars, and to the different parts of the world we inhabit. The progress of astronomy, which brought to light, from time to time, marks of a seeming independence of one heavenly body upon another, because the motions of those bodies were not comprehended, contributed greatly to the transformation of the pantheistic imaginings into polytheism. Before the Scythians had made their settlements in Dacia and Pannonia, the change had completely taken place. All the tribes inhabiting the country, between the fall of the Cimmerians and the coming of the Magyars, were worshipers of many gods. Their theology, it is true, was not as complicated

[1] In the reputed works of Orpheus there is a fragment, strikingly poetical, which gives the most ingenious and beautiful exposition of this original pantheism ever written. To the Cimmerians I have applied only so much of the passage as seems to belong to them. They were not as cultivated as the Thracians. Orphica, p. 138. Leipsic edition.

and perfect as that of their Roman and Greek neighbors; but it was less so merely because they were themselves less civilized, if not by nature less intellectual. There was a very great simplicity in their worship. They paid religious homage, indeed, to all natural objects, whether of the heavenly regions, or of the earth; but their ceremonies were extremely brief, though beautiful. A low bow of respect and of entreaty to the rising sun, or a look of gratitude toward his setting beams, or a glance of joy at the virgin brightness of the star of evening, or a wider and weightier consideration of the countless splendors of the night, were portions of their religious service. The plain, the river, the hill, the forest, every earthly object from which they derived advantage, received a peculiar token of their thankfulness. These, however, were but the immediate agents, by whose instrumentality the thousand benefits of life were conferred upon the worshipers. The original causes of these blessings were out of sight. Indeed, these early pagans, no less than the most enlightened and thoughtful Christians, who have lived under happier circumstances, saw clearly that the earth, with all its variety of powers, received its light, and warmth, and productiveness from sources entirely beyond itself. These sources were gods; they were gods with the faculties of men; and hence they were adored in human-like images of wood, of metal, and of stone.

The Magyars brought a new religion to this interesting land. Like most of the off-shoots of that vast people, which have dwelt so long on the Pacific shores of Asia, they were monotheists, paying no religious veneration to any being but their one almighty, omniscient and eternal God. Their altars were erected on the loftiest hills, or in the shade of remote forests, or within the precincts of neighboring groves. White horses were their choicest sacrifices. The name of their Great Spirit was Isten, a word of kindred origin, probably, with the Persian Izdan, or Izana, from whose beneficence they imagined all human blessings to be derived. They rendered a sort of grateful respect, not amounting to the lowest style of worship, however, to the earth, to the air, to water, and to fire, as the chief ministers of the Supreme Being, but especially to the sun as the principal messenger of his blessings.

The idea of an evil spirit, the author of sin, the source of all temptations to what is bad, they designated by the Persic name of Armany, which, in that language, is the word for intrigue. The diabolus, or devil, of Christian nations, from the title given him, is known as the opposer, or antagonist, of our nature in its upright condition, who performs his work by an open declaration of hostility. The Armany of the Hungarians, like the Ahriman of the Persians, whose Magyar cognomen was Urdung, or Ordög, was a wily spirit, who prosecuted his wicked purposes by guile.

They believed in the immortality of the soul, and, like all the oriental nations, indulged in glowing pictures of the future and better life. They buried their dead by the side of navigable rivers, rather than in the country, as if the passage of the departed would thereby be facilitated to the spirit-land. No mournful processions followed a deceased Magyar to his grave; but his relatives and friends spread their most sumptuous banquet over his buried body; and they sang over it their most cheerful melodies, as if the event were not one of sorrow, but of joy.

Nothing, however, was held more sacred by the Hungarians, than an oath. They surrounded it with every ceremony, and association, calculated to awaken awe. The perjurer was regarded as the perpetrator of the most daring and abominable of crimes. When about to take the oath, on a solemn occasion, they were accustomed to open a vein in one arm of each of the contracting parties, and let the blood flow out into a common vessel. From this vessel each of the contractors drank in turn till it was quite empty, and, at the same time, and in the same words, pronounced a heavy curse on him who should break the pact.

The priests of this religion, called magi, or soothsayers, were the counselors of the magistrates, as well as the poets, physicians and philosophers of the people. "In their festivals, and at the sacrifices, they sang heroic songs, which they accompanied by the lyre, in order to awaken in the people the love of glory, to pour strength and fortitude into the savage breast, or to melt them to gentler feelings. The people showed them unlimited esteem, but, nevertheless, would not allow them to violate or abridge the liberties of the nation, as the priesthood had done with many other oriental countries."[2]

When St. Stephen, the first king of Hungary, and the first princely convert from the religion of his fathers to the Christian faith, undertook, in the year 1000, to bring his nation into his new way of worship, he found it no easy task. Those in the habit of reasoning contended, that their ancestral belief was as sound, as rational, as useful as the one proposed; that, while both systems were monotheisms, partaking of the same general character, and based on the same fundamental principles, the new one was more complicated, more speculative, requiring faith to supply the deficiency of demonstration; and that the people professing it, though more contentious and uncharitable about their dogmas, were not at all more moral, more honorable, or more religious, than themselves. They quoted, as a proof of the political value of their religion, the energy, the good fortune, the unbroken prosperity of their fathers. They considered the proposed change as an apostasy,

[2] Horvath, Geshichte der Ungarn, Part First, sec. ii. § 4. From this work, translated from the original Magyar into German, and recently published at the city of Pesth, I have taken this sketch of the Hungarian national religion. The work will be of still greater use in some of the succeeding chapters of this volume. Written long after the publication of the great work of Fessler, it has corrected many of the errors of that well-known historian, and is now the standard history of Hungary with the Hungarians themselves.

committed in cold blood, from the faith of the Magyar nation, involving a total renunciation of their sainted dead. The whole population clung with filial fondness to the venerable worship handed down to them from the remotest ages. They openly resisted the authority, as they had argued against the example, of their respected sovereign. When pushed to extremities, they seized their trusty weapons, fled to the rude groves of their ancestors, and resolved to die in defence of the old religion, mingling their heroic blood with the ashes of the departed.

But the character, rather than the military forces, of their monarch finally prevailed against them. By nature a most upright and well-meaning man, in his life a paragon of every thing good and great, and his kingly heart beating with the pulsations of patriotism itself, his person was revered, his example was contagious, his word was clothed with almost the authority of law. He succored the missionaries sent to him from the See of Rome. He scattered them over all the country, gave them his royal seal and signature as a guarantee of their safety, and supported their influence and ministrations by all the prerogatives of his throne. Some of these apostles being learned, many of them eloquent, and all of them ingenious in their business, they at length prevailed in persuading the masses of the people to follow the footsteps of their beloved monarch; and the few nobles, who still persisted in their opposition, and seemed determined to rise or fall in battle, were met and humbled. The king was perfectly triumphant; and the banner of the cross was at once seen streaming upon the Hungarian breezes.[3]

From the eleventh to the sixteenth century, Christianity, as

[3] The last battle fought by Stephen against the rebellious nobles was to put down what is called, in Hungarian history, the conspiracy of Kupa. It was severe, bloody, protracted, but decisive. Horvath, Geschichte der Ungarn, Part Second, cap. i. sec. i. p. 31.

held by the Roman Catholics, was the religion of the Magyars; but a long time before the days of Stephen, before even the settlement of the Hungarians in this country, its Sclavic inhabitants had made marked approaches toward the doctrines and discipline of the Greeks. Charlemagne had made great exertions to introduce to its population the faith of Christ; and the conversion of the Moesians, Bulgarians, Moravians, Bohemians, and other Sclavic tribes, about the middle of the ninth century, had almost surrounded the Sclaves of Hungary with their kindred, who had submitted to the authority of the cross. Under the reign of the Greek emperor, Basilius, the inhabitants of Sclavonia and Dalmatia, jointly with the Arentanians, sent a solemn and public deputation to Constantinople, offering to renounce the rites and ceremonies of their pagan ancestors, if the Grecian patriarch would grant them teachers to instruct them in the truth. The overture was readily and joyfully accepted; Christian laborers were dispatched immediately to the fields thus providentially opened to the gospel; and, almost instantaneously, all the provinces of Lower Hungary, then inhabited almost entirely by Sclaves, were received into the pale of the Greek Church. The conversion of the Russians, toward the close of this century, completed the work which had been so promisingly begun. Nearly all the Sclaves in Europe, from the Baltic to the Bosphorus, from the valleys of Bohemia to the shores of the Euxine, were thus turned from paganism to a profession of Christianity, and, in company with the Wallachians, whose conversion happened about the same period, added to the communion of the Independent Greeks.[4]

But the schism of the Greek and Roman Catholics, which began in the fifth century and became settled at the over throw of Constantinople by the Turks, not only sundered the Christian world into two grand communities, but raised up

[4] Mosh. Eccl. Hist. Pros. Ev., 9th and 10th centuries.

a third party, possessed of no little strength. The Roman patriarchs, or popes, though legally recognised as the nominal head of Christendom, could not afford to lose the material support of all those rich and splendid countries, which, upon the division of the empire, had been acknowledged as dependencies of the eastern branch. The Greek patriarchs, on the other hand, failing to maintain their claim of equality with the Roman, and prompted to peaceful measures by several of the emperors, were constrained to offer and to accept, at different times, proposals for the reunion of the eastern and western divisions of the Church. As often, however, as these schemes were brought forward and subscribed by the high contracting parties, the body of the Greek clergy, supported by a majority of their communicants, would resist them with their might. Many large societies, nevertheless, scattered all over eastern Europe, served by a peace-loving or timid race of pastors, not only sustained these attempts at union, but, when the attempts proved unsuccessful, adhered perseveringly to their principles, and individually connected themselves with the Roman Church. They were not required to abjure any of their peculiar ceremonies or doctrines. They still adhered to the canons of their eight general councils. They still anointed the sick, as well as the dying, with extreme unction. They still immersed their converts, in the name of the holy Trinity, three times in water. They still offered both elements of the communion, mixed in a golden or silver spoon, to the faithful and devout membership. They still permitted their clergymen to marry virgins and rear their own households; and, it may be as truly added, they still fostered as real an enmity toward the peculiar heresies of their Roman brethren, as they probably would have done in a perfectly separate and independent state. With all their professions of peace, followed by a secret and bitter jealousy of the power and splendor of both their former and latter friends, they are known in Hungary, as in other countries, under the deceptive title of United Greeks.

The writings of Martin Luther carried the doctrines of the Reformation into Hungary. His character was exactly suited to captivate the Magyars. They looked with admiration upon his boldness, energy, and spirit. Though a pious and learned divine, there was something martial in him, which the Hungarians knew how to appreciate. His love of liberty, however, was the trait most attractive to them. He had his own ideas. He delivered them openly and freely. He would deliver them in spite of all men. All the rank Catholics of his city and vicinity combined against him; but he ceased not a moment in fear of the combination. The rulers of the church threatened him with an ecclesiastical prosecution; but he heeded not their threatenings. The head of the church fulminated a decree of excommunication against him; but he burnt the decree to ashes in the presence of his enemies. The emperor himself, who reigned over the largest and most powerful dominion of modern ages, summoned the reformer to stand before him, and before the assembled princes of the nations, to answer his royal questions at the peril of his liberty or his life; but, undaunted by every danger, the reformer went directly forward, met his majesty with perfect fearlessness, put the royal accusations beneath his feet, routed the whole body of his assailants, and stood forth to the world a conqueror, with his heel upon the heart of a corrupt church, with his grasp upon the throat of a superstitious and mercenary empire. That was the man, that was the attitude, to command the admiration of the Magyars. The doctrine, too, of personal responsibility and liberty, had always been their doctrine. They had contended for the right of private judgment in civil matters; and they were equally ready to accept it in relation to religious practices and opinions. They never had been Catholics as other nations had been Catholics. They had been coërced rather than convinced. Though, by a continued study and observance of the Christian religion for several centuries, they had become strong believers in its divine origin, and in its great value to the human race, they had never been very hearty papists. The papal system was too arbitrary to suit their temper. The dogma of pontifical infallibility had been to them an object of contempt. The custom of delivering up soul and body to the priest had never been their custom. They had ever been for liberty, individuality, equality. Luther, in their eyes, had broached no new doctrines. He seemed only to have espoused their principles. The first word from his mouth was to them the signal for re-asserting their national position. They did re-assert it; and the entire race, with the exception only of the great magnates, whose alliance with the government has ever been the means of their personal corruption, raised the banner of reform, and became stanch and open Lutherans.

The Magyars, however, had to undergo another revolution, before their religion could be entirely settled. The division between Luther and Zuingle was at once felt in Hungary. Luther, while stoutly denying the Catholic dogma of the real presence of the Savior in the elements of the Supper, by coining the barbarous word, consubstantiation, had introduced an unintelligible barbarism into his system of theology. Many of his warmest friends had declared themselves incapable of seeing any fundamental difference between this notion and the notion of the rankest Catholic. The Swiss reformer, in particular, strove manfully against it. Calvin, his successor, organized in Switzerland a new society of reformers, by making the bread and the wine of the eucharist merely the representatives of the body and blood of the Redeemer, and by purging the theology of Luther of several other half-catholic superstitions. His doctrine of decrees, which seemed to be but the revival of the old classic and oriental conceptions of fatality, was not at all unsuitable to gain credit with a people of eastern origin. When Matthias Devay began secretly to inculcate among the Magyars the opinions of the Swiss school, he found a large proportion of them, including the most intelligent and thoughtful, ready to receive him. Szegedin, a renowned Calvinistic preacher, quite equal in intellectual ability to any of the reformers, and resembling Luther in boldness and perseverance, followed Devay, and halted not in his great enterprise until he had succeeded in making a deep and general impression. The Lutherans of Hungary were divided by him into two great, irreconcilable, and even hostile parties. Time has not softened, but rather exasperated, their opposition. The Lutherans remain faithful to the theological system of the great German; but the Calvinists are, at once, the most liberal, the most enterprising, and the most powerful.

In the midst of all these religious revolutions, the Germans of Hungary, after the most liberal allowance for individual exceptions, have generally adhered fixedly to the church of the imperial government. The government is German; and they are German. The government is Catholic; and they are Catholic. That is the *rationale* of their position. It cannot be said that they dare not think. They do not wish to think. The government thinks for them. The priest is the paid and petted representative of the government. He sways his parishioners precisely as he lists. He teaches them to look down upon their fellow-citizens, belonging to the other communions, as so many damnable heretics, whose lives have been spared, not from merit, but from necessity.

Indeed, from this brief historical survey of the various ecclesiastical establishments of Hungary, it is evident, that, in that country, religion is by no means a bond of peace and amity, but a fountain of bitterness and discord. The different races, sufficiently separate and hostile by national attractions and repulsions, are rendered still more unfriendly by that which ought to have pacified and united them. In all countries, this multiplicity of faiths has ever been, and will always be, a source of many animosities; but, in Hungary, the evil is peculiarly aggravated. Each race has its own religion. The Sclave, to whatever subdivision of his family he may belong, as well as the Wallachian, is almost certain to be a member of the Greek Communion. The Magyar, with whom the Szeckler must always be connected, excepting only their official and titled nobles, is either a Lutheran, or a Calvinist. The German, by position quite as much as by preference, is naturally a Catholic. The remainder of the population is divided between the Jews and Gipsies, the former of whom have shown, in all countries and through successive ages, a memorable stubbornness of will, by which they have been an isolated people in whatever nation they have dwelt; and the latter, the mysterious descendants of an unknown race of men, are a tribe of heathen, upon whom Christianity has never made its mark.

In no country of the world, ancient or modern, has the population been so radically and perfectly divided in respect to religious faith. In no country have there existed more causes to render these divisions perpetual and bitter. Every Christian denomination, singular as it may seem, is the result of a religious quarrel. The Independent Greek Church quarreled with the Roman, separated from it, and then established both itself and its hatreds among the Wallachians and Sclaves of Hungary. The United Greeks, after raising a domestic feud, turned traitors to the Independent Church, and united with its rankest enemies. The Roman Catholics had a natural war with both these sects, and, though receiving the little band of returned prodigals with an ostentatious clemency, they have never granted them the affection and confidence, which had been promised and expected. The Protestants, whether Lutheran or Calvinistic, are the offspring of the bloodiest of all religious schisms; and they look down with a most hearty but justifiable contempt upon the superstitions, and ignorance, and degradation of both the Roman and the Greek Catholics. The Jews, of course, despise all these rebels to the faith of Abraham, and are as sincerely hated or pitied by all the rebels in return.

Thus, the Hungarian races are rendered tenfold more inimical to each other, by their profession of inimical religions; thus, these inimical religions, sufficiently opposite themselves, are rendered tenfold more opposite, by the quarrels in which they had their origin; and thus, from the beginning of its history, with increasing rather than abating turbulence, has the land of the Magyar been torn, and rent, and sacrificed by its religious denominations. An eternal, unappeasable, insatiable hostility exists between them. No word of love and peace, from one to another, is ever offered. No such word would be received if ever so freely spoken. Each is contending for superiority. The Sclave struggles against all the others, not only because he is a Sclave, but because he is a Greek Catholic, while the rest of his countrymen, in his estimation, are worse than pagans. The German contends for the supremacy, because he is a German, because the government of the land is German, but much more because he is a Roman Catholic, while every thing about him is regarded as the rankest heresy. The Magyar, though willing to grant equality of privilege to the other sects, is indignant at the corruptions brought into the bosom of the Christian Church—the church of his affections—by both Greeks and Romans. Century after century, while a religious peace has been gradually settling down upon other countries, the religions of Hungary, which, in general, are races as well as sects, have been nearly as distinct, as hostile, as irreconcilable, as if they had inhabited as many unfriendly and warlike countries.

The Hungarian religions have, also, become woven into the political movements of the several adjacent countries, whose races are represented in the mixed population of this kingdom. The present governors of Hungary, as has been seen, are Roman Catholics. They acknowledge the sovereignty of the Roman pontiff. The Greek Catholics, on the contrary, have their own pontiff, whose right of supremacy is not only maintained by them, but by the entire Sclavic family, over which Russia is now dominant. The Protestants, on the other hand, while they depend, from religious connections, upon no foreign people for support, renounce the jurisdiction of all pontiffs, and make the pure word of God the sole authority in religion. The state church, in all its ambitious projects, has been able to rely upon the help, not only of the Roman bishop, but of his Roman commonwealth. The Sclavic church, in its opposition to the Roman, has leaned upon the arm of the Greek bishop, and, through his agency, as well as by the license of a common interest, upon the more powerful support of imperial Russia. The Protestant cause, however, has had nothing to sustain it but its own intrinsic truth.[5] Indeed, in their religious character, they have ever been a peaceable, liberal, tolerant people, desiring the reformation of their Greek and Roman fellow-citizens, and sufficiently zealous in the propagation of their faith, but raising no fierce contentions in their country for religion's sake. The wars of opinion have been waged, not by their instrumentality or co-operation, but in spite of them and generally against them. To break them down, or to exterminate them from the country, Italy has sent swarms of Jesuits into their communities, armed with secret influences, guided by secret counsels, sustained by secret but abundant subsidies. With the same foul purposes in view, Russia has constantly tampered with the Sclavic tribes, sent political and religious emissaries among them, induced

[5] Once, it is true, the Protestants of Hungary, when suffering a most cruel persecution from the other sects, who threatened their annihilation, sought and obtained the succor of Great Britain. But, at all other times, in all their calamities, they have trusted entirely to themselves. It is a singular fact, that, at this day, the Bank of England pays an annual interest on a sum of money funded by Englishmen for the benefit of the Hungarian Protestants.

the priests and bishops to acknowledge the Czar as the head of their ecclesiastical establishment, and turned their hearts against all the remaining inhabitants of the country, and particularly against the Magyars. In this way, Hungary has been made the common battlefield of Austria, and Rome, and Russia, as well as of all the nations taking part in their respective projects. Three great races, three great religions, three irreconcilable and indomitable ambitions, have thus divided and distracted the inhabitants, as well as weakened the power, of this most unfortunate but most interesting country.[6]

These religious feuds have implicated, not only the politics of the kingdom, and the political designs of the most powerful and unscrupulous of the surrounding nations, but also the cause of popular education. Each race, each sect, each political interest, has made the most strenuous exertions to sustain itself by the agency of schools and colleges. In many other countries, in the most enlightened and liberal portions of the world, sectarian seminaries have existed; but, in no part of Europe, or of America, is there one educational institution, which can be compared with the majority of similar establishments in Hungary. Every school is sectarian. In every one of them, not excluding the schools for the miners, some sectarian theology is forced upon the pupils. The great national universities are Catholic; and no Protestant can send his sons to be educated in them, unless at the fatal risk of seeing them graduate as apostates to their paternal faith. The colleges of the Protestants, on the other hand, at Debreczin, at Papa, at

[6] "As political agents and spies of the Russian court," says Paget, vol. ii. p. 82, "the Wallach priests are said to be made use of, and I am fully inclined to believe it; for they regard the Archbishop of Moscow as their primate, and the emperor of Russia as the head of their church." Nearly all travelers in Hungary speak of the efforts of Rome and Russia, upon the Sclavic and German populations, to unite them respectively against the dominant race of people.

Poson, at Kesmark, at Oedenburg, are forbidden by law to the sons of Catholics. The few seminaries of the Greeks, Independent and United, are equally under the ban of the other denominations. By this means, the educated men of the country are rendered rank partizans of their respective churches. Education, which, in many other parts of the world, is a bond of union among the more enlightened and powerful portion of the population, here serves as an instrument of separation. Sectarianism is formed within the hearts of the citizens from their earliest childhood. Their toy-books teach it to them. Their text-books engrave it into their souls. The authority of the masters, and all those tender and resistless influences, which are felt at school, so weave it into the texture of their being, that it becomes and continues to be an inalienable attribute of their personality.

The same spirit is also carried into social life. In city and in country, the people are divided into religious cliques, or circles, whose members hold intimacies almost exclusively with each other. In Pesth, in Pressburg, in all the great towns, and with nearly equal uniformity in the more populous of the rural districts, Catholics associate with Catholics, Protestants with Protestants, Greeks with Greeks, Jews with Jews. All the little but important civilities of common life run in these separate circles. Trade is almost equally exclusive. Not only the aged, whose principles and prejudices are apt to be confirmed, but the youth, also, are so settled in their habits, or governed in their choices, that they seldom transgress this established regulation of Hungarian intercourse. The consequence is, that few friendships are formed, and few alliances take place, between the families of opposite religions. Intermarriages, in fact, have been legally discouraged, and sometimes positively forbidden, to young men and maidens of Catholic parentage. The government can not see, at least with satisfaction, the formation of any social connections, which would serve to abate the zeal of its adherents. So watchful has it been to preserve the exclusiveness of its partizans, that, whenever any contraband marriage happened to occur, they have refused to give legal sanction to it, thereby throwing the question of inheritance, where there might be property at stake, into a troublesome and terrifying uncertainty; and the priests of the state church, always obedient to the religious prejudices of their sovereign, because they were thus but giving succor to their own, have refused not only to perform the matrimonial service, but to have any farther intercourse with the family and friends of the recreant party. The children of these mixed marriages are, by law, divided between the parents, the father having the charge of his sons, the mother of her daughters. Thus, this lamentable spirit of disunion, of separation, of hostility, begins its unholy business with the cradle. Mournful indeed, in every way, is the social condition brought about by the religious intolerance of the Hungarians. The Magyars are the only people, who, consistently and perseveringly, have opposed the sway of this spirit within the limits of their country.[7]

Perhaps the most embarrassing circumstance, connected with the religious state of Hungary, is the fact, that, in respect to their power, the parties are so nearly equal. If either of them had a decided preponderance, though there might be more oppression, there would be less agitation, and, consequently, less political imbecility. The Catholics, though a minority of the whole people, are held up by the authority of the government; but the numerous dignitaries of their church, distributed carefully to all the important places of the king-

[7] The marriage of M. de Beöthy, about the year 1839, is an example of the bigotry and policy of the government. The bishop of the diocese refused to officiate on the occasion. A Protestant minister was employed to perform the service; and the enraged bridegroom, who had been a stanch Catholic, became one of the boldest and most successful defenders of Hungarian liberty.—*City of the Magyar*, vol. i. p. 288.

dom, would give their communion a formidable influence without the help of any legal privileges. The king of Hungary is himself the acknowledged head of Catholicity within his dominions; but his authority is divided between the bishops of Erlau, of Kalocza, and of Gran. Under them there are fourteen diocesan, and sixteen secular, bishops. Below the bishops there are eighteen metropolitan and collegiate chapters; two hundred and sixty beneficed and honorary canons; one arch-abbot, ruling over a hundred and fifty abbots; and, below them all, a numerous, ignorant, bigoted, intolerant, sensual priesthood, whose bread is guaranteed by the fostering government, whose services are always rendered on the side of tyranny and oppression, and whose lives would be a scandal to the most degraded classes of any enlightened country.

The Independent Greek Church is governed by two bishops, who, by the characteristic intrigue of the government, have been subjected to the Roman archbishopric of Gran. Under the jurisdiction of these bishops are two chapters, eleven beneficed canons, six titular or honorary canons, and about one thousand pastors. Though thus put under the surveilance of the state church, the Greek hierarchy support the government only when its measures are leveled against the Protestants; but, whenever they have any interests of their own to serve, they look to their natural ally and protector, the Russian Czar, for whose health and welfare they daily employ a most impressive and devout supplication, which is not only publicly pronounced, but openly inserted in their book of ritual. The priests of this religion, like the people served by them, are the most ignorant, debased, and superstitious in the kingdom.

The United Greeks, on the other hand, who are decidedly more numerous than the Independents, are not very warm in their attachments either to their German rulers, or to their Russian patron. Russia, while she bestows her bribes upon them with a lavish liberality, does so with desire, rather than with expectation. The bond of sympathy between the United

Greeks and the Russians is their common origin and language; but the ecclesiastical influence of this large body of religionists, where it is not itself otherwise interested, leans toward the Austro-Roman government of their nation; and they have been willing, for several centuries, to submit to the dictation of the Austro-Roman archbishop of Karlowicz, to whom Austria has committed the trust of keeping them in subjection.

It must be evident, therefore, that the Protestant Magyars are the only people of Hungary, whose entire interests begin and terminate with their country. The Catholics belong to Rome and Germany. The Greeks, both Independent and United, are the natural confederates of Russia. Should Hungary fall, the Catholics have a home, a country, a kindred on its western boundary. The Greeks, in the same event, have a still larger and perhaps safer refuge just beyond its eastern limits. The Jews and Gipsies are as much at home, as much at their ease, in one part of the globe, as in another. The Magyar alone, of all its population, has no interest, nothing he can call his own, nothing to which he would lay a claim, but Hungary. All the others derive their being, or receive their consequence, or draw their support, from foreign sources. To these foreign sources they, consequently, fondly look and gratefully pay their allegiance. The Magyar receives nothing, owes nothing, pays nothing of the kind, in relation to any land but Hungary. The Magyars are Hungary. All the rest are foreigners. These expect all things from Austria, from Rome, from Russia. The Magyars have no dependence but God, their country, and their valor.

Their religion makes them, at the same time, the friends of personal liberty. It has no hierarchy. Each congregation is wholly independent of every other. Every one of them is a miniature republic, in which each member has his voice, his vote, his individual responsibility and importance. Every one of them is a school for the study and practice of the great doctrines of human freedom. Every one of them is a place, where men learn to think, to resolve, to act, not as other men may dictate, but as the pure word of God, expounded by reason and enforced by conscience, may command them. With the Magyar, indeed, allegiance to God is the first and great commandment. The second is a sincere, perfect, hopeful, unfaltering self-reliance.

CHAPTER IV.

LANGUAGE AND LITERATURE OF THE MAGYARS.

It has been a question among philosophers, whether a language makes its people, or a people makes its language. The Greek, for example, not only contained a civilization within itself, but it had the power to impart that civilization to any people, who might adopt it. Such, indeed, is the actual history of the Greek, as it spread from its native seat to the many ancient countries, which it successively pervaded. It can not be maintained, perhaps, that there was any meaning, or potentiality, or creative power in the words themselves; but those words, when looked upon by the most barbarous tribes, were seen to be the exponents of human thoughts; and, therefore, into whatever land they traveled, they became active in stirring up the mind of its population to realize the ideas thus represented. In this way, more than by the valor of all her armies, did Greece gradually and effectually expand the compass of her nationality, till it was rendered almost universal.

Not only the Greeks, however, but the population of every country, convey their national character to their language. Their language, in fact, is only the receptacle of that character. It is the common treasury, into which they all pour their thoughts, their feelings, their peculiarities. When thus full of the mind of a nation, it reacts directly and powerfully upon that nation, forming the mind of each new generation as it rises. Their speech becomes, in this manner, the perpetuator of the people, just as the people are the perpetuators of their speech. Let a certain portion of them lose the use of their mother tongue, and learn the dialect of another conntry, and they will at once be transformed, in heart at least, and in reality if they can have their choice, into citizens of that country. Let them all be led or forced to abandon their tongue, or let their tongue be annihilated altogether, and the entire nationality, which they had before, will be laid off, and a new nationality will come to them from their new language.

Greece, in an early period of her history, happened to communicate her language, by the means of a few colonies, to the western shores of Asia Minor. The result was, that all that portion of the world became, in every particular, Grecian. The inhabitants talked Greek, and read Greek, and transacted all their affairs in Greek. To Greece, as their father-land, they looked, for their instructors in philosophy, their text-books in science, their models in the arts, their forms of government, their principles of legislation, and for every thing which molds the character and creates the condition of a commonwealth. Colonies equally large, and equally enlightened, were planted, also, on the plains of Italy and Sicily; but there were causes in existence, in these countries, which forbade the propagation of the colonial language within their limits. The Greek civilization, therefore, was confined to the Grecian cities thus transplanted in the west, though their political influence was paramount in south-western Europe, till they were subsequently overthrown by the towering enterprise of a native population.[1]

It has evidently been the conviction of all countries, which have had any reasons for giving attention to this subject, that a nationality is more inherent in the medium of a people's intercourse, than in their laws and constitutions. Spain, to defend herself against the Moors, fought for centuries to oppose the extinction of its own tongue by the diffusion of the Arabic. The old statute-books of Great Britain are full

[1] This topic has been ably handled by Heeren in his Politics of Greece.

of legislative efforts, made by successive parliaments, against the Latin and the French, which Cæsar and the Norman conqueror had respectively brought with them. Indeed, it was for a long period regarded as a hopeless task, by many English statesmen, to combine all parts of the realm under a homogeneous government, whatever might be the nature of that government, until the dialects of the Scotch, the Irish and the Welsh could be melted down into one common language. Their foresight was almost prophetic. Scotland, at this time, is divided, not only between the Scotch and English languages, but, as a consequence, between Scotch and English sympathies, predilections, and tendencies. In Ireland, too, the same prophecy has met with the same fulfilment. In her northern counties, the English is spoken almost exclusively by the native population; and it is in the north of Ireland, also, that the inhabitants look upon themselves, in all respects, as Englishmen, while the southern portion of the island, where the original Celtic still prevails among the lower classes, has ever been the hot-bed of Irish independence.[a]

Not only the governments, however, but the religions of mankind, have seen and recognised the stubbornly preservative power of language. The Jew, in all ages of the world, and in every region, has been able to maintain his mode of worship, against all the influences of all the countries where he has made his habitation. This he has done by clinging, with the tenacity of despair, to that majestic speech in which his venerable religion lies imbodied. Popery is perpetuated in modern Latin. The destruction of this form of the Latin, which makes repentance synonymous with penance, and in which the thousand other peculiarities of Romanism are in-

[a] If England wishes to Anglicise Ireland, let her take such steps as will effectually root out the Irish dialect, by which the clannish spirit of the Hibernians has been maintained, and will be maintained, in spite of all the laws of parliament.

separably interwoven, would be the annihilation of that ancient ecclesiastical establisnment. This object, however, will not be achieved without a struggle; for Rome well knows the position and importance of her citadel.

Within the limits of the American States we have several striking illustrations of the great fact now considered. Louisiana, while speaking the French, and employing it as the legal language, even after her cession to our Union, continued to be, for many years, as much in sympathy with France, as with this country. Her citizens, her science, her philosophy, her literary influences, even her system of jurisprudence, were imported from the land to which her speech allied her. Until very recently, the legislature of this republic enforced the publication of all state papers in the French, and, so long as this practice was maintained, in spite of its close geographical connection and organic incorporation with the other republics of this nation, it was virtually, in every thing but a general recognition of our style of government, a foreign state. No sooner, however, did the English become the authorized language, than the French influences were discarded; and the old Civil Law, which it had brought from the mother country in the codes and pandects of Justinian, and which had been the established common law till that moment, was abated. So true it is, here as everywhere, that the laws and language of a people come and go together; while it is the next thing to an impossibility to destroy a nationality, without first destroying that organized system of social intercourse of which the nationality is the life-receiving, as well as life-giving, spirit.

It cannot be thought wonderful, therefore, that the language of every country has been felt and acknowledged as a political question with those making use of it. Every people, as they cherish their own identity, must pertinaciously adhere to that, which, more than every thing else, maintains the identity of their nation. They will not only choose to think, to feel, to speak, in the dialect endeared to them from the days of childhood, but to read the enactments of their legislators and the productions of their writers in that dialect. The words and accents so familiar to himself, every parent delights to hear his children reproduce, and every citizen resolves to have them perpetuated in the schools of his native land, and in the intercourse of social life. No reward can bribe, no power can compel him to relinquish his vernacular tongue, and to see another one replace it. He will war against every such design at home, and against every effort to contribute to it from abroad, with that force that springs from a universal instinct. His reason, too, will stir up his patriotism against it. To defend his language, and thereby his nationality, he will submit to any sacrifice, and impose upon himself any amount of hazard.

Without denying the possibility, however, of one nation's passing over from their own to another language, the facility of its so doing, nevertheless, is identical with the facility with which it can pass from its own to another nationality. That this passage can be made is not a matter of speculation, but a fact of history. Yet, between nationalities widely different, and still more where they are exactly opposite, the attempt to make it will be difficult. Two republics, though characterized by different languages, may, by a great and mutual effort, run into each other, and so amalgamate; and either of them, by a much harder struggle at self-sacrifice, may possibly put off its personal characteristics, and put on those of its associate or rival. For a republic, however, to pass into a monarchy, or for a monarchy to become a despotism, is a feat inexpressibly more laborious and impracticable; while the transition of a despotism into a republic, or of a republic into a despotism, has ever been the work of force, and is attended by the terrible concomitants of war and blood.

In the same manner, the languages in which these nationalities are imbodied, are equally various in their individuality, their stubborn self-existence, their ability to resist aggressions, some falling under a few hostile strokes, others defying every combination of influences and of powers. It may be laid down as a general law, that those have the greatest vitality, which are the most developed, precisely as a man is less easily destroyed than a little child. They, on the other hand, are the most developed, which the people speaking them are the most free to use. The language, in other words, of a free people, has not only greater capacity, compass and perfection than that of a nation, whose mouth is half-closed with fear, but also a much greater tenacity of life. A race of men, who, under all circumstances, can utter exactly what they think, will think the more. Their more numerous thoughts will give existence to a more numerous vocabulary of words. The language of such a race is, therefore, constantly drawing into itself the elements of strength. With every such language the time may come, when, like the Roman, it will have the power to conquer those, by whom the population originally employing it have been conquered.

In making a reference of these general statements to the topic particularly under consideration, it must be remembered, that the Magyar is the speech of a free people, who have never been otherwise than free, and who, from their constitutional ardor, would be expected to pour, without restraint, all the rich and spontaneous productions of their free hearts into their social conversation. This expectation, it is said by those best acquainted with Hungarian, is entirely fulfilled; but a slight inspection of the language will be enough, so far as the present purposes require, to justify this opinion.

The Magyars, originally of oriental extraction, have dwelt so long in Europe, that their language is neither eastern nor western exclusively. It is both; and it shows the marks of its twofold parentage in its structure.[3] Like the Hebrew,

[3] "La langue Magyare," say Cheuchard and Müntz, in their excellent geography, "n'a de rapport, en Europe, qu'avec celle des Finlandais, qui sont probablement, ainsi que les dominateurs de la

and its cognate dialects, there is a prevailing tendency to unite the smaller words, with us called particles, as prefixes and suffixes to the larger ones; and there is, also, a great scarcity of abstract terms. We are told by an American historian, that, when the first missionaries to the Indians wished to translate the Christian doxology into the native tongues, they found it impossible to come nearer to the original than to say—"*our* Father, *his* Son, and *their* Holy Ghost"—because of the want of words for father, son and spirit to which the relative particles were not organically affixed.[4] This perfectly illustrates what is to be understood of the characteristic just expressed. The difficulty here encountered, however, would not be met with in the Hungarian, because, though born in the east, it has had a long European education. Nor, indeed, is any of the Semitic tongues as straitened, in respect to abstract words, as that of our unlettered Hurons; while the Magyar has not only a clear title to some relationship with the great family of European languages, but, in the quantity of its abstract words, is nearly equal to some of them, which have long been accounted copious and polished.

The Hungarian is rich in inflections, almost every relation existing between words, or things, being easily and perfectly expressed by modifications of the words themselves. As, in Latin, *caput* means *a head*, but *capitis*, *of a head;* so, in this language, *ki* signifies *which*, and *kik*, *to which;* and, in a similar way, nearly the entire vocabulary submits to the same changes for the same purposes. In some words, particularly in the pronouns, these changes are very marked; *my* and *magam*, for example, *our* and *I*, coming from the same root,

Hongrie, d'origine Mongole."—Universal Geography, Paris 1839, p. 458.

[4] Bancroft's Hist. United States, vol. iii. p. 258. The fact was first discovered by Brebeuf.

which is nothing but the letter *m*. In other words, there is no inflection whatever, the particle *te*, for instance, being either *you*, or *thou*, or *thy*, as the sentence may require, though the correlate of our word *thine* is *ti-ed*, which is only another form for *te*. The word *man* is *ember;* and the dative case is *emberhus*, which signifies *to a man*. The remaining cases are treated in the same manner.

The Greek and German have long been celebrated for their great facility in the composition and resolution of their words; but neither of them surpasses, nor even equals, in this quality, the Hungarian. It would almost seem to be, not a verbal, but a syllabic language, whose syllables are capable of an infinite variety of temporary unions, according to the innumerable requirements of thought, which, when these demands are met, are again distributed, like a case of type, to be used again in other combinations as endless as the workings of the mind.[5] With all this flexibility, however, it is singular that many relative words, which, it would be supposed in a language so accommodating, could be cut into almost any size and shape, have no abstract forms on which the relatives are based. The Hungarian, for example, has a vast number of modifications of the root-word *assom, woman*, embracing all the relations in which the term, or the being, can possibly be placed; but the simple word, *wife*, without qualification or connection, can never drop from Hungarian lips. The Magyar can speak of his own wife, by using the word *felesigem, my wife;* and, by certain easy changes upon the word, he can make it represent the wife of any person he may choose; but, to set aside all

[5] "In consequence of this joining together of words," says Paget, "the Hungarians can construct a whole sentence in a single word; and the following is often given as an illustration—not that such a word would be used in conversation, but as a proof of how far it may be carried: *Ha meg kö-penye-ge-sit-te-len-nit-teh-het-né-lek*. This signifies, in English—'If I could deprive you of your clothes!'"—*Hungary and Transylvania*, vol. ii, p. 277. Am. Ed.

idea of persons, with whom a wife may be connected, and to represent her as a being by herself, and yet as a wife, is a thing that he cannot do. But there is a more singular trait in the Hungarian than this. All those languages, which, like the Greek and German, make the gender of a great number of their words depend, not upon the objects they represent, but upon their respective terminations, have been long laughed at or admired for the marvellous confusion they produce in the natural division of the sexes. In Greek, *a man* is masculine, while *a little man* is neuter. The German commits the still greater absurdity of making the *wife* neuter. But the greatest absurdity of all is in the Hungarian, in which the word is neither masculine, feminine, nor neuter. The language takes no account whatever of the sexes.

The readiest and simplest way, nevertheless, to get at least a general conception of a strange language, is to inspect the style and structure of some passage in it, which, in his own, is familiar to the student. It is for this reason that the Lord's Prayer, rather than any other passage, should be adopted as the key to be commonly used for this purpose by comparative philologists. That Prayer, with a sublinear English translation, as near as it is possible, perhaps, to render an oriental into a western language, is as follows:

My At-yank ki vagi a mennyecben;
Our Father which art in heaven;

szenteltessek meg a te neved; jaeijaen-el
hallowedness be to thy name; come thou

a te országed; legyen meg a te akeratod
to thy kingdom; let be to thy will

mint mennyben ugi itt e-faeldenis;
as in heaven so in the earth;

ami mindennapi kenyerunket ad-meg;
and day-by-day our-bread give;

boksatunk azoknak a kik mi ellensunk
forgive all [things] to which we ourselves

vetunk; es ne vigy minket a kifertebö;
return forgiveness; and not lead us to temptation;

szabadies (meg) minket a gonosztul;
deliver (be) us from evil;

mert ti-ed az orszag, az hatolom, es a
for thine is kingdom, is power, added to

diesaseg, mind-aeraekke. Amen.
glory, all-forever. Amen.

The European, or Japhetic, relationship of the Hungarian will be sufficiently evident, by a comparison of the following twelve words, taken from this Magyar Pater-Noster, with their correlates in the Latin, German, French, Spanish and English languages, though the collation might be carried to any extent:

Hung.	Latin.	German.	French.	Spanish.	English
My	Meus	Mein	Mon	Mi	My
Mi	Meus	Mein	Mon	Mi	My
Ki	Qui }	formerly pronounced *kee* in Europe	Que	Que	
Kik	Qui }		Que	Que	
Meg	Machinor	Machen			Make [be]
Ad-meg	Do. with ad	Do. with ad			Do. with *to*
Neved	Nomen	Name	Nom	Nombre	Name
Legyen	Licet	Lassen	Laisser	Licito	Let
A	A	An	À	Á	At
Te	Tu	Du	Te	Tu	Thou
Ne	Non	Nicht	Ne	No	Not
Az	Est	Ist	Est	Es	Is

It is evident, therefore, that more than one quarter, at least, of the words of the Hungarian Pater-Noster are European.[6]

[6] Mr. Sandor Tokátz, a native Hungarian, now a resident of Cincinnati, true to the pride of character so natural to the Magyar,

Its affinity to the oriental, or Semitic, languages is naturally more remote, and less easily discovered, just as the characteristics of the child are apt to lose themselves in the more complicated habits of the man. This is particularly true of the vocabulary of the language, while its organic laws have been less liable to change. There are many striking analogies, nevertheless, between the words of the Hungarian and the Hebrew, with occasional resemblances to the words of other eastern tongues. The Magyar *kalap*, for example, which means *a hat*, forcibly reminds the scholar of the Hebrew *kelub*, which signifies any thing *woven*, or *plaited*, or *braided*, as we know the hats of the Hungarian peasantry, as well as the hats of the common people of the whole of southern Europe, have been from the earliest times. The word *nop*, which is our *sun*, also makes one think of the Hebrew *noph*, the term for *hight*. The Hungarian *chilák*, *star*, recals the Hebrew *kilak*, an old root with the sense of *beating*, *pulsating*, and hence *flashing*. The word for *water*, *wiz*, whose European relative is found in the German *wasser*, and whose Asiatic connection is plainly manifest in the Arabian *wadi*, belongs to that interesting class of words, found in the dialects of all

kindly furnishes books and advice to every one who is curious enough about his mother tongue to ask his assistance, but will not let himself out as a teacher of it, while he depends for his livelihood upon the business of his profession. I feel bound, therefore, to inform my reader, that I am greatly indebted to that gentleman for the very little that I have been able to acquire of his beautiful and rich language. Like every Magyar, Mr. Tokátz is a natural linguist. He has traveled extensively in Europe, in Asia, in Africa, and in America. He speaks with fluency Hungarian, Latin, German and Italian, and has some knowledge of the Arabic and Coptic, having spent quite a period in Egypt. In four months he learned to speak the English. If, as a country, we wish to make the best practical use of the misfortunes of unhappy Hungary, we should employ her gifted sons, who have fled to us for shelter, as teachers of language in our schools, colleges, and universities.

known countries, which demonstrate at once the unity of all systems of human speech, and of all the scattered tribes of men that employ them.[7]

The sound of the language, when pronounced as it should be, is clear, soft, musical, and yet grand. It abounds in vowels; nor is the tone of the consonants as harsh as in most European languages. The letter *s*, for example, which renders all the Gothic dialects so disagreeable, in a large proportion of their words, in Hungarian is reduced to a firmly enunciated *z*, or a moderate *sh*. The name of the great hero of Hungary, for instance, which, in America, is wrongly called *Kóssuth*, with the accent on the first syllable, with both the sibilants hissingly brought out, and with the rough *h* at the termination of the word, in the lips of the educated Magyar becomes *Kozzhóot*, in which every letter is both soft and sweet. At the beginning of a word the Hungarian generally repudiates the doubling of a consonant; and if, in any word, two consonants do come together, as in *szenteltessuk*, they are nearly always such as require a soft enunciation. Often, as in the adopted

[7] The Hungarian Pater-Noster I have superficially compared with the Pater-Nosters of ten eastern languages—the Syriac, Arabic, Persic, Coptic, Abyssinian, Malayan, Zanguebaran, Siamese, Bengalese, Malabaran,—which, with many others, are now before me. In spite of a very imperfect acquaintance with the laws of comparative philology, and of a still more imperfect knowledge of most of these oriental tongues, as well as an absolute ignorance of some of them, I have been able, by dint of some interest and perseverance, to make out a general parallel in their grammatical structure, and an occasional resemblance in their vocabularies. The common notion, maintained by recent writers, and particularly by Fejer, that the Hungarian bears no analogy to any known language but the Finnish, I trust is shown in the text to be incorrect; but it might be much more largely and elaborately demonstrated to be false, by a collation of the tongues above enumerated, were it consistent with the general object of this chapter to expand upon the discussion of so erudite a subject.

word *iskola,* from the Latin *schola,* a short supernumerary vowel is employed, as in the Greek and Hebrew, to make the pronunciation easy and euphonic. In this way the Turkish *kral* becomes *kiraly.* The simple vowels are seven in number—*a e i o ö u ü*—which, to form the prolonged vowel sounds, are modified by an accent—*á é í ó ő ú ű*—by which it is indicated that the sounds are lengthened. The addition of this accent not only affects the pronunciation of all words, and modifies the sense of many, but of some of them makes a complete revolution. The word *kar* means *arm,* and has its analogy in the Greek χεὶρ, which signifies the *hand;* but *kar* with the accent, *kár,* means *injury,* which is entirely another word. In the same manner, *kerek* is *round,* and *kerék* is a *wheel,* while *kérek* is the verb *to beg.* It is this power and importance of the accent, more than its grammatical structure, or even the very troublesome composition and combination of its words, that renders the Hungarian so difficult of acquisition. There are accents enough in Hebrew; but a scholar can read that language without any dependence on them. In several of the oriental languages, they are convenient, but not essential. In the Sanscrit, it is known, they have this Hungarian privilege of making radical alterations in the sense of words; and, to illustrate their occasional power in Greek, the wit of Demosthenes may be cited, who, wishing to make the Athenian multitude call his opponent a hireling, and render them vociferous in their condemnation, asked them, at the top of his voice, if the man were not a μίσθωτος. They, to correct his pronunciation, as he expected, cried out from every part of the assembly, μισθωτός, *misthotós;* upon which the wily orator, turning full upon his apparently convicted and shuddering victim, but now with the proper accent, exclaimed with prodigious emphasis—"Did I not tell thee, sir, that thou art a *misthotós?*"—a hireling![8]

[8] It may be necessary to observe that the word μίσθωτος, which the

The language of the Magyars, indeed, is among the richest and most beautiful; but its literature is far from being equal to it. The inequality, however, does not spring from any want of vigor, or activity, or enterprise in the Hungarian mind, but from the force of circumstances. There was scarcely ever a people, in this respect, so unfortunate. At the beginning of the eleventh century, just as they completed the settlement of their country, and conquered a peace with surrounding nations, the conversion of king Stephen to the Catholic faith gave admittance, not only to the priests of Rome, but to the Roman language. In the court and camp of the monarch, and, as a natural consequence, in the legislative chambers of the nation, the new tongue at once acquired the ascendancy. It soon passed downward to the masses of the people. In a short time, not only the laws of the land, but the business of the towns, and the conversation of the populace, were published and carried on in Latin. Thus introduced into the country, its position was secured by the erection of schools, in which the foreign tongue entirely displaced the native. Before the death of Stephen, numerous monastic and episcopal seminaries were raised up in Hungary; and, in the thirteenth century, a general institution for the cultivation of the liberal arts, as well as for theology and jurisprudence, was established at Vessprim. In the year 1367, Louis the First founded a new university at Fünfkirchen, which, in 1388, was followed by that of Buda. Matthias Corvinus established a third at Pressburg. In the sixteenth century arose the almost numberless schools, great and small, of the Hungarian Protestants; and, in the seventeenth, the Jesuits built those of Tyrnau, Pressburg, Kaschau and Klausenburg. The institution of Tyrnau subsequently became a university, which,

---

Athenians supposed Demosthenes to be using, might have been confounded by many with μίσθατις, which made bad grammar as well as a bad meaning.

on the expulsion of the Jesuits in 1784, was transferred to Pesth. The number of minor colleges, with one or two faculties, brought into existence during the seventeenth and eighteenth centuries, indicates a general and powerful ambition in the cause of learning; and the academies of Pressburg, of Kaschau, of Raab, of Grosswardein, and of Agram are still popular. It is lamentable, however, that, in all the institutions here enumerated, the Latin entirely displaced the language of the country.

The accession of the French princes, in the year 1307, began a new era in relation to the literature of the Magyars. In the court of the king, and in the army, the French language was at once spoken. From these sources it spread over all the nation. The schools, it is true, still maintained the supremacy of the Latin, not only in their own halls, but in the various departments of human learning. The books of the country, on almost every topic requiring erudition, were still written in it. The French, indeed, rapidly became the language of fashionable life. The Hungarian, however, yet slumbered in the low dwellings of the common people; and it is worthy of remark, that these princes of the house of Anjou, with all their natural admiration of the French, never made the first attempt to suppress the vernacular speech of their Magyar subjects. Several of them, on the contrary, studied, mastered, and employed it.

On the field of Mohacz, in the year 1526, the French period came to a sudden and final termination. It was followed by the ascendancy of the Germans, who, on the elevation of Ferdinand the First to the throne of Hungary, spread their language and literature over the whole kingdom. The French, it is true, remained; but it remained only among the more genteel classes of society, who still kept up their French sympathies and breeding through the instrumentality of books. They sent their sons to the great university of Paris, which, in those days, was more than what Oxford, or Cambridge, or Göttingen is in ours. In the presence of the king, however, the German was always spoken. The officers of the army, also, who were generally the countrymen of the monarch, carried the dialect of the court to the deliberations of the camp. Germans, always and everywhere a working and trafficking people, rushed into the cities and towns of Hungary, and soon made their language a necessity, even to the natives, in business and in trade. In the sixteenth century, the introduction of the reformed religion, which, from Geneva to Wittenburg, was found either in Latin or in German, gave a new impulse to this lingual revolution. In the seventeenth century the revolution was complete.

Thus, the Hungarian has been three times overwhelmed by the influx of foreign languages; and, at all times, it has been surrounded by the Sclavic, which is spoken by three-fifths of the population of the country. The force with which it has repelled these aggressions, the obstinacy of its adhesion to itself, are a proof of great vital energy. No similar example has been recorded. In England, the Celtic, the Latin, the Anglo-Saxon, and the Norman have given way to each other in succession, until, at this day, the English is almost the only language. In Spain, the original Basque, and, in central Italy, the Tuscan, were so entirely subverted by the Roman, that there is scarcely a word now extant of either. In the north of Europe, the French and German have nearly smothered the Dutch, the Danish, and all the Scandinavian dialects. Similar facts exist in all parts of Europe, as well as in Asia, in Africa, and in our own continent. In Hungary, however, the language of a single race, which constitutes a minority of the people, has held its ground in spite of all opposition. The opposition, too, has been more general, more frequently repeated, and more determined, than ever has been raised against any other language. Yet, there it is, as vigorous, as obstinate, as fresh for the battles of self-defence, as ever.

The literature of the Hungarians, nevertheless, it must be

confessed, is not so flattering. There has been native talent enough, certainly, to have produced any amount of books in every department of human learning; but, from causes operating alike in all countries, the Magyar authors have too generally been compelled to send out their works in a dead, or in a foreign, language. Had they not done so, at certain periods in their national history, their productions would never have been read. If not read, they certainly would not have been sold or bought; and it may be safely presumed, that authorship in Hungary is not so easy and natural a business, as to have lived without support. The historians of Hungary have given to the reading public long lists of works, published since the art of printing was introduced into their country in 1473, chiefly in Latin and German, as the leading productions of their press; but not only are the majority of them the works of foreigners residing in their land, but a great proportion of them are destitute of any general celebrity in the literary world.[9]

The Lutheran Reformation, while it helped to spread the

[9] In history and its collateral sciences they give us the following names: Bonfinius, Galeotus, Ranzanus, Ursinus, Brutus, Taurinus, Laszky, Werner, Lazius, Ilicinus, Sommer, Gableman, Typotius, and Ens, all of whom, I think, excepting Laszky, were foreigners. Among their native authors, on the same subjects, may be reckoned Jo, Thurotzius, Tubero, Flacius, Brodericus, Zermegh, Listhius, Verantius, Forjacs, Olahus, Sambucus, Schesaus, Zamosius, Istvansi, Petrus de Réwa, Parmanus, Inchoferus, Nadasi, Frölich, Ratkai, Johannes and Wolfgangus, Counts Bethlen, Lucius, Toppeltinus, Haner and Szantivanyi.

In medicine, and its cognate studies, occur most frequently the names of Clusius, Kramer, Perliczy, Moller, Jessenius, Torkos, Molmar, Mitterpacher, Piller, Köleseri, Weszprenyi, Naygar, Parispopai, Benkö, Poda, Born, Hedwig, Lumiczer, Kietaibele, Grossinger, J. B. Horvath, Domin, Pauhl, and Ichraud.

In the philosophical and mathematical sciences may be set down the names of Petrus de Dacia, Peurbach, Dudith, Boscovich, Szenti-

German language among the Hungarians, did still more to call out the native Magyar. The papal party, not being acquainted with the language of the people, were compelled to write almost entirely in Latin; but the Hungarian reformers, taking advantage of this ignorance, addressed their arguments and appeals to the populace in their cherished vernacular. The result was, that a new life was breathed into it. Discussions, letters, books appeared in it, one after another, in rapid succession. The Bible was frequently translated into it. The religious struggle soon became patriotic. The papal party, seeing the power of the vernacular in the great contest, rose with one voice with the determination to suppress it. The nation rose with equal unanimity to defend it. All manner of works, historical, literary, and religious, poured from the Hungarian press, and filled the dwellings of the native population. Reading became a sort of duty; and every Magyar, who could write a book in his mother tongue, was sure to find any extent of patronage. This, in a word, was the dawning period of native literature in Hungary.[10]

vanyi, Berenyi, Segner, Hell, Makó, J. B. Horvath, Pap Fogarasi, Handerla, Mikovinyi, Rausch, and Rozgonyi.

In poetry and eloquence the Hungarian student sees oftenest the names of Janus Pannonius, Johannes Vitéz, Bartholemew Pannonius, Jakob and Stepan Piso, Zalkan, Olahus, Franciscus Hunyadi, Szentgyörgyi, Bekenyi, Schesaus, Lang, Werner, Uncius, Sambucus, Túry, Kassai, Filitzky, Dobner, Bajtai, Zimányi, Szerdahely, Somsich, Nicolaus Révai, Desöffy and Karlooszky.

[10] Next to the religious productions of this period, which are too numerous to be mentioned, orations, histories, codes of law, philological works, as well as popular songs and even epics, are the most abundant. Among the orators, who appeared between 1558 and 1738, the following are the most noted: Goal (1558), Juhac (1563), Davidis (1569), Kulczar (1574), Bornemisza (1575), Telegdi (1577), Decsi (1582), Karolyi (1584), Pasman (1604), Kecskemeti (1615), Zvonarics (1628), Kopcsanyi (1630), Kaldi (1630), Margitai (1652), and Alvinczy (1738). The principal historians were Szekely (1559),

The efforts of the papal party, however, to suppress the language and literature of the Hungarians, were at length almost victorious. The Magyar press was more and more shackled. Magyar productions nearly ceased to flow from it. The Latin was revived again. A Latin era followed; and, what is worthy of distinct observation, it was between 1702

Temesvari (1569), Heltai (1572), Petho (1660), Bortha (1664), and Lisznyai (1692). The Latin code, written by the hand of Stephen, was translated into the Hungarian by Blasius Veres (1561), Kaspar Heltai (1571), and Okolisczanyi (1648). In philology are included the Pesti Nomenclatura (1538), Ordösi's Grammar (1539), Calpin's Lexicon with Hungarian notes (1587), the dictionary of Kovácz (1590), Molnai's Grammar (1610), the grammars of Geler Katona, Ksipkes Komáromi, Pereszlenyi, and Kovesdi, and the dictionary of Párizpapai with Tzeczi's principles of Hungarian orthography. Unnumbered ballads fell from the pens of Tinveli (1540), Kakony (1549), Valkai (1572), Tzerényi, Szegedi, Illyfalvi, Szetary, Faszkas, (1577), Balassa, Illosvai, Gosarvrai, Veres, Enzedi, Szöllösi (1580), and Tzakoranyi (1592). Epics were produced by Count Nicolas Zrini, (1652), Ladislaus Listhi (1653), Christoph Pasko (1663), and Count Stephen Kohary (1699). The intellectual efforts of the noted Stephen Gyöngyösi (1664–1734), as well as the lyric attempts of Rimai, Balassa and Beniczky, belong to this vigorous era. Of the several translations of the Scriptures into Hungarian, the following are the best known to European scholars: Komjati (1533), Pesthi (1536), Erdösi (1541), Heltai (1546), Szekely (1548), Juhacz (1565), Felegyházi (1586), Karolyi (1590), Molnar (1608), Kaldi (1625), an association of reformed theologians (1661), Kzipkes Komiáromi (1685), and Totfalusi (1685). Many of these translations, though made in Hungary, were printed in foreign cities, among which Cassel, Utrecht, Nuremberg, and Brieg may be mentioned. It is impossible, in a note, and it would be foreign to the object of the text, to enter into any criticisms of this list of works, which I have compressed to its closest form; but a bare inspection of it will be enough to impress the reader with the vitality and energy of the Hungarian language, when once roused to action, in spite of its having been so long overwhelmed by the languages of Germany, of France, and of imperial and papal Rome.

and 1780, after all these great deeds of the Magyar mind to disenthral itself, that the Latin reached its greatest purity and power in Hungary.[11]

This Latin period terminated at the accession of Joseph the Second to the Hungarian throne. That monarch, falling in with the Catholics, did every thing in his power to give the German the ascendancy in political and common life, though the Latin was still allowed to linger in the schools. Again the nation stood up against this attempt. Its patriotic feelings were completely roused. It resolved, with an energy truly Hungarian, that its own language, instead of being crowded down to a third or fourth-rate place, from that moment should hold the first. The resolution was, at the beginning, merely political, being confined to the National Assembly and the county meetings. It soon became national and universal. In 1781, the noted and talented Matthias Róth established the first Hungarian journal at the city of Pressburg, which, though weak and feeble at the first, grew at length to great popularity and power. During the agitations of the French Revolution, from the rise of Roland to the fall of Napoleon, this and other Magyar newspapers kept the Hungarian public well informed of the real state of Europe, while the Austrian journals, according to their character, mistified and misled their German readers. The successes of

[11] The works of Hidi, Hevenesi, Kzwittinger, Kazy, Tarnozy, Bel, Prileszky, Huszty, Szegdi, Decericius, Stilting, Bajtai, Timon, Peterfsi, Kaprinai, Kollar, Lod, Thuroczy, Schmitt, Bod, Szaszky, Schier, Severini, Benczur, Pray, Cornides, Cetto, Ganoky, Novak, Salagi, Katona, Kerchelich, Palma, Wagner, Schönwisner, Kovachich, Wespremi, and Hovanyi are regarded as the great ornaments of this Augustan age of Hungarian Latin. The Magyars, however, were not entirely idle. The close reader of the literary history of this era will learn the names of Franz Faludi, Barczai, Lorenz Orczy, George Bessenyi, Baroczi, Teleki, and of Daniel and Paul Anyos, who still adhered, with no trifling reputation, to their native language.

the French armies in Austria so shattered its imperial strength, that, with all its subsequent boastings, it has never since had the power of domineering over its subject provinces and kingdoms, as it had had for nearly all time before. Hungary had the sagacity to see her day. Without harboring, however, the remotest intentions of separation or revolt, she again renewed her resolution to protect herself. Her nationality existed in her language. This she plainly perceived; and, in 1820, she began to pass laws tending toward its complete emancipation. It was ordered, that all the acts of the Assembly, all the proceedings of the courts, and all the governmental business of the country, should be published and transacted in the vernacular. Prizes were also offered for native literary works of merit; and, by the same authority, the Hungarian was taught in all the schools, from the lowest to the highest. Lecturers were also sent out, to traverse the country, to awaken an interest in the subject, and to deliver addresses on the language in all the academies and colleges. Literary periodicals, of no small pretensions, sprang up in every quarter. A Hungarian theatre was opened at Buda, and another at Pesth, for the purpose of perfecting the pronunciation of the mother tongue, and of teaching it to the higher classes, who, in the universities and in their residence at court, had almost forgotten it.[12]

The poetic, and particularly the dramatic department of the national literature has had so much to do in developing the talents and the taste of Hungary, that it deserves the most

[12] To this period belong certain names, which, dryly as they may appear in a simple enumeration, should be given to the curious reader, who may wish hereafter to make some farther acquaintance with the language of this newly-opened and interesting nation. On grammatical and philological subjects, he may inquire for the works of Izabo, Rajnis, Beregszaszi, Gyarmathi, Aranka, Höldi, Beukö, Kassai, Pethe, Szentpali, Böjthi, Versegi, Virag, Revai, Marton, and Stephen Horvath.

marked attention. The oldest poet of the Magyars, so far as there is any record, was Demetrius Tszanadi, who sang the conquest of Hungary.[13] He was followed by Stephen Szekelyi, Nagy Batzoy, Temesvori, Bogoti, Valkai, and Ilosvai, who wrote the glorious chronicles of their country in inglorious rhymes. Valentine L. B. Balassa is looked upon at home as the Hungarian Pindar. Erdösi endeavored, but without much success, to introduce the hexameter into his language. His subjects, if there had been no other obstacle, would have defeated him; for they consisted chiefly of foolish attempts, at the end of each book of the New Testament, which he had just translated, to give a poetical summary of its contents. The seventeenth century was quite prolific in poetical composition. The works of Simon Petsi and of Petrus Benitzky continue to be read. Stephen Gyöngyösi, who filled up the entire space between 1620 and 1704 with his life and labors, did much to enrich his native language, though his style is stiff, unnatural, and diffuse. George Tranowski, who wrote sacred songs, which were partly original and partly translated from the German, is reverenced as the Luther of Hungarian verse. Ladislaus Listhi was an epic poet belonging to this period. He treated the defeat of Mohacz, at the same time that the fámous Nicolas Zrini celebrated the deeds of his more famous ancestor, the defender of Szigeth. The most of these poets manifested a crude taste in the choice of topics. The English Armstrong has been ridiculed for treating the Art of Health in verse; but George de Vizaka Baracz, a Hungarian poet, had preceded the Englishman in his folly, and greatly surpassed him in ill success. His theme was the vascular system of the human body; and his poem sets forth the wonders of the secretory and excretory vessels very much as a madcap of a medical professor would teach them to his class. At an earlier date, Oroszeghyi had tried his skill in

[13] He flourished about 1527.

rhyming the utility of cultivating the fir-tree; and, with an equal stupidity, Onadi had made the elements of arithmetic dance, or hobble, in didactic verse.

The eighteenth century was ushered in by the songs of Count Stephen Kohary, a lyric poet of some eminence, who was succeeded by Florinda, in whose works the geography and history of the modern empires and nations are combined. Count John Lazar, known as the Dacian Janus, and Samuel Hruskovitz, a sacred poet, attained no small distinction, among their countrymen, before 1748. About the same time, the popular effusions of George Verestoi and of Benjamin Szönzi, who were the Burns and the Berenger of the Magyars, seized upon the patriotic spirit of the people and carried the nation in a sort of triumph.

The French school of Hungarian poetry was founded by George Bessenyi, whose career began in 1740 and closed in 1811, and to whom his native land owes a deep debt of gratitude. In 1773 he established the Hungarian Spectator, in which he stated and defended his peculiar views with great eloquence. His command of language was the wonder of his generation. He not only made for himself an undying reputation, as a polite scholar, but fixed his opinions as laws of taste to a great proportion of his countrymen.

The classical school may be traced to a very early period; but its power was first felt in the works of Szilagyi, and of Szentiobis, two recent but successful imitators of the style of Horace. The social humor of the great Roman is said to have been remarkably well mimicked by the latter of these writers, while his sentimental manner was most conspicuous in the productions of the thoughtful and melancholy Paul von Anyos. The very learned John Baptista Molmar, and the didactic poet, Kalmar, were in the eighteenth century the ornaments of this school. They were followed by Alexander Baroczy and Nicolas Revai, who, in their classical tendencies pursued the beaten path of the Germans and the French.

Gabriel Dayka, the Anacreon of Hungary, took the erotic odes of Horace as his models. The school was continued by Gideon Raday, and by the epigrammist, Benedict Virag, whose works were much read and quoted at the beginning of the present century; while Franz Verseghi, the last of the classical Hungarian poets, died but a few years ago.

After the French and the classic, the composite school of Magyar poetry arose. It began with Franz Kazinzy, a native writer of considerable originality and talent, though not very deep. He is celebrated for his skill in versification. He wrote in the lyric and the epigrammatic style. He followed neither the French nor the classic taste exclusively, but whatever seemed to him best suited to the topic he had in hand; and generally, indeed, the influence of all the reigning modes was at once exhibited in his songs. His principal supporters and successors were Michael Vitez Esokonai, a popular song-writer, Andrew Fay, the humorous fabulist, Paul Szmere, the delightful singer, Daniel Berzsenyi, a most talented and glowing writer of high lyric poetry, and Alexander S. Kisfaludy, who, as a composer of ballads, is regarded by the Hungarians as their Thomas Moore. Kisfaludy, like Walter Scott, had acquired a universal popularity in his native country before his real name was known. His amorous songs, collected under the anonym of *Himsys*, are yet sung by the peasantry, as well as by the nobles, all over Hungary. Taken together, they constitute a sort of ballad epic, in which he sings his unsuccessful love to a certain Lisa, who listens to the soft petitions of another, and thus drives the poet to the wars. The soldier-bard, however, lives to see his Lisa again, after he had passed through many a bloody battle; she, conquered at last by the singular perseverance of his devotion, gives him her hand and heart; and, the moment they are joined in happy wedlock, the lyre of the lover becomes more sonorous than ever, and rings with a melody, a variety, a power of expression, which it had never known before. The husband becomes more sober.

He studies the legends of his country, and lends them the charm of his rich verse; and the close of his eventful life is devoted to another lyrical epic, the "Gyula Szerelme," of ten cantos, which, with us, may have something like a counterpart in the Canterbury Tales.

The genuine Hungarian school took its origin, perhaps, from the works of Daniel Berzenyi, in which is to be found a tone of decided patriotism, of profound nationality, which spurns at every thing foreign, not only in the thoughts, scenes and sentiments, but even in the choice of words. He was succeeded and emulated by Andreas Horvath, the author of a didactic poem in hexameter—"the Recollections of Zirez"—which, however, is greatly surpassed by his epic entitled "Arpad." The cotemporaries of Horvath, and poets of the same style, were Aloys Szentmiklossy, and Gábriel Döbrentei, two graceful lyric bards, one of whom, the latter, has acquired a European reputation. The fabulist, Michael Vitkovics, attained to popularity by making the animals, birds, reptiles and insects of Hungary employ the words of wisdom, while he seemed to forget that such men as Æsop and La Fontaine had ever had existence. After the death of Vitkovics, in 1829, such a host of patriotic poets sprang up in Hungary, the greater part of whom are even now just ripening into manhood, that it will be impossible to name them all. Among the most eminent is Guadanyi, who, in comic narrative, is surpassed only by Alexander Kisfaludy. Karl Kisfaludy, the publisher and editor of the "Almanac of the Muses," is a young writer of decided promise. A young poet of the name of Kölcsey, of real genius, has recently made himself known as the introducer of the romance-ballad into Hungary. To these must be added the sonnet-writer, Bartay, the high lyrist, Baiza, a disciple of the German Göthe, Szenvey, a philosophical poet after the style of Wordsworth and of Schiller, and Michael Vörösmarty, a very successful miscellaneous writer, whose "*Foti-Dal*" has become one of the national ballads, and may be heard from every hill-top and valley. Next to Vörösmarty, Gergely Ezuczor is the greatest epic poet of the nation; and his numerous works, among which are his "Battle of Augsburgh," his "Diet of Arad," his "Arpad," his "Defeat of the Cumanes," his "Siege of Erlau," and his "Magic Valley," are at this time the pride and boast of every patriotic Magyar. The most popular lyric poet, of the present day, is Sandor Petöfi, whose several ballads, the "Pearls of Love," "Cypress Leaves," and "Starless Nights," remind the American reader of our own Longfellow, though the Hungarian is scarcely a rival to the author of the "Voices."

Though the Hungarians have raised up no Shakspeare, no Corneille, no Racine, to impart a world-wide celebrity to their drama, they can mention some names, whose plays would do no dishonor, perhaps, to the royal theatres of London and of Paris. Mimics were known in Hungary at a very early period. The oldest national dramatic poem is the "Melchior Balassa," by Paul Karadi, of the year 1569, which was followed by the Clytemnestra of Bornemisza, a close imitation of Sophocles' Electra. In the year 1692, the Emperor Leopold gave to a citizen of Klausenburg the privilege of performing melo-dramas at the sessions of the National Assembly, in the camp, and at all festivals and fairs, with the proviso, however, that they were first to be submitted to a censorship. A work of this character is still extant, under the title of Comico-Tragedia, which treats of the contest between good and bad principles. Another, bearing the title of a "Tragedy of the Dispute between Jupiter and Plato," written by George Felvinczi, is yet read, though seldom performed, in Hungary.

In the eighteenth century this original drama sank intc oblivion, and a new era arose, which was not only ushered in but supported by the Jesuits. Plays were written for the colleges and schools; and they were performed by the pupils and professors for the amusement of the public at the examinations, as similar trifles are occasionally exhibited, in our own country, at the present time. Though moral in their tendency, as works of genius they had no character, and they deserve no praise. Many of them, however, are still extant; and the names of their authors are preserved.

In 1790, the first licensed Hungarian dramatic troupe was organized; and, in 1792, another received the royal sanction in Transylvania. Just prior to the recent revolution, in addition to the great national theatre at Pesth, there were not less than twenty companies, perhaps as many as twenty-five, strolling through the country and dragging the car of Thespis from one village to another. By the Magyars, they were regarded with great satisfaction, and welcomed even by the most religious, because, whatever else they may have done, they were contributing powerfully to a resuscitation of the native language. It was at Buda, that the first building was erected expressly for the accommodation of a Hungarian theatrical company; and, in 1834, in spite of the neglect of the National Assembly and the opposition of the imperial court, the second was reared at Pesth by the enthusiastic patriotism of the people. In 1839, when visited by an English traveler, this structure was lighted with gas, well furnished with stage-scenery, and occupied by a most successful and artistic troupe, of which La Schodel, the Lind of Hungary, was the acknowledged queen.[14] The pieces acted are chiefly the productions of their native writers, among the earlier of whom the names of Simai, Sos, Szentjobi, Endrödy and Dugonicz are the most conspicuous. The drama of the present day, if not rivaling that of England, of France, or of Germany, has certainly

[14] This traveler, Miss Pardoe, speaks of Schodel as "the very incarnation of soul;"—and says, in her lofty admiration, that the *cantatrice* "pours out her voice as if by inspiration." And it must be remembered that the writer was accustomed to visit the best theatres in the world.—*City of the Magyar*, vol. ii. p. 143.

been creditably sustained by the works of Bessenyi, Alexander and Karl Kisfaludy, Vörösmarty, and several others of almost equal reputation. The greatest tragic writer of modern times, among the Hungarians, was Ezako, who died in 1847, and whom his countrymen compare with Shakspeare; and his cotemporary, Esato, who, at the last accounts, was yet surviving, is the author of the finest comedies in the language. In his "Tiger and the Hyena," Petöfi, it is thought by critics, has passed over from the pure dramatic style to a sort of romance; and Eötvös, who has written some plays, is regarded as the living link between the fiction of the stage and the fiction of the closet.[15]

The Sir Walter Scott of Hungary, however, is the much-read, much-admired, and justly-celebrated Nicolaus Josika, to whom even his German critics award the very highest talent. His skill in technical composition is universally applauded. He makes his characters speak, not his language, but their own peculiar dialect. From the shepherd to the prince, he seems to understand, not simply the passions and principles of every clan and class of his numerous countrymen, but exactly the words which every one of them would use on every supposable occasion. His fancy is equal to his knowledge; and he works up his materials in a most effective manner. His predecessors in the same department—Kourgi, Dugonicz, Guadanyi, Kuthy and Kovacz—have been entirely eclipsed by him; and Joseph Eötvös, who, in his "Village Notary," has finely painted the life of a small officer, as well as Ignaz Nagy, whose "Secrets of Hungary" has vividly portrayed the unchangeable character and habits of the Jews, are not to be

[15] Literatur-Geschichte der Welt, von Dr. Johann George Theodore Grässe, Bibliothecar seiner Majestat des Königsvon Sachsen. Leipsig, 1848. The article on the Hungarian Drama excellently translated by that elegant scholar, Professor William Wells of Cincinnati, to whose paper, on a kindred subject, in the Feb. No. of the Ladies' Repository for 1851, I am also somewhat indebted.

compared with their great rival. Josika is a name to be remembered.

In almost every other country, ballads and romances have been the earliest of their literary efforts; but, in Hungary, though songs are ancient, novel-writing is the very latest form, which has been assumed by the literature of the nation. Late as it is, however, it has risen rapidly to the first place in quality, quantity and importance. Novels are now more read in Hungary than all other styles of writing. In 1838, there were two hundred and twenty-one works, from the paper-covered pamphlet to the full-bound volume, published in the native language, of which eighty-five were works of taste and fancy.[16]

It must not be imagined by the reader, who has had interest enough in this new and untrodden field of literature to work his way through the wilderness of names and dates, which, to be just to Hungary, it was necessary at least to point out to him, that the land of the Magyar, in spite of what has been hitherto said of it, is a land of the highest literary cultivation. It has produced names and works enough, it is true, to give it a marked position among the most enlightened countries; but there is only here and there an individual, out of the untold number of its writers, whose performances have had sufficient power to break the barriers of the nation and its language, and thus pass into general notoriety. Of the first class of authors, such as Milton, and Shakspeare, and Addison, Hungary has as yet produced not even one. Of the second class, in which our Dryden, and Pope, and Johnson, and Irving, and Bryant may be found, she has produced a few. Of the third, which, in every country, embraces the mass of its respectable writers, she has produced many of deserved renown. Between this very honorable class, who deal in books, and the very lowest, who get their names into the lists of authorship for

[16] City of the Magyar, vol. iii. p. 92.

having published a pamphlet, a play, a poem, an essay, a sermon, or a speech, she has produced a countless multitude, who, when taken in the aggregate, show well for the literary spirit of the nation.

It is not the authorship of Hungary, however, that gives her the highest claim to regard as an associate in the republic of letters. It is rather that she has acquired a taste for this profession and an ambition for this fellowship. If she does not now produce the first class of books, she has reached the point next below this lofty elevation. She reads them. The works of Göthe and Johnson, of Corneille and Camoens, of Burns and Byron, of Schiller and Shakspeare, are as much known in Pressburg, and as correctly criticised, as in London, Leipsic, or Lisbon. At Pesth there is a grand Casino, or reading-room, supplied with all the great quarterlies, magazines and newspapers of modern Europe; and on the hights of Buda, where the soldiery of Trajan were once mustered, the speeches of Cass and Canning, of Webster and Wilberforce, have been and are yet as commonly discussed, as in Westminster, or in Washington.

Decidedly the most promising trait, nevertheless, in the literary character of the Hungarians, is the one which constitutes the salient and closing topic of this chapter. It has come to see its own political importance. The great writers, in poetry and in prose, in philosophy and in science, in history and in belles-lettres, now fully understand, that the existence of the nation is only a part of the existence of its literature and language. They clearly perceive, that, should their language ever go out of use, the Magyars would instantly become Germans. We shall hereafter witness the connection of this feeling with the revolutionary history of the kingdom. One thing we can easily appreciate at this moment. We can behold the wonderful vitality of a language, which, in the very midst of a maelstrom of other languages, and repeatedly overwhelmed by successive waves and floods of them, has been able to hold on to life, and recently to put forth the manifestations of unabated activity and strength. As the nation, also, is now unanimously determined to preserve and perpetuate the language, so, if this determination is successful, the language will infallibly preserve and perpetuate the nation.

CHAPTER V.

THE HUNGARIAN CONSTITUTION.

The Hungarians, while living in their north-eastern home among the tribes of the Caucasus, are described by their native historians as a gentle, temperate, pastoral people, giving offence to no one, and taking it only after sufficient provocation.[1] Before their emigration from that country, however, they were compelled to become more warlike by the frequent attacks made upon them by the natives; and, in their subsequent wanderings toward the west, and particularly by their frequent encounters with the Alani and other fierce nations of the European forests, they progressed so rapidly in their military education, that, on their entrance into Hungary, they were regarded by the inhabitants, as well as by the Greeks, as the most martial and savage of barbarians.

The Greek emperor, Leo the Wise, has given a very graphic sketch of their appearance, manners, and spirit at that period. "The Hungarians," says the imperial historian, "are from their childhood horsemen. They do not like to walk. On their shoulders they carry long lances and spears—in their hands the bow; and they can use these weapons very skilfully. Their breasts, and the breasts of their horses, are protected by a breastplate of iron or of skins. Accustomed to fight with the arrow and the bow, they do not willingly come into close contact, but make battle from a distance. They attend carefully to every thing about them, but keep their own intentions very secret. They place numerous watches before their camp,

[1] Geschichte der Ungarn, by M. Horvath, Pesth, 1850, Part First, sec. ii. § 4, p. 14.

one quite separate from another, on which account it is difficult to surprise them. In battle, they divide their army into small companies, each containing about a thousand men, to which they give positions not far distant from each other. They have also a reserve corps, with which, if it is not brought into action, they lay snares for the enemy, or give needful succor to the yielding or thinned battalions. Their baggage they leave a mile or two on one side of the army, under the protection of a small detachment. It is a principal care not to extend their lines too much in breadth. Their single battalions are consequently deep, their front straight and dense. Their snares are laid by spreading the two wings of the army, and encircling the enemy, or by feigned retreats and quick returns. If the enemy flees, they pursue him as long as their horses can keep up the pursuit, or until they have annihilated their antagonist. Afterwards, they seek the booty. If the flying enemy retreats into a fortress, they watch for the succors to be sent him, and compel him either to surrender or capitulate."[2]

When not in war, the Hungarians spent their time in fishing, in hunting, and in pasturing cattle. With agriculture they had no acquaintance; and they knew only enough of mechanical trades to make their weapons and their clothing. When the pasturing grounds at any place were run over, they abandoned them for fresh localities, taking with them their tents, their herds, and all their property.[3]

So true were the ancient Magyars to the spirit of civil liberty, that, just as they were about to enter upon the subjugation of their new country, they called a general assembly of the people, discussed the political wants of the nation, and laid down the foundation of a free and popular constitution.

[2] Tact. cap. ii., Leo Sap.

[3] Horvath enumerates smiths, sword-makers, shoemakers, and manufacturers of bows. Part First, sec. ii. § 4.

The whole immigration, consisting of about one million of souls, had been divided by their first leader, Lebed,[4] into one hundred and eight tribes; and these tribes had been subsequently distributed into seven grand divisions, which, though entirely independent of each other in their private affairs, lived together as one people in the form of a general confederation. Each grand division acknowledged the supremacy of one principal leader, or duke, called a *woiwode;* and a convention of the woiwodes constituted the highest assembly, and exercised the supreme authority, of the nation. When met for the transaction of business, one of their number was elected temporary Oberhaupt, or chief, to whom this election gave no new powers as an officer of the government, but whose duty it was merely to preside in the assembly while in session. The convention of the woiwodes was not, in the usual sense, a legislative body; for it could make no laws, or regulations, binding upon the divisions, which affected their private business. Each division had its own municipal institutions; and each woiwode, when sitting in council with his equals, represented the predetermined wishes of his constituents. A majority of suffrages, however, in the assembly of the dukes, always gave direction to the federal operations of the nation, which embraced every question in which all the divisions were equally interested.

This republican mode of government, to which the Magyars seem to have been strongly attached from the very beginning of their history, with all its high value to a people sufficiently civilized to enjoy it, needed, in those warlike and barbarous times, a central power above that of a mere chairman of a chief assembly, and above the authority of a modern president, to give it promptness and energy of action. Necessity,

[4] The Greek historiographers, as well as the Hungarian Thuroczy, make Arpad the first leader; but Fessler, Horvath, and all the remaining Magyar historians give this distinction to Lebed.

which has been the creator and finisher of all constitutions, soon taught the Hungarians, that, unless some such central force was added to their popular confederation, their hoped success in the great undertaking of the nation, of searching out and subduing a new fatherland, in the face of vigilant and powerful enemies, would be impossible. Accordingly, just prior to their great irruption into Hungary, in a special convention of the woiwodes, and in the presence of the whole people, the deficiency was supplied by the election of a perpetual and hereditary Oberhaupt, or first duke, with whom the electors made a covenant in the most sacred and solemn manner. Each woiwode opened a vein in one of his arms. The blood thus shed, caught in a convenient vessel, was drank by the contracting parties. The ballots were then thrown, probably into the same vessel, for the new officer. The lot fell on Almos, one of their own number, whose bravery in battle, whose sagacity as a counseler, and whose virtues as a man, had marked him out as the one most fit for the enviable position. "From this day," said the woiwodes to Almos, "we elect you our head-chief and commander; and, wherever your fortunes lead you, we will follow."[5]

While the authority of the newly-elected officer was yet recent, and before it could become forgetful of the source from which it had arisen, the woiwodes took care to mark out distinctly the principal features of this reformed constitution of the Hungarian nation. In another convention of their number, with their Oberhaupt before them, they agreed upon and ratified the following stipulations: 1. That, from that day, the Oberhaupt should forever be elected from the family of Almos. 2. That, whatever should be acquired in their military expeditions, should be divided among the woiwodes, as the representatives of their respective divisions, according to their merits. 3. That the woiwodes, who had voluntarily elected

[5] Horvath, Geschichte der Ungarn, Part First, sec. i. p. 8.

Almos their Oberhaupt and commander, as well as the descendants of the woiwodes, should never be excluded by Almos, or by his successors, from the council of the commander, nor from the government of the fatherland. 4. That, should any of the woiwodes, or their descendants, break this covenant with the commander-in-chief, or sow discord among the woiwodes, his blood should be shed as the blood of the covenanting parties was then shed, while ratifying the national compact. 5. That, on the other hand, should the descendants of any of the Oberhaupts, or commanders-in-chief, or the descendants of any of the existing leaders (Stammhäupter) of the tribes, break this mutual pledge, the curse of outlawry should at once seize them; the curse should never be removed from such criminals, but rest on them eternally; and, of course, they were not only to be degraded from their offices, but excluded from the commonwealth by an act of irrevocable banishment.[6]

Under this modification of the original constitution of the country, there would seem to have been at least four classes, or estates, recognised by law. The Oberhaupt, or commander, the woiwodes, the officers under the woiwodes, who were the leaders of the tribes, and the common soldiery, are expressly mentioned. It is probable, also, from what appears to be inevitable to a nation passing from one country to another, that the soldiers by no means constituted the whole, if they did a majority, of the migrating horde; but that, led onward and defended by the warriors of the tribes, the great mass of the population, for various disabilities not prepared to fight, performed what other services they could, and were glad enough to be acknowledged as the useful, though somewhat servile, kindred of their armed and victorious brethren. While in the act of emigration, this portion of the people would feel themselves sufficiently compensated for any thing they could

[6] Horvath, Geschichte der Ungarn, Part First, sec. i. p. 8.

do, by receiving their necessary food, clothing, and protection. They would not claim any right of giving directions, or making rules and regulations, or performing any of the functions of government, or of legislation. By the force of their circumstances, without any thought on their part, and without any design on the part of their superiors, they would naturally acknowledge themselves to be simply peasants, or countrymen, who claim none of the rights of sovereignty, because they can do nothing of consequence for the sovereign.

The National Assembly would, therefore, be divided into two branches, though, in the transaction of business, they might meet together. The commander-in-chief, and the woiwodes by whom he was elected, would make one division. The leaders of the tribes, who were also officers of the army, and who were undoubtedly chosen by their military subordinates, would constitute the other. The inferior but more numerous branch, coming more directly from the body of the people, would naturally be regarded as the popular portion of the Assembly, while the king and his constituents would be looked upon as the aristocratic.

Arpad, the successor and the son of Almos, was the Joshua of the wandering Magyars. He led them into their country. For five years he fought the natives, and, at last, conquered them. He divided the land among his followers. But he had no sooner taken possession of the subjugated region, than he saw the impossibility of maintaining the supremacy of his race, without making radical improvements in the constitution of the nation. Consequently, calling in all the armies, which had been carrying the terror of the Hungarian name to the confines of Europe, he made a grand assembly of all the heads of the tribes on the Pustza Szeren, a beautiful plain near the banks of the Theiss, and, after a consultation of thirty-four days, gave to his people the third revision of the great charter of their liberties and institutions. Only one ancient author has spoken definitely of the results of this long deliberation;

and he is not known by name, though his extant productions are familiar to modern historians under the signature of the "anonymous" or "secret writer." He expressly declares, that, in the assembly here mentioned, "the rights and duties of the people, as well as the relations existing between them, the nobility and the prince, were more accurately set forth than they had been; that judges were appointed; and that the execution of the laws, and penalties for infracting them, were established."[7]

Though this account is extremely brief, it is long enough to convince the native historians of the country, that the division of the whole territory then conquered, as well as the entire system of municipal self-government, were at this time particularly secured to the Hungarian nation. It was the special care of Arpad, also, in the distribution of the lands, to raise up a class of servants capable of defending him and his successors against the heads of the tribes, and against the woiwodes, who, not forgetting how the commander-in-chief came by his great authority, had always conducted themselves toward him with too much independence, and sometimes with insolence. Without directly breaking any one of the five stipulations of the national compact, he effectually reduced the importance of these princes, by giving princely possessions to the most worthy and faithful of the people, who, not hoping to rival his influence, but looking to him for protection against the heads of the tribes and the woiwodes themselves, by whom the people were more directly governed, would have no interest opposite to his power and grandeur. All the castles of the country, with the extensive circumjacent regions belonging to them, Arpad took into his own hands, as the rightful property of the commander, whose duty it was to defend his subjects against domestic and foreign enemies. These numerous and valuable state domains he could not expect to hold in his own

[7] Horvath, Geschichte der Ungarn, Part First, sec. ii. § 3, p. 12.

person; nor could he deny the justice of the claim set up by the woiwodes and leaders, that, as the castles were seized by him as military fortresses, the possession if not the property of them was rightfully due to themselves, as his representatives in peace, and his adjutants and officers in war; but he was careful under what title he gave them the occupancy and management of such vast estates. He acknowledged them only as his agents, subsequently called *comites castri*, empowered to hold these national properties in his name, but claimed for himself the prerogative to change his representatives at pleasure, whenever he should find a change necessary to the public good. Thus, without saying so, he made all the castles of the country really his own property, and the property of his descendants, by which his and their authority was secured and established for all time to come.

If the castles were to be the *points d'apui* of the Hungarian system of defence; if the officers holding them were to be regarded, in a period of war, as the military representatives of the reigning commander, the soldiers ought to be settled near at hand, that they might be ready when an emergency should arise. Such was the order of the great Arpad; but, not satisfied with the existing establishment, which he had received from his father Almos, he instituted another army, by granting lands to those of his subjects, who were willing to become soldiers. This new army, which received its being and consequence from him, as well as the means of their individual subsistence in times of peace, though not set off into a separate corps, was ready to consider itself, nevertheless, not only as the defenders of their country, but as the special supporters of their prince.

This artful commander raised up another class of personal friends, whose descendants would be equally friendly to his dynasty, by giving lands to such worthy foreigners as had been found in the country at the conquest, and by offering similar grants to all others, of free and gentle birth, who might wish to leave their respective homes and become his subjects. In this way, he enriched his fatherland by the introduction of many thousands of the most enterprising citizens of the surrounding countries, at the same time that he added great strength and perpetuity to his own position.

Arpad, however, was as just and humane, as he was politic and ambitious. While engaged in subduing the mountains and the plains of Hungary, the majority of its population, it is true, had opposed him; they had fought hundreds of the bloodiest of battles to break his progress; they had protracted the struggle to a five years' war, and exercised a ferocious disposition towards the advancing Hungarians. A portion of the inhabitants, however, had made no resistance. To these, who, by the undiscriminating victors, were all known as Sclaves, he awarded personal freedom and their former properties and possessions. Such of them as had been magnates, were to be magnates still, whether they were really Sclaves, Goths, Scythians, or Romans. None, indeed, were reduced to servitude, but such as had actually fought against him, together with such persons of his own army as had been convicted of treason to his authority.[8]

Such, however, was the extent of the conquered country, compared with the number of those among whom it was thus distributed, that each recipient obtained a much larger grant than he could himself occupy. Nor, in fact, did he need to cultivate his own grounds; for, by the very side of him, though below him, there was a numerous class of his countrymen, who, as explained before, offered no claims to the territory into which they had been conducted. The land-owners, therefore, had only to cut up their respective tracts into con-

[8] When the Hungarians entered the country they found serfdom in general practice, the serfs being, probably, the subjected inhabitants of the successive conquests. Fessler's Die Geschichte der Ungern, Erster Band, sec. 323.

venient sections, and invite the unlanded population to settle down upon them. The terms of settlement were not, at that time, onerous. The doing of a little homage to the landlord, and the payment of a small rent-tax, gave the poor tenant a hereditary right to the usufruct of the soil he cultivated.

In the year 907, of the Christian era, Arpad, the most celebrated of all the Hungarian dukes, was carried to his grave amidst the regrets of a prosperous and contented people. Three of his successors, Sultan, Taksony, and Geisa, made no essential changes with the constitution thus established. The fourth, however, who was no less a personage than the renowned St. Stephen, may be regarded as the Solon of his nation. In the seventh year after his election, which took place in the autumn of 993, he became a convert to the Christian faith, and acknowledged the supremacy of the reigning pontiff. That pontiff encouraged his disciple to discard the old name of Oberhaupt, or duke, and put on the splendor of the regal title. Stephen was not an unwilling auditor to the arguments bestowed upon him; and he may not have seen the papal design of using him as a petted ally of the Vatican against the unchristian ambition of the German emperors. A golden crown, fabricated by the hands of angels, and sent to the pious successor of St. Peter by a celestial messenger, was delivered by human hands to Stephen. The royal novitiate received the gift with becoming gratitude; and, supported by the influence of the pope, as well as by that of his countrymen, who had made a profession of Christianity, and against a violent opposition set up by his pagan subjects, he undertook and completed a thorough revision of the Hungarian constitution.

Under his predecessors since the time of Arpad, the power of the magnates had been greatly weakened, while the royal authority had become more and more robust and settled. Still, it was quite evident to Stephen, as it must have been to any one having to perform his duties, that a yet greater contralization of power was demanded, unless the government should go back to that unlimited democracy, which, from actual necessity, had been willingly relinquished to his ancestor, Almos. Such a democracy, in a country the majority of whose population were ignorant and quite barbarous peasants, would have been certain ruin to every thing bearing the name of government; and if a monarchy was to exist at all, or meet the condition of such a heterogeneous and uncultivated people, it must have power enough to command the respect and obedience of all classes. When it is considered, also, that the era of this revisal of the Hungarian constitution was the same as that in which a feudal tyranny was established in Great Britain, the reader will be prepared to respect, rather than criticise, the charter of Magyar nationality, of which it is not difficult to give the leading propositions:

1. The throne of Hungary was secured forever to the family of Arpad. The king was to be the head of that portion of the Christian church which had been, or should be, established within his dominions. He was to possess the power of vetoing every enactment of the National Assembly, or Diet, without the designation of his reasons. He was to be capable of declaring war and peace. He, alone, could grant patents of nobility; and whatever property fell, by confiscation, to the state, was to be again given out by him to such persons as he might select to be the recipients of the royal bounty.

2. The judicial system was very simple. The king, by virtue of his office, was to be supreme judge throughout the kingdom. There was to be no appeal beyond his decision. To assist him in the administration of justice, as well as to represent his entire authority where he could not be present, he created a new officer, unknown to the constitution of Arpad, called by the Latin name of Palatine, because he was to be the first minister of the palace. The Palatine was to accompany the monarch, in all his judicial expeditions, to give him such aid as might be needful; and when the king should be

otherwise employed, or sick, or too infirm for active life, his place on the bench was to be supplied by the presence of his chief servant. The kingdom, however, might so increase in magnitude and population, and the business of this department might be so greatly multiplied in consequence of this growth, that the Palatine himself would not be sufficient for the demands of speedy and equal justice. An assistant judge, recognised by the German historians of the country under the name of *Hofrichter*, but more familiarly known to the Magyar lawyers by the Latin title of *comes curiæ regiæ*, was, therefore, appointed for each grand subdivision of the kingdom, called a county. For all trivial causes arising within a county, which were beneath the dignity of the higher judges, or too numerous for their personal attention, two inferior magistrates, entitled *judices regales*, were created. The course of appeal was always from the lower to the next higher court, till a cause had reached the ears of majesty, beyond whose supreme tribunal it was impossible to go. The royal decree was final.

3. The National Assembly, or Diet, originally composed of all the woiwodes, leaders and officers of the nation, was now to consist of the nobility, of which there were three orders. The first rank had been conferred, by the grateful and pious king, upon the ministers of the new religion, who, as missionaries from Rome, had endured incredible hardships in their glorious work of converting a country of pagans to the gospel. Next to the clergy were the descendants of the woiwodes, leaders and officers of the tribes—Volkshäupter and Stammhäupter—who are known in the decrees of Stephen, as well as in the modern nomenclature of the law-books, as *seniores domini*, whose nobility descended to them with their blood.[9] The third order, called *nobiles servientes regales*, included all other freemen, who were to exercise the right of suffrage.

[9] In Hungarian Latin they are styled *jobbagyones regis*. Geschichte der Ungarn, Part Second, c. i. sec. i. p. 34.

The practice of electing delegates to the assembly, however, was at that time unknown. All the noblemen, of every rank, could claim their place, when the nation met for the purposes of legislation; but it was not the custom, nevertheless, in that early day, to hold so general a convention of legislators. Wherever the monarch, or the Palatine, happened to make any stay, in the course of their official progresses, it was their habit to call together as many of the members of these three estates, as lived within a convenient distance, and lay before them such questions as might have arisen in their respective neighborhoods. This mode of legislation, though extremely inartificial, was quite equal to the wants of a simple, upright, and unsophisticated people; and, under a wise and good king like Stephen, it was as likely as any other to result in judicious arrangements, as no decision of the Assembly could become a law without the sanction of the monarch.

4. To perpetuate the existence and powers of the nobility, the new constitution protected their persons, by express statute, against all arbitrary arrests, though such arrests might be issued by the crown itself. In France, at a much later period, a royal *lettre de cachet* could put under custody, for a given time, the highest nobleman of the kingdom, without carrying upon its face the reasons of the act. In England, the personal liberty of the citizen was not secured till the year 1215, more than two centuries after this right was established in Hungary by the constitution of Stephen; and, in spite of the Magna Charta, by which the immunity was acknowledged to all English subjects, it was practically nullified by the kings of England till the beginning of the seventeenth century. The arbitrary imprisonments by the privy council, in the reign even of Elizabeth, have been lamented by modern historians and civilians.[10] In Hungary, on the contrary, there never was a

[10] Hallam's Constitutional History of England, vol. i. pp. 307–320, and Kent's Commentaries, vol. ii. part iv. pp. 26–37.

time when the citizen could be deprived of his personal liberty, excepting for an open insult to majesty or for treasonable conduct. The property, also, of the citizen was made absolutely inalienable, unless forfeited to the state by the crime of treason. The lower nobility, who had hitherto been subject to the Volkshäupter and Stammhäupter, or leaders of the tribes and people, were hereafter to be amenable, like the higher nobles, only to the monarch and his official representatives.

5. The military settlements, which had been made by Arpad around the castles, were to receive justice from the hands of a distinct class of officers, called *comites castri*, or by the synonymous but inelegant German appellation of Burggrafen; and for the defence of both the castles, and their circumjacent colonies, he raised up an order of knights, which the Hungarians entitled *jobbaggyones castri*, but to whom the Germans have given the characteristic cognomen of Burgunterthanen. They were to be entirely equal, in their privileges, to the other orders of nobility. Large properties were assigned them, out of the lands pertaining to the castles, the usufruct of which they were to have forever, by the payment of half of the produce to the Burggraf, who, after deducting a third part of this moiety for himself, delivered the balance to the king.[11] For their privileges, this class of noblemen were to be obligated, for all time, to defend the castles, and the lands and people belonging to them, from foreign invasion; and the better to carry out this purpose, they were arranged into battalions of one hundred, and these into companies of ten, under the general leadership of the Burggraf, whose subordinate representatives, called *comites parochiani*, controlled the smaller sections, and attended to the details of the command both in peace and war.

[11] If the Burggraf cheated the monarch of his dues, he was compelled to pay, as penalty, double the amount of the injury, besides making restitution. That is, he restored *threefold.* Stephani Decreta II. c. xlii.

6. Under the same jurisdiction were placed all those, who cultivated the domains belonging personally to the king, and of whom there were several grades. One class, denominated by the Magyars *Udvannok*, by the Germans Hofdiener, as rent-service for their lands, were to serve the king in whatever way he might desire, whenever he should visit the districts where they lived. Another class were the *Tarnok*, or Aufbewahrer, who had charge of the king's granaries and magazines, and were bound to pay implicit and perpetual obedience to his word. A third class were the royal grooms, or Pferdehüter, who were to keep the king's stables, and, it is probable, were to have the general oversight of his flocks and herds. The last of all were the *vinitores*, or vinedressers, who, in addition to the duty of furnishing the monarch with his supplies of wine, were to provide his table with every thing necessary to a royal board.

7. That portion of the population, which lived on the estates belonging to the nobility, were to be subject to their own landlords, though the property of the castles and the jurisdiction of the Burggrafen might, in some cases, extend beyond them. The nobles, imitating the manners of the king, were to hold their own courts, try whatever causes might arise among their tenants, and execute justice in their own way without the slightest interference from higher powers. Difficulties might occur, it is true, between the tenants, or peasantry, and the landlord himself; but such were to be settled as disturbances are allayed between a father and his children. There was no tribunal established by the monarch for the adjudication of such causes. The tenants were to share the produce of the lands cultivated by them with their masters, attend them in arms when commanded to do so, and do many other services, of a menial character, which might be called for at the courts and palaces of their manors.

8. Besides those inhabiting the possessions of the king and nobles, there was a large and respectable class of people, who

were denominated *freemen.* It consisted of persons manumitted from servitude by their landlords, called *duschenici*, and of immigrants from foreign countries, who were regarded as the guests—*hospites*—of the nation. They might hold any kind or any amount of property, as if they were the highest nobles of the country, by paying a small tribute—*liberorum denarii*—into the royal exchequer. Their persons were as inviolable as that of the wealthiest, or mightiest, nobleman. They were a much favored class. From the first, a uniformity of condition, as well as a common interest, induced them to settle down in groups, wherever they could find localities favorable to business. From these settlements have arisen the Hungarian cities.

9. It was the policy of Stephen to propagate Christianity, not by the sword, or by any open force, but by incorporating it into the constitution of his country. An outward homage to it, which passed for a profession, was the basis of the right, even in the noble, of holding landed property; and the chapters of the various episcopal dioceses were allowed to try certain civil causes, particularly those pertaining to inheritance and doweries, which properly belonged to the ordinary tribunals. As noblemen, therefore, the bishops had a seat in the National Assembly, and had great influence in making the laws of the land; as judges, they held a most conspicuous and powerful position, having the prerogative, in the most important topics of litigation, to determine the meaning and application of the laws when made; as large land-owners, with a vast number of the peasantry directly under them, they were equal to the highest magnates as citizens of the country; and, as ministers of the gospel, who were then supposed to have the authority to bind or loose the lofty and the low alike, and that for time and eternity, they exercised a power over and above the powers of all the other classes.

10. The mode established for trying causes in all the courts, but especially in that where the king presided, was very singu-

lar. A suit was opened by listening to the private statements of the parties. The points of agreement between the two statements, when closely compared by the judge, were stricken out. The next business of the bench was to increase the points of agreement, as far as it was possible, by putting questions and cross-questions to the litigants. The disagreements left, after this process had been carried to its utmost, were then examined, each party being allowed to sustain his report of facts by the testimony of sworn witnesses. The witnesses, however, could not be picked up at random. Only a freeman could give evidence against a freeman; against an ecclesiastic, only an ecclesiastic; and the same of every rank of the entire population. When a suit was acknowledged by the judge to have a genuine foundation, but, after all the testimony had been rendered, was regarded as yet doubtful, the disputants were allowed to decide it by what were then called God's judgments, which had been recommended to the king by the pope's ministers. He, who could hold a hot iron longest in his naked hand, or stand longest in a cauldron of hot water, or sit longest on some sharp instrument of torture, was declared victor. It was an unusual but perhaps salutary provision, that the lower judges had to answer for their decisions, if complained of by either of the parties at any time litigating before them; but, in case their sentence should be confirmed by the higher court, the complainant had to pay them a heavy sum of money.

11. Nothing was more singular, however, than the punishments fixed by Stephen for offences. The general principle followed by him seems to have been the *lex talionis*, which he had found in the works of Moses, and to which popery had given a revived existence in nearly all Christian countries. Some crimes, nevertheless, it is impossible to punish by retaliation. It was, therefore, ordered by the monarch, that traitors, calumniators of the king and nobles, and thieves who had been caught the third time in the act of stealing, should suffer death. Murderers, excepting one class of them, were not

hung, or punished capitally at all; but they paid the penalty of their crimes with money. The class excepted were those who took the lives of their victims by the use of swords; for the papal missionaries read the mandate to the king, which, according to their custom, they interpreted literally, "he that taketh the sword shall perish by the sword." For murdering his wife, a count paid fifty oxen; a nobleman, ten oxen; a Burgunterthan, five oxen. For the murder of a citizen, the freeman paid one hundred and ten pieces of gold to the nearest relatives. Incendiarism, perjury, the disturbing of the public peace, and stealing other men's wives, could be atoned for by the payment of fines, by fasting, and by passing through the prescribed penances of the church. The right of asylum, that bane of civil society in the middle ages, was extended to all crimes, excepting treason. The murderer, the robber, the thief, after perpetrating his iniquities, if pursued by the officers of the law, had only to flee to a church, to the king's court, or to some sacred place, and no law could touch him.[12]

12. In return for being entirely exempted from taxation, excepting as the products of the soil contributed by the peasantry were in part the landlord's property, the nobility were to be wholly responsible for the defence of the country against internal and external enemies. Every nobleman was by ne-

[12] This right of asylum is a pagan institution, and was recognised by the Greeks and Romans, who, when determined to punish the culprit taking refuge, would starve him to death by cutting off all supplies of food, as in the memorable case of Pausanias, or even burn down the building into which he had fled for shelter. With many other pagan ceremonies, the practice was adopted by the Catholics, from whom it spread into all modern countries. Pope Pius the Seventh was compelled to abolish it in his dominions; but his successor, Leo the Tenth, had the courage and the power to revive it. It was at once banished from most Protestant nations by the genius and spirit of the Reformation.

cessity a soldier. He was not permitted to employ a proxy. At the command of the king, he must equip himself, and go off to the field of battle. While his tenants were tilling his lands, and procuring the means of his support, he was justly held responsible for their safety. In this way, and not very unequally in that martial age, were the burdens of society distributed. If there was any difference, it was decidedly in favor of the peasant, who, unless he held lands in connection with a castle, or under a special military obligation, could expect to live in peace, and quietude, and plenty, even when his superiors were fighting, and toiling, and starving in the camp, or perishing by the hand of his country's enemies. The clergy themselves were bound to the same hard duty. Two armies, the royal and the national, were established by the monarch. The royal army consisted of the Burgunterthanen, led to the field by their Burggrafen, of those immigrants to whom the king had given lands on the condition of their performing military service, and of all others who had received substantial favors from the monarch, whether in the shape of property or of titles, with a similar understanding. These, in every way, were the king's troops. They were bound to him by personal obligations. They had acquired their social position from him; and they were, consequently, held under obligation to defend him and his kingdom from domestic or foreign injury. The national army, on the other hand, was made up of all those nobles, who had derived their estates from the national conquest, which, as we have seen, consisted chiefly of immense districts about the castles, and of all other noblemen, not belonging to the royal army, who thus paid for their personal freedom, and for all the privileges pertaining to their order. The royal army had for its special duty the internal protection of the country. The national army was to defend it against its enemies while they should be beyond its borders. Both, however, when an emergency demanded, were to be united into one body, or under one command, of which the king was to be forever the supreme commander.[13]

Such, in few words, was the constitution of Hungary, as established by the celebrated Stephen. If, in studying its details, the American reader should feel disposed to complain of some of its leading features, let it be remembered, that it was drawn up to meet the peculiarities of a people, whose position was without a parallel in the history of any nation; that, in most respects, it did meet those peculiarities better than they could have been met by the best constitutions of more recent and more enlightened countries; and that, in all respects, it was infinitely more wise, more liberal, more free, and better adapted to promote the happiness of the subject, than any constitution then existing. Indeed, in no other country, in the age now under consideration, can we find a methodical and written constitution of any kind, or character. When France and England were feudal monarchies, whose sovereigns were as absolute as the autocrat of the Russias, Hungary had led the way, and set the example to Europe and to the world, by raising up a constitutional state, in which every man knew his rights and duties, his relations and obligations, his condition and his prospects. And this knowledge has ever been considered, whatever be the form of society, as the chief advantage to be derived from civil governments.

For a little more than two centuries and a half, after the

[13] Horvath, Geschichte der Ungarn, Fessler Die Geschichte der Ungern, Paget's Hungary and Transylvania, Smith's Parallels between the Constitution and Constitutional History of England and Hungary, together with various articles published in the European and American magazines, particularly a splendid article in the Christian Examiner by the lady of the Rev. Dr. Putnam, of Roxbury, Massachusetts, are the principal sources from which I have derived the materials of this abstract of the Constitution of St. Stephen. Horvath, however, is my chief authority. Geschichte der Ungarn, Part Second, cap. i. sec. i. pp. 31–37.

death of Stephen, the Hungarian constitution, as last described, was administered by the king and higher nobility. The lower nobles, including the freemen of the cities, though members of the National Assembly, by virtue of their rank, never claimed to exercise their privilege, so far as history can ascertain the facts, till the year 1298, when Andrew the Third, by the advice of the archbishop of Kalocza, summoned all classes of the nobility to meet him on the famed Rakos' Field, which skirts the modern city of Pesth, now the capital of the nation.[14] The object of the monarch was to set bounds to the almost unlimited influence of the Burggrafen, or Grafs, as they had begun to be called, and of the titled nobility, or Barons, who, though they had received every thing from the beneficence of the crown, had gradually settled down into a complete sympathy and union with the Grafs. This united body of magnates had exercised too great an authority in the kingdom. The constitution of the great lawgiver had all the while been developing itself, as one emergency after another had presented demands for changes and additions; but the larger part of this growth was entirely aristocratic, giving more and more consequence to the higher nobles, but no new importance to the lower. Both the king and the lesser nobles, indeed, had been great sufferers. Andrew, however, at the period mentioned, found himself in a position to raise an open and direct opposition to this dangerous tendency of the constitution. He was the particular friend of the House of Hapsburg. He had formed a private alliance with Albert, the son of the celebrated Rhodolph. He had espoused the beautiful Agnes, Albert's daughter, whose charms were as powerful at court as

[14] Engel speaks of a similar Assembly in the year 1061; but all other historians, so far as I have been able to consult them, regard the one mentioned here as the first on record, of whose object and proceedings we have any definite information. Paget, who seems to have taken some pains to study the subject, agrees with their opinion Hungary and Transylvania, vol. i. p. 147.

the sceptre of her father. When the Hungarian nation, at the call of their lawful sovereign, flocked to the field of Rákos, they found there a prince determined to give the inferior class of citizens the place of power in the future direction of the government. The magnates, it is true, called a separate council of their order; but the smaller nobility, supported by the king and clergy, asserted their rights with such emphasis, that the magnates were compelled to yield, and consent to share the responsibilities of government with their more numerous and more democratic brethren. From that moment, in fact, we are to date that remarkable and indomitable spirit of democracy, which has shown itself triumphant in all the subsequent history of the country. Indeed, at the time here designated, the three estates of the kingdom—the king, the magnates, and the gentry—took their independent positions, and made the first distinctly visible manifestations of the Hungarian constitution, as it has existed for the five centuries preceding the late revolution.

During these five hundred years, the National Assembly has been composed of the three orders, whose powers, prerogatives, and privileges have been, in nearly all respects, very clearly stated and understood. The general duties and objects of the Assembly itself have been summed up by a native writer, whose works, until recently, have formed the principal source of information respecting the manners and customs of his country: "To maintain the old Magyar Constitution; to support it by constitutional laws; to assert and secure the rights, liberties and ancient customs of the nation; to frame laws for particular cases; to grant supplies and to fix the manner of their collection; to provide means for securing the independence of the kingdom, its safety from foreign influence, and its deliverance from all enemies; to examine and encourage public undertakings and establishments of general utility; to superintend the mint; to confer on foreigners the privileges of nobility, together with the permission to colonize the country, and to enjoy the rights of Hungarians, are the important functions of the Hungarian Diet."[15]

This National Assembly, as it existed prior to the recent revolutionary struggle, may be studied as the most actual and reliable exponent of the constitution in its modern form. Its supreme head, no longer a Magyar of the house of Almos, or of Arpad, but an Austrian of the family of the Hapsburgs, was still known by the title of King of Hungary, whatever he might be called in any other countries under his dominion. Though no more, as his predecessors had been till a comparatively recent date, an elective prince, but claiming his seat upon the throne as a hereditary right, he was, nevertheless, sworn to administer the government of the nation according to its constitution, laws and usages. Though a foreigner, he was looked upon, in virtue of his office, as a native citizen; and since, according to the fundamental idea of the government, as held by his subjects, every enactment must be ratified by the whole nation, no act of the National Assembly could become a law without his approval. Indeed, the nation could not meet for legislative purposes without his consent; as he exercised the power of calling and dispersing the Assembly at his will. Until new laws were made, however, the king was sworn to administer the affairs of the country according to those already existing; and hence this prerogative of royalty amounted only to this—that the monarch could hinder the nation from making progress in its institutions. When the laws were made, he was their sole executor, since all the executive officers of the government represented him, and existed by his appointment; and, therefore, whenever any enactment of the legislative body was opposite to his interests,

[15] In this nearly complete enumeration of the powers of the Assembly, Fessler merely transcribes the language of the Assembly itself, employed at different times and under various circumstances. Every item mentioned has a separate history.

he could do much to alter, or weaken, if not to annihilate its sense, by the manner in which he might please to enforce it. But the meaning of the laws was much more at his disposal, since, by the theory of the constitution, he was acknowledged to be the *fons et origo jurisdictionis* in all the courts of justice. The presiding judge and all the councillors of the Supreme Court, or Curia Regia, received their dignities and the measure of their duties from him; and the district courts, which arose from the tribunals of the Burggräfen, and which are distributed over all the kingdom, were almost equally at his dictation. His wishes, therefore, had only to be signified to his judicial representatives and servants to insure such a degree of subserviency, in the interpretation of the laws, as would best support his objects. The people, it is true, in any such case of royal iniquity and oppression, stood all around the throne ready to make resistance; but, on the other hand, by the constitution of the country, the man sitting upon that throne, as commander of the army, could defend himself by calling upon the entire military establishment of the nation to maintain his authority. The support of the army, however, it may be replied, was in the power of the people, who, by resolution of the National Diet, granted all supplies and subsidies; but, as if to meet and check this popular reservation, the king was sole master of the mint, and, for a time at least, could control the hoarded treasure of the nation. If he chose to be an arbitrary sovereign, indeed, he was possessed of other powers, which could not fail to give him such personal wealth, as would make him a dangerous opponent to the whole people. He had the right to nominate every officer of the government, excepting only the Palatine, who was chosen by the Diet, the lieutenants of the counties, fifty-two in number, and the two officers into whose hands had been entrusted the crown and other regalia of the kingdom. As no persons, besides those thus nominated, could be raised to office, a despotic and peculating prince could secure immense revenues,

12

almost enough for his worst purposes, by selling the exercise of his prerogative, as has often been the practice, to the highest bidders. By the law entitled the *jus successionis*, the king inherited all the estates of the nobility, on the extinction of the male heirs of their respective families; and, if a bad prince, he could acquire vast pecuniary influence, and indeed possessions, from another royal privilege, by which he was made the legal guardian of all orphans. The means of popular intelligence were, also, very much at his disposal; he claimed a censorship of the press and the entire management of the post-office system; so that, in the event of any design, on his part, against the liberties of the people, he could greatly hinder, if not entirely suppress, all public expression of disapprobation, as well as the general circulation of the facts on which any disapprobation might be grounded. If, however, discontent did happen to spread among the population, he had the means, as lawful head of the state church, of swaying popular opinion in a manner, and to an extent, at all times alarming. He gave to every bishop, and high ecclesiastical dignitary, his position and his bread; and he thereby made himself felt, and that most effectually, in every pulpit; and the pulpits themselves, over all the kingdom, constantly echoed his voice, and taught the masses to mingle his authority with the authority of Him, whom all men are bound to reverence. At his own pleasure, without even asking the opinion of the nation, he could, at any time, declare war and make peace; and all moneys raised by vote of the Assembly, as well as the ordinary revenues of the kingdom, to whatever purpose they may have been granted or applied, were, when raised, completely in his power. He could devote them to what ends he would. It is, therefore, plain, that, against an officer clothed with such manifold authority, it would be generally impossible to make resistance, should he be set toward despotic measures, without the most evident approaches, at least, to a revolution.

The Palatine of Hungary was chosen by the Diet out of four magnates nominated by the crown. He was, consequently, as much the officer of the people as the representative of the king. In all his duties, indeed, as president of the upper chamber in the National Assembly, and as first judge of the Curia Regia, he was justly looked upon as a constitutional mediator, at all times of necessity, between the nation and the throne. His position, however, was one of great difficulty. Both parties were liable to suspect him. He never dared to assume any regal splendor, even when representing the monarch at the seat of government, for fear of exciting the jealousy of the court; and his prudent submission to the suspicions of the court rendered him an object of popular distrust. But if really just and impartial, his administration was always successful in winning the gratitude of the Hungarians, who, in that event, always covered the memory of his name with their heartiest blessings.

The superior department of the National Assembly, called the Chamber of Magnates, was composed of the higher clergy, the barons and counts of the kingdom, and those who were magnates by birth and title. Thirty-five bishops and archbishops of the Catholic Church, headed by the powerful and and princely archbishop of Gran, and one bishop of the Greek Church, constituted the clerical portion of this chamber. Fourteen of the highest officers of state, and the fifty-two official counts of Hungary, sat there with the title of *barones et comites regni*, and made up the second section. The third included all titled princes, barons, counts, not holding office, but whose right to a seat in parliament had descended to them from their ancestors. The character of this chamber was entirely regal, since all but three of its proud members—the Palatine and the two Guardians of the Regalia—were nominated by the monarch, and sat there to watch and defend his interests. Its powers, however, were quite restricted. It could initiate no measure, nor propose amendments to measures, but only approve or disapprove of such bills as came to it from the popular branch of the Assembly. Though its prerogatives as a body were well determined, the comparative rights of its three classes of members had not been entirely settled, as it was yet disputed whether the titular magnates had the privilege of voting on certain questions. By some of the Palatines, while presiding over its deliberations, the general maxim had been laid down and observed—*vota non numerantur, sed ponderantur*—but by what principle this *weighing* of votes was to be conducted, or by whom the scales were to be held, were topics not fixed by any decrees or statutes of the kingdom. The positive power of this chamber, therefore, though it represented at least three-fourths of the wealth and aristocracy of the country, was really small in any great discussion, which concentrated the attention of the public. Its reputation, too, had been greatly humbled by the reckless avarice of the Austro-Hungarian monarchs, who, it is well known, had not scrupled to fill their coffers, as well as to support their ambitious schemes, by selling patents of nobility to all those willing and able to pay the price ![16]

The President of the Chamber of Deputies, called the Personalis, was appointed directly by the king; and, besides his duties as presiding officer, he was expected to understand, and to represent to the people, the wishes of the crown. Of the remaining members, one hundred and four were the representatives of the fifty-two counties of the kingdom, each

[16] Austria has always been fond of selling her imperial honors without much regard to the previous dignity of the purchasers. All Europe had the pleasure of laughing, only a few years ago, when Stultz, the London tailor, was made a Baron for £10,000. The common price of the title is only £2000; but Stultz, poor fellow, had to pay five prices in consideration of his being raised so high from so low a rank. It has not been recorded, I believe, whether Baron Stultz made any better breeches after than before his elevation! Paget, vol. i. p. 244.

county having the right to send two delegates. The boroughs and towns, also, as well as all the provinces attached to Hungary, had a just proportion of representatives in this chamber. All came there by popular election. They were bound, by the oath of office, to express and carry out the wishes of their constituents, according to such instructions as those constituents had given them.

The National Assembly was generally opened by a speech from the throne, or from the Palatine, in which the crown presented such propositions as it wished to have come up for deliberation. Before proceeding to the regular and official business of a session, the lower department of the legislature were accustomed to hold informal meetings, called Circular Sessions, where the questions to be determined by legal vote, in its subsequent and constitutional meetings, were discussed with great freedom. Each deputy had a right to speak, on every measure, as often as he could get a hearing. When these preliminary debates were over, and the affairs of the nation had been put into some proper shape, the house resolved itself into its more legal form, and undertook the reexamination of each question, under the more stringent rules which governed its regular proceedings. Upon the passage of a bill, in this chamber, it was sent to the Chamber of Magnates for their approval. If not approved in the upper house, it was returned to the deputies, who might continue to discuss and pass it, as long and as often as they might hope, by this means, to bring the magnates to their opinion. It could not, however, go before the king, until it received this superior sanction; and when it did receive it, the monarch might reject it, and throw it back upon the Assembly, without assigning any reasons to justify his disapprobation. If, notwithstanding these obstacles, it obtained the assent of the magnates and the signature of the king, it had another difficulty to encounter, before it could be enforced, which, properly to understand, will require a brief exposition of the last resort and absolutely impregnable bulwark of the liberties of the Hungarian nation.

From the earliest period of its history, beyond which "the memory of man runneth not to the contrary," the counties of Hungary have enjoyed all the rights of private municipal independence. According to the original customs, which were not disturbed by the constitutions of Almos, of Arpad, and of Stephen, the one hundred and eight tribes of the people were entirely independent of each other; and, though it is impossible now to tell precisely how these tribes became fifty-two rather than fifty-four counties, it is certain that the counties have always been more like an assemblage of small but perfectly free republics, than merely political subdivisions of one common country. The principle by which they have been held together, under a general head, has been that of a constitutional confederation. Each of them has ever had a distinct existence, and exercised all the important functions of an independent state. Within the limits of the county, thus free as a whole, all the inhabitants, whether noble or not noble, Magyar, Sclave and Saxon, excluding only criminals, vagrants, and captives taken in battle, which are excluded in all countries, have always stood, at the bottom of the social organization, on one common level. As the kingdom is divided into counties, so the counties are made up of villages; and the magistrates of the villages, who have a more immediate bearing upon the daily welfare of the population, than all the other officers of the government together, have been elected to their posts, not by the nobles only, but by the universal suffrage of all the people, from the wealthiest prince down to the most needy peasant. The peasants, therefore, to a very great degree, have had the government of their neighborhoods and homes at their own discretion; and their wishes, conveyed to the county meetings by their own magistrates, have generally had a due influence upon the deliberations of those larger gatherings.

The constitution of the country was, consequently, at the foundation, absolutely democratic; and the aristocratic and monarchical elements, according to the original theory of the government, were combined with the democratic with almost a mathematical symmetry and order. The officers or representatives of the countless villages were elected by all the people; the representatives of the fifty-two counties were elected by those called nobles, who, by this title, were known simply to enjoy the freedom, or suffrage, of the county; the representative of the legislature, the centre and executor of its authority, was elected by a still smaller number, called magnates, who may be said to have exercised the freedom of the capital. Originally, all the officers of the country were elective; and each class of the people appointed its own officers, or agents. The majority of the inhabitants were simply countrymen, who were to cultivate the soil, and to live in peace, under the protection of those bound to military service; and hence only such questions as affected their flocks and herds, their trades and traffic, their homes and firesides, were submitted to the disposal of their magistrates. The question of defense, on the contrary, with all its relations to revenue and to general legislation, was the question of the defenders, or noblemen, who could rightly claim to have the management of their own business. The supreme command of this martial force naturally belonged to the whole body of those having the inferior command; but these soon found it necessary, or convenient, to delegate this high authority to some one individual of their number, either by frequent election, or for the term of life.

The whole people, therefore, through their village officers, could speak directly to the assembled noblemen of the counties; the counties, by their representatives, were listened to in the National Assembly; and the National Assembly, by means appointed for the purpose, could address words of authority to the king. It was easy, therefore, for power to run from the many to the few, and from the few to the one, till, from the most distant circumference, it had reached the centre. It was impossible, however, without the consent of the different circles of the population, that power should proceed from the centre to that circumference. It is to be distinctly understood, that the king could only lay his *propositions* before the National Assembly; the National Assembly could transform those propositions, as well as its own motions, into legislative *enactments;* but, what was the grand security of the liberties, freedom and happiness of the people, no enactment could become a *law*, within the limits of a county, until acknowledged and ratified by its own inhabitants.

Thus, the constitution of the Hungarian nation, at first entirely democratic, successively assumed to itself, to meet new wants, aristocratic and monarchic powers; and these, in the maturity of its being, before it had been tampered with by foreign tyrants, were more fittingly combined, more nicely mixed, than in any nation they had ever been before, or have been since. It was emphatically a free constitution, because, though recognising the existence of aristocratic and regal powers, the whole people were acknowledged as the last tribunal, before which every wish of the king, and every motion of the legislative body, had to pass to obtain the authority of a legal regulation.

CHAPTER VI.

EXTERNAL RELATIONS OF THE COUNTRY.

When the Hungarians crossed the Carpathians and entered into their present country, and from that period to the corona tion of St. Stephen, all Europe was in the act of passing from under the yoke of Roman despotism, and of creating for itself new states and empires.

In Italy, the Romans had submitted to the Ostrogoths, the Ostrogoths to the Lombards, the Lombards to the French, and the French to the Germans, who, at the beginning of the eleventh century, took possession of the entire country, as far south as the States of the Church, excepting the territories belonging to the Venetian and Genoese republics. These two cities, however, were rapidly rising to importance. Genoa, shaking off her servitude to France, could not be conquered by the Germans. Venice, driven from the land by successive bands of barbarians, had fled to a little nest of neighboring islands, and was extending her dominion over the bays and bosom of the Adriatic. The territory of the Church, which had been usurped by the See of Rome, when the empire was falling, had been legally recognised by the French, as well as by the Teutonic, sovereigns. Constantinople, also, was still standing; but it was standing as a monument to discord, and tottering to its dissolution. East of it, on the banks of the Tigris, sat the city of Bagdat mourning like a captive, as she beheld the hand of the Turk, whom she had hired as a servant, grasp and brandish the still powerful sceptre of the Arab, while the glory of her Caliphs was departing. On the north-east of the Hungarian fatherland was the country of the

Rossi, or Russians, but their name was better known to geographers than to statesmen. West of this region of the Rossi was the land of the Poles, which, in the very year of Stephen's coronation, was erected by Otho the Third into a separate and independent kingdom. Germany itself, however, with the spoils of the empire of Charlemagne, and with nearly as large a territory as ever cowered beneath the domination of the Cæsars, was comparatively feeble. When Arpad set his foot in Hungary, the name of his race was a terror to all these nations; his three successors, Soltan, Taksony and Geisa, compelled both the Germans and the Greeks to pay them tribute, as a reward for their promised quiet; and, throughout the west and south of Europe, the liturgy of the churches taught the devout worshipers to pray—"Good Lord, deliver us from the Hungarians."[1]

These Hungarians, it must be admitted, were at that time very barbarous; but the inhabitants of nearly all the European countries were almost as much wanting in knowledge and refinement. The era of this singular immigration was the gloomiest period, the very midnight, of the middle ages. The Catholic religion, corrupt enough in itself, had been still more corrupted upon the conversion of the savages, by whom the Romans had been conquered. The simple rites of the apostolic church, after their first aggrandizement by being made to put on the pomp of the Jewish temple-service, had been degraded by the indecencies and vulgarities of the Celtic, Teutonic and Scandinavian worship. Many of the new ceremonies, which had been thus incorporated into the Christian system, were as scandalous as the mysteries of Elusus, or the

[1] From Almos to Stephen there were six dukes inclusive. Their reigns were these: Almos, 885–889; Arpad, 889–907; Soltan, 907–946; Taksony, 946–972; Geisa, 972–997; Stephen, till he assumed the regal title, 997–1000. Horvath, Geschichte der Ungarn, Part First, pp. 2–30.

orgies of the drunken Bacchants. At the very time, when the sanctimonious papists were supplicating Heaven's favor against the savages of Hungary, they were annually celebrating what they styled the Feast of the Ass, in the oldest and largest of their cathedrals. The object of this festival was to commemorate the flight of the virgin into Egypt. The ceremony will serve to manifest the darkness of that epoch. A beautiful young lady, dressed in a Jewish habit, with a young child folded in her arms, was seated upon an ass, which was adorned with the most gorgeous trappings. The animal had been practiced for the part expected of him. Going quietly along, from the place appointed for the gathering of the people, toward the door of the church, he entered the sanctuary of God in solemn order, while the assembled thousands followed him in one vast procession. While the multitude were thronging to their seats, below and above, the beast went forward, bearing the damsel and the child, and stood before the altar. The services of high mass now commenced. At the ringing of the little bell, which was the signal to the worshipers to fall upon their knees, the beast knelt with them. He arose, also, with the uprising of the people. At the conclusion of the service, which was full of all sorts of blasphemy and indecency, the priest dismissed the assembly, not by the usual benediction, but by braying three times like an ass, in recognition of the three persons of the holy Trinity; the people brayed three responses; and often the ass himself, either by the lessons given him, or catching the fit by a spirit of imitation, united his own bellowings to the inhuman chorus. This was Catholicism, this the civilization of central and western Europe, when the Magyars settled down, under their first king, on the soil purchased by their valor.

The regal dynasty of the house of Almos, or of Arpad, on the male side, which followed the dissolution of the ducal sovereignty, lasted from the year 1000 to 1301, when it came to a close by the death of Andreas the Third, in whom the male line of his family became extinct.[a] Among all the princes, who filled up this wide space in the history of their nation, not more than five or six of them did any thing worthy of special record. Bela the First is celebrated by the Magyars as the king who introduced the coinage of silver into Hungary. He also made regulations concerning weights and measures, fixed the prices of the leading agricultural products, and established a system of internal commerce. It was his reign, in fact, which transformed his countrymen from a race of herdsmen to a nation of agriculturists and merchants. Ladislaus the First, who, in our day, would be recognized as a statesman, had he not been in his own age canonized as a saint, is famous for having perfected the civil and social institutions, which Stephen had begun. Stephen, as we have seen, was the founder of the Hungarian constitution. Ladislaus the First developed and expanded its various provisions into laws. He has been almost equally renowned, by the religious of every succeeding generation, as the royal apostle, by whose piety and discretion the last remnants of paganism were subdued. When he died, the country went into sincere and solemn mourning, scarcely rivaled in the history of any monarch. For three whole years, there was not a festival, nor the sound of any instrument of music, in all the land which he had blest

[a] This dynasty embraced twenty-one monarchs, whose reigns began and terminated thus: Stephen, 1000–1038; Peter I., 1038–1040; Samuel, 1040–1044; Peter II., 1044–1046; Andreas I., 1046–1061; Bela I., 1061–1063; Salamon, 1063–1074; Geisa I., 1074–1077; St. Ladislaus, 1077–1095; Koloman, 1095–1114; Stephen II., 1114–1131; Bela II., 1131–1151; Geisa II., 1151–1161; Stephen III., 1161–1173; Bela III., 1173–1195; Emrich, 1195–1204; Andreas II., 1205–1235; Bela IV., 1235–1270; Stephen V., 1270–1272; Ladislaus II., 1272–1290; Andreas III., 1290–1301. These dates are made out by a comparison of several Magyar and German historians. Horvath, however, where he uses figures, is my leading authority till the reign of Koloman.

and left. His successor, Koloman, a person of very mean appearance, in intellectual and moral qualities was truly great. He undertook to carry out the unfinished designs of his predecessor. He is worthy of all admiration for his magnanimity, for his patriotism, and for his legislative talent. He seemed to have, in all his efforts, the highest of purposes in view. He wished, above every thing else, to make the spirit of the Christian religion the basis of the government, to secure the independence of the country by guaranteeing the liberties of the people, and, as a final support to all the blessings of a free nation, to give all needful power to the requirements, and to the representatives, of law. In many of his regulations, as well as in the general tenor of his administration, he was several centuries before the temper of his times. In one of his statutes it was decreed, that no more prosecutions should be made against witches, not because such proceedings were unnecessary, or inhuman, or impolitic, or beyond the reach of civil government, but simply because "there were no such beings as witches in the world."[3] Rather than involve his country in a religious war, he resigned to the pope the right of nominating priests and bishops, which he had exercised, without personal benefit, before. Such was the wisdom of his policy, that Hungary began to be regarded with admiration, or with envy, by surrounding nations. He introduced her, indeed, to the fellowship of the European countries; and, as a help to the external commerce of his subjects, to which his own administration had given birth, he levied the first tax ever known in this tax-hating land. It was a tax of five per-centum on imports and exports. It was followed by the

[3] It is known, however, that the practice was not entirely abolished. A witch was burnt, at Szegedin, so late as the reign of Maria Theresa. The son of the unhappy victim of superstition became first a *monk*, and afterwards a *novelist!* His name was Dugoniez. Pulsky's Introduction, p. 38.

tributum fori, or market-tax, and by direct taxes on freemen and on foreigners. Such was the honor in which this king was held, that his very taxes added to his popularity!

The limits of the kingdom were extended by the valor of this race of princes. Ladislaus the First, whose sword was as ready as his pen, conquered Sclavonia and Croatia in the year 1089; and, in 1102, Koloman took Dalmatia from the Venetians, who, in that age, were beginning to be one of the great powers of Europe. The Rossi, who then inhabited the territory next north of Hungary, now known as Gallicia, had previously been humbled by Salamon and by Ladislaus. The people of Moravia, too, who were also Sclavic, in attempting to foment disturbances between their kindred in Hungary and the Magyar government, were severely punished by more than one of these patriotic and powerful monarchs. At the death of Koloman, in 1114, Hungary had entirely passed the line that divides the Asiatic from the European style of civilization, and begun to enter into the system and fellowship of the European states.

This era, however, was followed by a long period of weakness, servility and disgrace. From 1114 to 1205, the country of the Magyars was ruled by the policy, as well as by the whims, of Constantinople. The Greeks, always a deep and facile people, repining over their eastern losses, wished to make amends by extending their influence toward the west. Not daring to attack so brave and warlike a race, as that of Hungary, they courted the princes and flattered the vanity of the nation. The Magyars were welcomed to the great metropolis of Christendom. The schools of the city, the marts of trade, and the places of amusement, were freely opened to them. A young Hungarian looked upon it as the last goal of fortune, if he could leave the rustic plains of his native land, proceed to the seat and centre of all splendor, initiate himself into the graces of some Grecian family, and either settle down among his benefactors, or return to his home the husband of a lady, whose eyes sparkled with the fire of her proud ancestry, whose lips dropped the accents of Aspasia, and whose heart claimed alliance with Pericles and Plato. Hungary, during all this time, turned her eyes as much as possible from every other part of Europe, and looked to the banks of the Dardanelles as the El-Dorado of the nation.

Andreas the Third, however, the last of this family of princes, was an exception to this general statement. He was by no means a Grecian. He saw with regret the tendency of his people toward the temptations held out to them at Constantinople. Himself nursed by a Venetian mother, and educated under German and Italian influences, he looked to Italy, or to Germany, for sympathy, for friendship, for alliances. He formed a close connection with the German emperor, made frequent visits to his imperial residence, and, in 1296, married Agnes, the beautiful daughter of the Austrian Albert. The nation, indeed, inclined toward the Greeks. The government of the nation was rather German.[4]

During the existence of this dynasty, and mostly between the reigns of Ladislaus the First and Andreas the Second, Hungary was united to Europe as it had never been before, and as it never will be again. The time spoken of was the period of the crusades. Those vast hordes of men, flocking from every European country to the Holy Land, took the road, which all travel and all commerce, between the east and the west, would be sure to take, were it not closed and guarded by the jealousy of a short-sighted and despotic rule. They went to Asia over the plains of Hungary. On reaching the boundaries of the kingdom, they were ordinarily met by an army headed by the monarch, who undertook to conduct them across his dominions, as much to defend his subjects against

[4] It is a notable fact, not mentioned, I believe, in English history, that Bela III. married Margaret, sister to the French king, and widow of one of the Henries of old England.

lawless violence, as to do honor to the object of their enter prise. This royal escort was not always sufficient to keep in subordination the rampant soldiers of the cross. Massacres, battles, encampments, and other military delays, occurred, by which the inhabitants of every part of Europe gained the opportunity of becoming personally acquainted with the people, position and products of this new Eden of the world. Many, indeed, tired of their pompous and empty undertaking, on their return from Palestine, some on their way to it, relinquished a life of religious but bootless chivalry, to settle down upon the soil of this enchanting land. They brought with them their languages, their predilections, and their foreign associations. Having friends in other countries, their epistles and messages were filled with information respecting their new home, and their urgent invitations brought many of their kindred to join them in their new career. Hungary, so long an unknown region, a *terra incognita*, to many countries of Europe, was in this way revealed to all.

When the last of this race of monarchs took his position upon the throne, Europe was in a very different condition from that in which it was at the opening of the eleventh century, when this dynasty began. For one century and a half, it may be truly said, Europe had been away from home. She had been abroad in Asia. On the way there, she had mingled her multiplied populations into one common mass, whose object, spirit and sympathies were the same. In this manner, Europe had become acquainted with herself. While residing in Asia, she had made the acquaintance of many new people, of people never dreamed of before. She had found, too, that the Asiatics, including the Mussulmans and Turks, were not the barbarians she had supposed them to be, but even more learned, more civilized, more elegant in their style of life than the Europeans themselves. Both going and returning, while the great hordes had marched through Hungary, several of the smaller and selecter bands, led by some of the first characters of that age, had taken their route through Rome, where, by personal observation, they had acquired a conviction that popery at home was far from being what popery was supposed to be abroad. Religious fanaticism had thus declined. The intercourse thus originated, between the inhabitants of different countries, had given to national fanaticism a mortal blow. The craft of kings had been wounded at the most vital part. To raise funds for the sustenance of their huge armies, the princes had sold charters of liberty to many towns and cities, which, not only by tens and scores, but by hundreds even, had risen up in France, in Germany, in Italy, and in every European land. Hungary, which had united in the movement, by which the three known quarters of the globe had been roused and brought together, shared, also, in its beneficent results. At this moment, and by this instrumentality, for the first time in her history, she became strictly and fully European.[5]

The third of the several lines of Hungarian sovereigns may be termed the female dynasty of the house of Almos. When the male heirs of the crown became extinct, by the death of Andreas the Third, who was taken off by poison, the noted Charles Robert, duke of Anjou, grandson of Bela the Fourth on the female side, was elevated to the vacant throne; and eight of his ten successors, who constitute the dynasty he began, had the blood of the first Hungarian Oberhaupt, derived exactly as Charles Robert himself had derived it, running in their veins.[6]

[5] The reader, who wishes to trace the influences of this grand period more minutely, than would be consistent with my limits, may consult Abel Rémusat's "Memoires sur les Relations Politiques des Princes Chretiens avee les Empereurs Mongols," pp. 154–157, and Guizot's History of Civilization, p. 206, where the leading passage of the great orientalist is largely quoted.

[6] The following are the names and reigns of this female line: Charles Robert, 1307–1342; Louis the Great, 1342–1382; Maria,

With this race of kings a new era in Hungarian history takes its rise. By the talents and virtues of her native princes, Hungary had been raised from a horde of barbarous nomades to the settled and civilized condition of a state; and some of the last of these princes, carrying the work of civilization still farther, had made her a respectable member of the system of European nations. She is now, however, to be ushered at once into the arena of empires, where she is to perform a most conspicuous part. Charles Robert was the grandson of the king of Naples; and he was raised to the throne of Hungary by the influence of Boniface the Eighth, the Roman pontiff at that time. He was the son of Charles Martel, a French duke, who was a reputed natural descendant of the famous Mayor of Paris of the same name. His mother was the beautiful Clementia, daughter of Rodolph, the celebrated founder of the Hapsburgh house. Thus, the new king was at once an Italian, a Spaniard, a Frenchman, a German, and a Hungarian; and he brought with him a debt of gratitude, and therefore a bond of alliance, to the bishop of Rome, who, in that age, was the centre of the European world. His policy as a monarch accorded exactly with his origin as a man. He was not, in his own mind, either a Hungarian, or a German, or a Frenchman, or a Spaniard, or an Italian, but all of them at once. He was, in other words, a European. The leading element of his character, nevertheless, was French. The French ideal of a government, which is that of glory and grandeur, rather than that of liberty and happiness, was the ideal of his life. He wanted to make his kingdom blaze with

1382–1385; Charles Martel, 1385–1387; Sigismund, 1387–1437; Albert, 1437–1437; Uladislaus, 1437–1445; Ladislaus Posthumus, 1445–1457; Matthias Corvinus, 1457–1490; Uladislaus II., 1490–1516; Louis II., 1516–1526. The Magyar historians have been puzzled to give this dynasty a characteristic name; but I have proposed the one stated in the text, by which a great deal of circumlocution is avoided, for the sufficient reason, as I trust, there assigned.

all sorts of splendor. The throne particularly must dazzle the eye of Europe. The people are to be transformed, by a stroke of his magic sceptre, from honorable and high-minded husbandmen to a nation of gentlemen and courtiers. The homely old customs are to be utterly abandoned. The graceful dress of the natives, which flowed most magnificently and characteristically in rich oriental folds, is to be laid aside for the narrow dimensions and tight fits of the latest styles of France. The French language must be spoken at court and by the people. French manners and ceremonies, French fashions of domestic and of public life, French luxuries of every sort, and, worse than all, French ideas of the decencies and indecencies of social life, must be imported for the benefit of a race of beings, who had ever been renowned for the purity and simplicity of their habits, for the frankness and integrity of their conduct, and for the many but nameless minor virtues, which make up the character of a natural, rather than an artificial, man. Vice and fashion came into the country hand in hand. So changed was Hungary, at the close of Charles Robert's life, that the natives scarcely knew whether they were Magyar or French. Not only the language and books of the higher classes, but the ideas of the common people, were entirely French. Simplicity was gone. The old matrons of the land could hardly tell what was meant, when their daughters asked them to their own tables to breakfast, or to dine. French cookery, with all its vocabulary of names, had transformed the well-known and seasonable repasts of the former ages into *dinès, soupès* and *dejeunès*. The nobility had their balls *paré* and their balls *masquè*. The towns, small as well as great, boasted of their *assemblées* and *redoutes*. Gentlemen played at cards with the ladies; and ladies, covered with *poudre à le Marechale*, vapored and had fits. Husbands kept an *ami de la maison* for their wives; and the wives as pliantly allowed a *fille de chambre* to their husbands. Every city was overflowing with *maitres d'hotels* and cooks; every hall resounded with ballets, operas and comic plays; and, at the same moment, the whole country, covered with true French splendor, was overwhelmed with degradation, debauchery and debt.[7]

Hungary was now emphatically European. Self-development was no longer the doctrine of the country. All eyes were turned abroad. Extension, magnitude, magnificence, were the words most current, even with the masses. Louis the Great, son of Charles Robert, spread the dominion of the Magyars to the shores of the three neighboring seas. He introduced the doctrine of a standing army into Hungary, and into Europe. With his brave soldiery, and its black flag, he twice traversed the heart of Italy, twice attacked Naples, twice conquered it, and twice banished its warlike princes from its throne. With this same bloody band, he waged war against the powerful republic of Venice, discomfited her ablest generals, cut down her mightiest armies, and recovered the greater part of Dalmatia, lost by some of his unfortunate predecessors, and hung it as a jewel upon his crown. In 1370, as a tribute to his martial talents, and without any agency of his own, he was unanimously elected king of Poland by the free electors of that realm. Hungary, Southern Italy and Poland were thus temporarily combined.

But the same world-wide policy went on during his daughter's reign. That daughter, the fair-haired Maria, had been married to the German Sigismund, who, after the death of his father-in-law, became both king of Hungary, by his wife's right, and emperor of Germany, by the election of his peers. He brought the kingdom of the Magyars again before the world. Under him it was looked upon, though in reality a distinct and independent country, as one of the great family of nations, which acknowledged the supremacy of his crown. After the death of Sigismund, and the assassination of Charles

[7] Riesbeck's Travels through Germany, Letter xxxi., Pinkerton's Collection.

Martel, who was only a pretender to the throne, Hungary again submitted to Maria, whose alliance with Italy and Germany made her strong.

In 1437, Elizabeth, the daughter of Sigismund and Maria, had been espoused to Albert of Austria, who, after Maria's bloody death, was elected king of Hungary through the title of his wife. He was subsequently created emperor of Germany, but, to present a barrier against the Turks, he made his Magyar kingdom the leading member of the empire, to whose necessities he caused every other interest to bow. That race of robbers, rising up in eastern Asia, had gradually migrated westward, spreading death and desolation on every side, till they had become the dread of every Christian throne. Now, when they were about to strike their last and most deadly blow, Hungary became the hope of all the western nations, the centre of the European world. Albert fell nobly and bravely fighting the battles of humanity and of man.

Uladislaus, the successor of Albert, was at the same time king of Hungary and of Poland. His life is only a demonstration that a man, great by position, is not always great in fact. He was the grandson of Louis the First, in the female line, and died in battle while waging a Quixotic war against the Asiatic Turks. He left the Hungarian throne to Ladislaus Posthumus, son of Sigismund and Elizabeth, a weak and contemptible monarch, but whose reign is immortalized by the heroic deeds of John Hunyady, the Transylvanian chief, whose name will ever live in history, in story, and in song. He was the Cid of that martial age. The Turks had now entrenched themselves in Europe and erected their tents about the walls of the metropolis of the Christian world. The Roman empire, reduced to a single city, was a prisoner within that city's walls. The Greeks could not stir abroad. They had no resource, no succor, no expectation in themselves. Hungary was almost their only hope; and Hungary was governed by a feeble and fickle king. But the king's general was a general indeed.

He defended the country against the Turkish hordes; and to Germany, which basely wished to take advantage of the presence of the infidels, and reduce the country of the Magyars to a German province, he administered a military lesson, which the empire had reason to remember for many a year. In 1453, the followers of Mahomet, assisted by this treasonable diversion created by the German emperor, seized and sacked the city of the Cæsars. Flushed with victory, the conquerors of Constantinople rushed to the plains of Hungary, expecting now to be able to sweep every opposition from their path. Hunyady met them at Belgrade. The slaughter of the Turks was terrible. They quailed, and turned, and fled. Christendom had been saved by the prowess of a single arm. But in twenty days after this memorable achievement, the glorious chieftain, mourned by the whole nation, was carried to his grave; and in a few months afterwards, the worthless monarch of the Magyars was deposited by his side.

Matthias Corvinus,[8] son of Hunyady, but a youth of only sixteen years, was raised by the gratitude of his countrymen to the Hungarian throne. He was the first of the Magyar sovereigns in no way connected to the Arpadian line; and he was, in all respects, the mightiest that ever wielded the sceptre of his native land. The greatest statesman, the ablest general, as well as the most powerful king, that his country had ever raised, his reign was one round of battles, victories and renown. He condemned the original military system of the Hungarians, which he considered useful only for defence, and raised up the nucleus of a standing army, called the Black Legion, whose valor shed a peculiar glory on his name. For the support of this army, he prevailed upon the nobility and clergy to lay

[8] When it is remembered, that the *v* in European words is usually pronounced like our *w*, and that the *us* is nothing but a Latin termination of declension, *Corvinus* is at once transformed to *Corwin*—a name not unfamiliar to Americans.

taxes, not upon the impoverished peasantry, but upon themselves. Pushing towards the east, he gives battle to the Turks, and imprisons them, as they had the Greeks, within their city walls. Turning northward, he subdues Silesia and Moravia, which had been meddling with Hungarian affairs. Proceeding westward, he declares war against the whole German empire, whose imperial head, Frederick the Third, had frequently insulted his weak predecessors, captures all the cities of Austria, and marches up to the entrenchments of Vienna, and takes the proud capital of the Hapsburgs by storm. Sweeping round toward the south, he settles the turbulence of his southern provinces, Dalmatia, Sclavonia and Croatia, and returns to the seat of government, covered with glory as with a garment, to raise up schools, colleges and libraries, and to spread over his country the light of a higher civilization than Hungary had ever known.

Under the successor of Matthias, Uladislaus the Second, king of Bohemia, whose election was secured to him as a remote descendant of Almos and of Arpad, on the female side, Hungary continued to hold a conspicuous position in European affairs. By his general, John Hunyady the Second, son of the late king, he prosecuted the war of his great predecessor against the emperor of Germany, and, by another able captain, John Zapolya, he punished Poland for certain insults offered to the independence and majesty of his crown. Toward the close of his administration, however, he committed an error, which Hungary has had cause to lament for three full centuries of time. Wishing, after all his hostility to the Germans, to strengthen his hands by a friendly alliance with his enemies, and flattered by the promises held out to him, he consented to form a double union with the House of Austria, which, from the little ducal principality of Hapsburg, had begun to stand up as one of the European powers. Actuated by these motives, he married his son to Maria, and his daughter to Ferdinand, the grandchildren of the celebrated Maximilian.

In this way, while linking the fame and fortunes of his country with a branch of the mightiest empire of the world since the fall of Rome, he ran the risk—the fatal risk—of subjecting that country to the sway of a foreign land. He died soon after the performance of this unwise and unpatriotic act; and his son Louis the Second, the husband of Maria and consequently brother-in-law to the emperor Charles the Fifth, was suddenly cut off while flying from the bloody field of Mohacz, where, in 1525, he left the Hungarian throne without an heir having the most distant relationship, by male or female consanguinity, to Almos, to Arpad, or to any of the old royal line.

For two hundred and seventeen years this female dynasty of the House of Hungary had continued. During its existence, Europe had passed from darkness to light, from infancy to manhood, from the bigotry of the Crusades to the universal liberty and charity of the Reformation. Between its beginning and its termination, the most memorable events had occurred, the most wonderful discoveries had been achieved, the most incredible advancement in civilization had been realized, that the race of humanity had ever known. The power of the Romans, which had filled the page of the world's history for more than two thousand years, had expired beneath the hostile tramp of a nation of oriental robbers. A new power had been planted, in a world but recently discovered, which, in no distant period, was destined to throw an eternal shadow over the glory of the Roman. The Church of God, purged of its corruptions, had risen up from the depths of its misery, dashed in pieces the shackles that had bound it, reasserted the design and dignity of its mission, proclaimed freedom to the captive faculties of mankind, and shed the glory of the Bible upon a multitude of nations. Schools had been everywhere erected. The arts and sciences had begun to flourish. The first paper-mill had been set to work in Germany. Post-offices had been established among the French.

Painting in oil-colors had been invented by the Dutch. India had been discovered by doubling the Cape of Good Hope. Magellan, with the newly invented mariner's compass, had made the circuit of the globe. Petrarch, by welcoming the Greeks, had laid the corner-stone of modern literature, and given the first-fruits of it to the world. The art of printing, discovered by the Germans, had been carried to all the great cities of all the great countries of the day. Every thing, in a word, had been in motion. Every man in Europe, stirred by the mysterious impulses of his times, had been roused from sleep. Every power of society had been at work. The secrets of nature, hid since the body of the globe was built, seemed to have been brought to light. The splendors of a new era, unrivaled and unapproached, had broken upon the countries of modern Europe, with which Hungary had held the most intimate connections for more than two hundred years. Now, at the close of her third dynasty of native sovereigns, she is about to sink into an insignificance, from which it will be the object of many a heroic struggle to reappear.

The last of the Hungarian dynasties, which covers the course of more than three centuries, made a most ominous beginning.[9] The National Assembly, which had openly remonstrated against the double alliance concluded by the intermarriages between the heirs of Uladislaus and of the German Maximilian, now resolved not to acknowledge Ferdinand, the

[9] The names and reigns of this dynasty, as far down as the year 1832, when a distinct period of Hungarian history takes its origin, are the following: John Zapolya, 1526–1540, and Ferdinand the First, 1526–1564 (rival kings); John Sigismund, 1540–1571, and Maximilian, 1564–1574 (rival kings); Rhodolph I., 1574–1608; Matthias II., 1608–1618; Ferdinand II., 1618–1636; Ferdinand III., 1636–1657; Leopold I., 1657–1705; Joseph I., 1705–1711; Charles III., 1711–1740; Maria Theresa, 1740–1770; Joseph II., 1770–1790; Leopold II., 1790–1792; Francis I., 1792–1832.

husband of their late king's daughter, but crowned John Zapolya, his general, on the 9th of November, 1526, by a unanimous election. Ferdinand, however, was not to be set aside so easily. Mary, widow of Louis the Second, was his sister, and zealous in his interest. Charles the Fifth, emperor of Germany, was his brother, with the will and the means to give him a powerful support. Zapolya, too, who had been a valorous and successful captain, became a weak and vacillating monarch. He was soon driven into Transylvania. Ferdinand, pushing into the country from the west, was elected and acknowledged on the 16th of December. A war of succession now arose, which, for almost half a century, raged with unceasing energy. The Turks were called in, by both parties, to aid in the settlement of the quarrel; and they, when once admitted into the country, from which they had been manfully excluded by the native sovereigns, pursued a double policy, till they had made themselves masters of the kingdom. For two centuries, with occasional intermissions, the Turks swayed the destinies of Hungary. The Austrian monarchs, who were generally emperors of Germany as well as kings of Hungary, were willing to see the Magyars reduced and humbled, as they would thus become more subservient to foreign domination. The introduction of those barbarians, therefore, as well as their continuance in the country, were the result of this perfidious policy. Eight of these German rulers, from Ferdinand to Charles the Third inclusive, in this way bled and subdued the nation, and forged the chains for binding it in eternal slavery at Constantinople. Germany, which professed to be the revival of the Roman empire of the west, and the sworn and sole protector of Christianity, to get possession of a people, who had ever been the champions of freedom, stooped to employ the avowed enemies of our religion through whom to effect its wicked and bloody purpose. Hungary, though nominally connected to an empire, whose history was the history of Europe during the two centuries in question, was really left to sink into obscurity, and welter in its own blood, shed by the hand of the barbarians.

Charles the Third, thinking that this foul work had been sufficiently accomplished, raised an army and expelled the Turks, about a century ago, after a few decisive battles. Hungary was again brought into notice as a member—a bruised and bleeding member—of the great Germanic system. The House of Austria, once the head of a little Swiss principality, now giving successive rulers to nearly one-half of Europe, was again willing to record the name of Hungary on its proud escutcheon. Hungary, however, during these two ages of treason and oppression, had acquired no willingness now to come forth from her long night of suffering, and stand before the gaze of the world, as a manacled and mutilated slave. Nor did the monarchs succeeding Charles the Third so treat her as to inspire her with any greater willingness. The three sovereigns between Charles and Francis—Maria Theresa, Joseph the Second, and Leopold the Second—though quite unlike in their natural temperaments and personal characteristics, pursued the one unchangeable policy of their house—self-aggrandizement by centralizing in itself the powers of the several states; and when Francis the First expired, in the year 1832, while the National Assembly was in session, he left his kingdom just on the point of opening for itself a new and more glorious career, by reasserting its original constitution, its liberties and its independence.

At that period, Hungary had settled down within the limits, which nature and necessity seem to have assigned it. It no longer maintained any organic connection with Italy, with Poland, or with Bohemia. The old provinces of Pannonia and Dacia, or Hungary and Transylvania, together with Croatia and Sclavonia, which had been acquired originally by conquest, and the Military Frontier, which stretched for nine hundred and twenty miles between Hungary and Turkey, completing the chain of the circumjacent mountains by an insurmountable but artificial barrier, constituted at that time the kingdom. Its relations to the surrounding countries, in the course of more than eight centuries, had become greatly changed; and many of the nations, flourishing and powerful when this kingdom was established, had been blotted from the map of Europe, while others had sprung into existence in a manner, which, in some ages, would have been regarded as miraculous. There are several of these neighboring states, which, though their names have been frequently employed in the foregoing pages, have so close a connection with the position and prospects of the Hungarian nation, and their histories are in themselves so marvellous, that some slight memorials of their origin and strength, at the death of Francis, are essential to a clear and complete exposition of the present topic.

In the sixth century of the Christian era, along the banks of the Irtish, on the steppes of north-western Asia, dwelt a small band of robbers, who, when pursued, fled to the steeps and solitudes of the Altay mountains. While the empires of Cæsar and of Mahomet were in annual conflict, disputing the mastery of the world, these corsairs of the land sold their services to the one or to the other party, according to the value of the bribes offered them. Not far from the middle of the eighth century, when their power had been humbled and their territory dismembered by the combined armies of the Chinese and the Saracens, they professed the religion of the Prophet, and were at once employed as the body-guard of the reigning Caliph. From servants they soon became masters. Every successive convulsion and revolution in Asia served to increase their power. The Seljooks and the Mongols swept over them for a time; but, in the end, the robbers were found to have acquired new strength from the sediments of these vast inundations. One of the captains of this band, by the name of Osman, with only about five hundred followers, looking with a greedy eye on the rolling landscapes, the hills and valleys, of the lesser Asia, sprung to his horse with a sudden resolution, took his course toward the shores of the Mediterranean, forced the passes of Olympus, and finally made a powerful settlement on the plains of Bythinia, within the acknowledged limits of the Roman empire. He soon conquered a large part of western Asia. The Greeks and the Romans, divided and contending with each other, could make no serious resistance. This daring adventurer was succeeded by eight military leaders, whose genius was equalled only by their triumphs. On all sides of them, wherever they went, to raise the sword was the same thing as to conquer. Their successes, instead of satisfying their ambition, only fed it. The celebration of every victory was only the sumptuous beginning of one still greater. Conquest was the road to conquest. Every year, every day, every hour, they were pressing westward. Europe trembled. Cutting off one province of the Roman empire after another, they finally reduced it to the single city of Constantinople; and this, in the year 1453, they entered and sacked, thus making themselves masters of the world's metropolis, and planting themselves at the world's centre. This band of robbers, in 1832, though stripped of some of its fairest dependencies by the Greek and Egyptian revolutions, still swayed a territory of more than nine hundred thousand square miles, and a population of over twenty millions. Being of Tartar origin, they held about as near a relation to the Magyars, in blood, in physical traits, in mental characteristics, as is held by the Germans to the Anglo-Saxons. The Turks, indeed, are the most natural friends and allies, which the Magyars have in Europe.

Such is one nation to which the Hungarians are externally related. For the rise and progress of another, we turn our eyes to that long and cold strip of territory, which constitutes the eastern boundary of the Baltic. There, hovering about the numerous bays formed by that inland sea, or ranging far out on its wind-swept surface, arose a race of pirates, whose name first appeared in history at about the middle of the ninth century. Not entirely satisfied with their uncertain and predatory life, a portion of them, under the conduct of Ruric and his two brothers, migrated eastward into the interior of the country, conquered the Sclavic tribes then inhabiting it, and formed the nucleus of a kingdom. The government of this new state was a military despotism. The captain of the pirates was king, commander, lawgiver, and judicial magistrate. Every thing submitted to his sole authority, as if he were still commanding his piratic fleets upon the water. His successors continued his mode of government and his victories. In the tenth century, the reigning sovereign, happening to be at Constantinople, embraced Christianity, and adopted the creed of the Greek confession. The nation prudently followed his example. The great-grandson of Ruric married Anna, a Greek princess, concluded a treaty of alliance with her nation, and added many tracts of country to his possessions. The fall of the Greeks contributed more to the success of the Baltic pirates than their friendship. They had been often attacked, by the Mangols, by the Teutons, by the Swedes, by numerous tribes of northern savages, but they had not been conquered. Every attempt had only rought vengeance upon the head of the aggressor. Sometimes, it is true, the freebooters appeased their opponents by a little tribute, but, watching their opportunity, they generally repaid themselves in full by the most terrible reprisals. At the close of the fifteenth century, they had annihilated all opposition, excepting an occasional attack from the side of Poland. In 1553, they made a treaty with Queen Elizabeth of England, when their name and power first became known in western Europe, through the enterprise of some British sailors, who had discovered the passage from England to Archangel. Treaty after treaty, with the leading Powers of Europe, followed. On, and still onward, went the empire of the Baltic pirates. In 1552, they conquered Kasan, in 1554, the kingdom of Astrakan, and, in 1587, the whole of north-western Asia. Next, they spread their conquests westward to the boundaries of Norway and Denmark. The whole of Finland was then added to their dominions. A third of Poland soon widened their authority toward the south. From the Turks they took Kinburn, Asoph, Kabarda, and a large portion of the Crimea. On, and still onward, went the empire of the Baltic pirates. In 1783, they took possession of Little Tartary, which made them the arbiters of south-eastern Europe. In 1793–7, they seized nearly another third of Poland, by which this rival was brought to the very brink of dissolution. In 1800, the Republic of the Seven Islands was erected and occupied by their garrisons, by which means their power was planted upon the bosom of the Mediterranean, from which it could menace at once the shores of Asia, Africa and Europe. In 1812, they acquired possession of the mouths of the Danube, with the adjacent provinces; and, in 1813, they completed their title to Georgia and to the exclusive navigation of the Caspian. On, and still onward, went the empire of the Baltic pirates. In 1815, at Vienna, in 1818, at Aix-la-Chapelle, when the crowned heads of Europe were partitioning the world between them, the power of the pirates was predominant; and, at this moment, it is supreme over the half of Europe, the whole of northern Asia and north-western America, and one-seventh of the habitable globe. With a population of sixty millions, and a standing army of one million, the empire of the Baltic pirates, whose subjects are different Sclavic tribes, are the nearest neighbors and most natural allies, not of the Magyars, but of the Hungarian Sclaves.

The third great nation, with which Hungary has an external relationship, is equally wonderful in its origin, and in its rise to power and prominence. Toward the close of the twelfth century, within the bosom of one of the great armies of crusaders, then occupying the kingdom of Jerusalem, arose a class of fanatical soldiers, under the title of Knights of the Teutonic Order, whose exploits are equally famous in history and in epic. The order was dedicated to the Virgin, the earthly dwelling-place of whose Son they bound themselves to rescue from the unbelievers, and defend against all opposition. Their purpose was at least a great one; their ambition was very lofty; their valor was undoubted; and their personal appearance was attractive. Being all of them noblemen by birth, and possessing sufficient wealth to support their affectation of magnificence, their entrance upon the stage of public life, as a banded brotherhood, marks an era in the annals of that chivalric and martial period. Their under-dress was a suit of jet black, over which was thrown a cloak of the purest white, on the back of which was the figure of a black cross shaded with an edge of silver. The head-quarters of these Knights were first at the Holy City; but, when the Turks had again taken possession of Jerusalem, they retired to Venice, and thence to Marburg. In the year 1229, they were invited by the Poles to give them their support against the Prussians, who were then pagans. After a struggle of fifty-three years, the Prussians were compelled to acknowledge the supremacy of the Order, which, without stopping to celebrate its triumph, at once proceeded to spread its power along the southern borders of the Baltic. Before 1525, a great part of the central section of northern Europe was held by these Knights, by paying a nominal homage to the crown of Poland; but, in that year, it was conferred by the Polish sovereign on Albert of Brandenburg, grand-master of these Teutons, who was to govern and transmit it as a duchy of this kingdom. In 1657, the *republic* of Poland acknowledged the independent sovereignty of one of the successors of Prince Albert over all the territory at first granted to his house, and over other large possessions acquired since the grant was made it. Frederic, the third of the dukes, in 1701, put upon his own head the royal crown, having taken the title of Frederic the First. The kingdom was at once established. Its influence was widely felt on the surrounding nations. Military in its organization, and imbued from the beginning with the military spirit, the end and aim of every enterprise, the object of every wish, was conquest. Frederic William the First, the successor of the first king, established a military government, with a standing army of sixty or seventy thousand; and the next successor, Frederic the Great, transformed the little kingdom into one of the great monarchies of Europe. In art, in science, in philosophy, in all the works of modern civilization, the small dukedom of the Teutonic Knights has become the soul and centre of the German empire, wielding an influence to the ends of the world. That influence has a threefold and even contradictory relation to the Hungarian kingdom. As a Teutonic influence, it is naturally allied to the interests of the Hungarian Germans. Its opposition to southern Germany, however, would cause it to take into its embrace the entire Magyar country; but its constant and close connection with the empire of the Baltic pirates, the head and champion of the great Sclavic family, neutralizes its natural affinities, nullifies its more liberal policy, and makes it the instrument of that imperial despotism of the north, which, for its own purposes, incites and supports the Sclave against the Magyar, which always stands opposed to a nation having any tendency toward the doctrine of human freedom, and which resolves, sooner or later, to crush the last relic of civil liberty in Europe.

There is one more great European nation to be marshalled into being, and set in its true position, in relation to the Magyar kingdom. Its history is not less wonderful than that of its three predecessors. On the banks of the Aar, in Switzerland, toward the close of the eleventh century, a Christian bishop, by the name of Werner, built a fortified episcopal palace among the broken crags of a very lofty eminence. To those down in the deep valley of the river, the bishop's residence seemed no bigger than a speck, and reminded the rude peasants of that Alpine region of what they had often seen among the mountains. The occupant of the airy dwelling, by the manner of his life, may have added something, in the way of association, to the resemblance. The peasantry called it, in their own language, Der Habichtsburg, which, in our tongue, is the Hawk's-Nest. If, at the first, this title was justly applied to it, it is certain that the successors of Bishop Werner gave ample reason for the application. They were as hawk-eyed, greedy, rapacious a set of priests, as ever rose up in any country. Seated in their high and inaccessible aëry, far above the reach of either law or punishment, they watched the neighboring valleys with the keenest vigilance. Seizing their opportunities with the vulture's precision and penetration, they pounced upon every moving object, from which they expected to draw nourishment for their craving appetite. Power was the object of their ambition. Their own particular district was at once reduced to absolute fear, dependance and subjection. The adjoining districts, or dioceses, next became the victims of their rapacity. In that barbarous age, when social distinctions were not nicely drawn, the lines of separation between ecclesiastical and secular authority were very irregular and faint; and the bishops of the Hawk's-Nest found it not difficult gradually to annex a civil to their religious influence. The little town that sprung up under their feet, which, from the name of their own residence, was also called Habichtsburg, by the natives corrupted into Hapsburg, was made the centre of several dioceses, of which the occupant of the high castle became the count. Still uniting the two kinds of sovereignty, the counts of Hapsburg, never for one moment forgetful of the sole object of their existence, and constantly adding to their power by making themselves the self-serving ministers of the pope, at the opening of the thirteenth century, began to draw the attention of the German states. The north-east of Switzerland had submitted to their dictation. Commanding the head-waters of the Rhine, as well as one of the principal passes of the Alps, both Italy and Germany were often under obligations to their politic generosity, or were stung by the severity and obstinacy of their power. Their territory, small as it was, defended by its Alpine walls, could defy the proudest barons of the land. Rhodolph, who became Count of Hapsburg in 1240, spread all over Switzerland the terror of his name. He sought to make quarrels with his friends, that, as in the case of young Hugh of Tuffenstein, he might have occasion to attack them and get possession of their estates. He raised the sword against his uncle and guardian, and, when the strife was over, demanded and received a strip from his relative's inheritance to repay him for the expenses of the war. Having borrowed money from another uncle, and being denied when he wished to borrow more, he paid the debt by endeavoring to seize the whole of his kinsman's patrimony and conveying it to himself. Interfering with a civil war in Strasburg, he took possession of the city, and compelled its lawful ruler to purchase a restoration to the throne. As guardian to his cousin Anne, instead of defending and preserving her vast inheritance, he boldly and openly added it to his own. Full of all intrigue, he conquered many cities, among which was that of Zurich, by stratagems and ambuscades. Espousing the cause of the citizens of Basle, who had risen against their magistrates, he was about to batter down the walls of the town, when, at midnight, a fleet messenger brought to him the intelligence, that the count of Hapsburg had been elected emperor of Germany by the unanimous suffrage of the states.[10] The emperor by no means put off the count. Ottocar, the duke of Austria, refused to acknowledge the elevation of the new sovereign, when Rhodolph, who could not be satisfied with any common penalty, grasped the scepter of his opponent by force of arms. That scepter never was restored. The provinces adjacent to Austria—Styria, Illyria, Corinthia and Carniola—were soon annexed, by warlike means,

[10] The bishop of Basle, on hearing the news, is said to have exclaimed—"Sit fast, great God, or Rhodolph will occupy thy throne!" Coxe's House of Austria, vol. i. p. 16.

to this ever-growing and ever-ambitious house. Bohemia, with its dependencies, Moravia, Silesia and Lusatia, soon met with the same inevitable fate. Hungary was obtained by a marriage supported by the sword. Parts of Poland were acquired by unlawful force. Always grasping after the imperial crown, and frequently with success, the Hapsburg sovereigns ultimately reached a height of authority, by the use of which it became easy for them to settle in their own family the succession to the German throne; and when the crown of the Cæsars had been worn by them for many generations, Francis the First ostentatiously resigned a bauble, no longer the ensign of power, declaring himself the emperor of Austria, which, indeed, under the ambitious rule of a long line of unscrupulous robbers, had swallowed up the German empire and grown to be almost as large, quite as powerful, and decidedly more magisterial and intolerant, than that of ancient, iron-hearted, iron-handed Rome. The Castle of the Hawk's-Nest had become one of the capitals of the world.

Such, then, are the external relations of the Magyar nation. At home, the Magyars are surrounded on all sides by Sclaves, in the midst of whom, hemmed in and hated as they are, they have maintained their supremacy for more than nine hundred years. The four great monarchies just described, Turkey, Russia, Prussia and Austria, all of them tyrannic governments, constitute another wall—a wall of despotism averaging a thousand miles in width—by which they are entirely enclosed. Beyond this there is still another irregular circumvallation of monarchical and despotic states, Asiatic, African and European, the most of which are but partners or dependants of the four, whose historical positions have been portrayed. Thus imprisoned, at the centre of a vast system of confederated despotisms, these friends of freedom, the champions of civil liberty, have borne up against every influence, have defended themselves against nearly all aggressions, have maintained at least the name of their historical and constitutional independence, since their original settlement in the land. The name of independence, however, it must be confessed, is about all they have been able to preserve. Successful against all nations, by whom their country and institutions were openly attacked, in the earlier periods of their history, they have at last been compelled to yield to the perfidy, diplomacy and intrigue of a monarchy, which, from its origin on the banks of Aar, has known no object but self-aggrandizement, no scruples but those of ambition, no means better than treachery and war. If ever they have dared to demand their rights, to ask for the restoration of their liberties, for the real as well as nominal acknowledgment of their happy and almost republican constitution, they have failed of success, for the last three hundred years, for the want of a sufficient European sympathy on which to lean in their day of need. Every patriotic effort was sure to rouse the hostility of the surrounding countries. Turkey, though their kindred in origin and in blood, could not favor a country of republican institutions. Russia, in every commotion, was certain to take the side of her Sclavic kinsmen against the people, whose liberal constitution she additionally despised. Prussia, ever since the fall of Poland, has been generally the secret or open ally of the Russian government. France and England, since the days of the French Revolution, have been maintaining the balance of Europe by a close connection with Austria and Turkey against the dreaded ambition of the Russias. The other states of Europe are no longer powers. They are nothing but dependants. Hungary, therefore, for three centuries, has been a forlorn captive, chained in a mighty prison-house of nations, without the means of self-liberation, without the hope of foreign interference, but in no way giving up to despondency, or relinquishing her faith in a happier and a better day. It is no dishonor, when her unfortunate position is carefully considered, that she has been in chains so long. It is her glory, that, in spite of her outward captivity, at heart she has been always and forever free.

CHAPTER VII.

ATTEMPTS TO OVERTHROW THE HUNGARIAN NATIONALITY.

We are told by the historian of the House of Austria, that Frederic the Third was accustomed to employ his leisure in the composition of a royal diary, and in the construction of enigmas and unintelligible anagrams. One of these anagrams was extremely curious. It was based upon the five vowels of the Roman alphabet. These letters, during the life-time of the emperor, were engraved upon his plate, and upon all the articles of his household furniture. His visitors used to be perplexed in seeing them at the table, in his halls, on the covers of his books, and everywhere throughout his palace. Thousands made the attempt to interpret them. All attempts, however, proved fruitless. They continued to be, till the day of his death, an unsolved mystery, the wonder of his generation. After his demise the riddle was explained. On one of the leaves of his diary, his executor found the following singular inscription:

A	E	I	O	U
ustria	st	mperare	rbi	niverso.
lles	rdreich	st	esterreich	nterthan.[1]

It seems, therefore, that, years before the Hungarian monarchy was united to that of Austria, one of the leading members of the Austrian family of kings had expressed the well-known policy of his house, though the time for making it public had not arrived. It did not originate, however, with Frederic. It had been the actuating spirit of every one of his predecessors. It was born in the breast of the first occupant of the Hawk's-Nest. From the priest it had descended

[1] Coxe's House of Austria, vol. i. p. 277, and Fugger, p. 1080.

to the count, from the count to the duke, from the duke to the king, and from the king of a single nation, and that a small one, to the sole monarch of half a score of realms. It had grown with the growth of power. All that can be said of Frederic is, that he wished to see how it would look in words, but, the better to conceal it from the jealousy of other nations, and still to preserve it in a memorable form, for the benefit of his own subjects, and especially of his successors, he vailed it in the manner above mentioned. Whether he expected, when writing out the resolution of the imperial riddle, in his secret journal, that it would ever be given to the world, is not a question. He evidently intended it only for those, whom it was designed to prompt to greater energy, in the only business of his family. But whoever will now read the bloody and ambitious history of this family will not need the riddle, or the resolution of it, to point out to him the one, unalterable, untiring purpose of every member of it, crowned and uncrowned, since it was brought into being among the Alpine crags. This plain and positive declaration of the emperor is proof enough, it is true, of the ruling object of the Hapsburgs, in all their relations to other lands; but their recorded acts, through a long line of princes, and through the space of many centuries, in respect to the race and country of the Magyars, furnish a better and clearer exposition of that object, than any royal enigma could afford.

Hungary, as we have seen, was originally an independent country, bound by no allegiance to any foreign power. The conquest, gained by Attila and his Huns over the Sarmatian, Gothic, and Roman inhabitants of Dacia and Pannonia, was complete; and the Magyars, by conquering the Huns, acquired as good a title to the whole land, as had been vested in their predecessors.

It has been said, however, that, in either case, a military title is an imperfect tenure; but, should the present generation undertake and effect a revolution upon this subject, not only Hungary, but every other settled and civilized nation, in America and in Europe, would have to relinquish their existence. It would be utterly impossible, on this or the other side of the Atlantic, to find the remnants of a people, to whom the sovereignties of the several enlightened states could be, with historical and legal accuracy, resigned; for, though it would not be difficult to discover, in all these states, some fragments of our nearest predecessors, it is now well known, that they were themselves the conquerors of other peoples, who held prior possession of the countries. In England, it might be possible for the present rulers, who represent the Norman conquerors, to yield their supremacy to the living descendants of the original Anglo-Saxons; but, by the same theory, the crown could not easily pass backward, through the Danes, Saxons, and Romans, to the present race of Britons. In America, we should be compelled to dissolve the existing republic, and call back the red men of our eastern and western forests, to exercise dominion over us; and even these, before they could take command, would be bound to quit their claim in behalf of that unknown people, who, ages prior to their captivity or annihilation, by the modern Indian tribes, enjoyed the possession of our hills and valleys. In Hungary, the task of retro-cession would be still more difficult; and the Magyars, who have held their country more than three times as long as we have held our own, and by exactly the same title, have always been, and are yet, a sovereign and independent people. Though surrounded by their conquered countrymen, the Sclaves, they are no more bound to abdicate in their favor, than the English are bound to deliver their sceptre to the Welsh, or the Americans to the descendants of Red Jacket and King Philip. The instincts of humanity, and the practice of all nations, as well as the laws of necessity, establish the validity of the Magyar claim to all the territories and dependencies of Hungary.

The land of the Magyar is not only legally and justly his

possession, according to the law of nations, together with all its associated provinces, but his title has been ratified, in the usual form, by the surrounding states for a long course of ages. The supremacy of the dominant race has been thus legally established. It has received, also, a still higher ratification. It has been acknowledged, for many centuries, by the Sclavic provinces themselves. Not only their constitutions, but their statute laws, as well as every thing pertaining to their local governments, have constantly recognised themselves, during all this time, as dependencies of Hungary, of which the Magyars have ever been the ruling people. The French in Canada might as rightfully throw up their connection with the Provincial Parliament, in which the Anglo-Saxon influence is justly paramount, or with the Imperial Parliament of Great Britain, as the Sclaves of Hungary could renounce their long-standing and legally-established relations to the race that conquered them.

Nor can it be denied, indeed, that the victorious people have granted much greater liberty to the subject race, ever since their subjugation, than it has been convenient for England to grant to the French in her North American possessions. This is a part of the domestic history of Hungary, which, by nearly all foreigners, has been too little understood, or too partially considered. The Sclaves of Croatia and Sclavonia, which are united in their local administration, have always enjoyed a municipal independence. They have their own General Assembly, or Diet, which meets at their capital of Agram, where all their private matters are discussed and settled according to their own wishes. The National Assembly has ever been characteristically generous and high-minded in its liberality toward them. These Sclavonic provinces, in their separate capacity, have borne about the same relation to the Hungarian kingdom, that the counties of Hungary, properly so called, have had to the same general government. They have been cordially admitted into the common fellowship of the nation.

Transylvania, too, which forms a still larger portion of the kingdom, has its own Diet at Hermanstadt, its capital, and there exercises all the functions of self-government, in all affairs of a merely provincial interest. Never, perhaps, in the history of conquests, has a conquering race been more magnanimous to the conquered.

This local independence of the provinces and counties is one of the most remarkable features of the Hungarian constitution, having no parallel, perhaps, excepting in the independent but united states of our own great republic. There is no difference among these constituent parts of the nation, whether their inhabitants are Magyars, or Sclaves, or Saxons. Not only do all of them elect their own officers, in their own way, and send delegates to the National Assembly to represent their interests according to the instructions given them, but they have the sole management of their municipal affairs, in which the national government has asserted no right to interfere. They assess and collect their own taxes, make and repair their own roads, erect their own bridges, cut their own canals, and perform all other acts of private sovereignty not inconsistent with their relations to each other as one confederated government. The king himself can execute the laws of the National Assembly only through the county and provincial officers, who, responsible to their constituents only, cannot be compelled to serve a mandate not acceptable to the people. By the Bulla Aurea, too, of King Audreas the Second, the legal voters of the counties have a right to take up arms against a monarch, who attempts to violate the constitution, without incurring any legal blame. So thoroughly democratic is this Magyar kingdom, that, in one particular, if not in more than one, the people have retained a prerogative dangerous to the efficiency, if not to the integrity, of the general government. When a county sees fit to resist the execution of any unpopular enactment of the Assembly, or mandate of the king, should it know of any neighboring states friendly to its private views, it has the privilege of concluding treaties with those states, offensive and defensive, as if it had no connection with the monarchy of which it professedly forms a part. This excess of democracy, however, is a sufficient proof of the republican spirit of the nation.

According to the fundamental laws of the country, therefore, Hungary has always been a popular government, and, in every thing but the name, a republic. It is true, in the two provinces of Upper and Lower Hungary, the Magyars at first asserted certain political privileges, which they did not grant to their conquered fellow-citizens; and the same is true, as we have seen, and with still greater emphasis, in our own country respecting our aboriginal inhabitants. The distinction, however, has long since been regarded as a dead letter; while, in no part of the kingdom, has there ever been so wide a difference as exists between the two races in our southern States, where no conquest can be quoted, but whose republicanism has always been legally and universally acknowledged. In all the other provinces, the Magyar has never claimed any more rights, than he has freely and fully granted to his Sclavic and Saxon brethren. All over the kingdom, from the earliest times, the superior state-officers have been almost entirely raised to their respective posts by popular election; the exceptions to this general custom have been less numerous than in the states of the American Union; and the king himself, as well as the duke before him, elevated by the same means, has not only been thus the responsible representative of a free nation, but the possessor of less power, by the original constitution, than is exercised by an American President. The National Assembly has ever had less authority than our Congress. The people of Hungary, always a liberty-loving people, from the time when their first Oberhaupt was elected till the total extinction of his lineage, have ever maintained more of the forms and functions of local self-government, than have the people of our own republic.[2]

So jealous, indeed, have the Hungarians always been of regal domination, and so determined to secure their popular institutions against every possibility of the centralization of their powers in the hands of their sovereigns, that, when first transferring their crown to a foreign prince, they caused him to swear, in the presence of God, to maintain the integrity of the country and of its constitution. This oath is one of the most solemn and emphatic ever taken upon the lips of any mortal. It is too plain for the least opportunity of misunderstanding or equivocation. It has been pronounced, under the most open and imposing circumstances, by every Austrian king of Hungary since the coronation of the first Ferdinand. Alas! it is the oath by which every one of them, without an exception, is guilty of the blackest perjury. Let us proceed to enumerate the several charges, which impartial history has to bring, in this relation, against this line of princes. We shall see whether the anagram of Frederic was an unmeaning riddle.

It must be remembered, that the same man, who, as king of Hungary, is a limited monarch, checked on every side by the constitutional liberties of his subjects, as emperor of Austria is possessed of a regal authority entirely absolute. This right of absolute domination is, of course, his darling attribute; and the provinces of his empire, where his will is irresistible, are his darling provinces. So far as it can be possible for such a ruler to confer lasting favors upon a people, so far would the Austrian despots very naturally exert themselves to give a greater apparent prosperity to the im-

[2] Paget's Hungary and Transylvania, vol. i. chap. xviii. *passim*, and J. Toulmin Smith's Parallels between England and Hungary, pp. 18–58 inclusive. Smith is particularly to be examined on this subject.

perial, than to the royal and constitutional, parts of their dominions. Could the subject be made to believe, that his fortune is easier, that his success in life is more certain, in those portions of the wide realm, where the emperor is sole master, than where his prerogatives and powers are restrained by popular limitations, a decisive work would be accomplished on the side of tyranny, and a sure step taken toward the ultimate establishment of his despotic sway over the other portions. This, indeed, is the first article in a system of policy, by which the House of Austria has been endeavoring, for more than three centuries, to subjugate the Hungarian nation, and to rob it of its liberties, of its constitution, and of its independence. A most glaring and iniquitous favoritism, respecting all the branches of human industry, in the encouragement of talent and ambition, and in the assessment and collection of the revenue, has been practised. In Hungary, agriculture, manufactures and commerce have been discouraged, while, in the imperial provinces, such rewards and bounties have been offered as always develop the resources of a nation. On those immense tracts of land belonging directly to the king, particularly on such as were within the boundaries of Hungary, every mode of expenditure has been lavished, by which the happiness and contentment of their inhabitants, and an invidious comparison with the lands held by the other part of the population, could be secured. In the Banat, for example, where whole counties are the personal property of the monarch, this system of royal partiality has been carried to the highest pitch.[3] All over Hungary, however, wherever the Hapsburg monarch has had possessions, these substantial and powerful though sophistical arguments have been stamped upon the soil, upon the public improvements, and, as far as possible, upon the convictions of a poor, short-sighted and

[3] Paget's Hungary and Transylvania, vol. ii. p. 60, American edition.

superficial people. In all other portions of the country, the iron sway of a foreign rule has repressed all enterprise, discouraged all improvement, and so loaded the laboring classes with an illegal system of indirect taxation, that they long since sank into an almost hopeless poverty. The internal taxes of the kingdom the monarchs could not touch; but they could make every article imported into Hungary, and every article exported from it, pay the most enormous duties; and, thus doubling their malice, they could not only wrench a vast revenue for themselves by the first of these cruel practices, but by the second actually prohibit and annihilate the productive operations of the country. The hard-working peasant of Gallicia, beyond the north-east border of Hungary, over the Carpathian mountains, has been compelled to import his scythes from the Austrian province of Styria, beyond the south-western limit of the kingdom, though the Hungarians have been manufacturing a superior article at Gömär, almost within sight of the green valleys where the demand for them has existed.[4] All joiner-work, done in Hungary, has had to pay a duty of one hundred per centum, while many other trades and professions have been, by the same means, prohibited. The capital and talent of other portions of the world have been industriously discouraged from seeking employment in the doomed and desolated country; for not only have the foreign monarchs, their servants and their subjects, united to slander the opportunities, which it holds forth to enterprising strangers, but German political economists, like the well-known List, have been paid for writing and publishing against it the most false and serious libels. For the last fifty

[4] Pulsky, vol. i. p. 5. The Banat is known to be full of coal; and yet, owing to this system of partiality, it is as dear at home as that brought from England by the way of Constantinople! Paget, vol. ii. p. 54. The duty on salt is a still worse specimen of maladministration. Paget, vol. ii. p. 170.

years, whenever an inquisitive traveler has arrived at Vienna, and proposed to visit and explore the interdicted region, he has been clamorously informed, that Hungary is a land of wolves and other wild beasts, and of a still wilder and wickeder population; where there are neither roads, nor bridges, nor means of travel; whose inhabitants wander, in forlorn groups, either naked, or clad in the coarsest and dirtiest sheep-skins; and in which a man's life would be taken for a cup of Karlowicz, or the value of a kreutzer![5]

But the Austrian kings have not limited their aggressions, against the liberties and independence of Hungary, by such a peaceable though contemptible opposition. Ferdinand the First, it will be remembered, acquired the crown of St. Stephen by a long and most bloody war, which he waged against John Zapolya, the rightful heir, whom the Hungarian Diet, in 1526, as well as the estates of Sclavonia, had unanimously

---

[5] City of the Magyar, and Pulsky's Memoirs, *passim*. The newspapers of Vienna are *now* holding the same language. Paget opens his great work with the following passage:—"The reader would certainly laugh, as I have often done since, did I tell him one-half of the foolish tales the good Viennese told us of the country we were about to visit. No roads! no inns! no police! we must sleep on the ground, eat where we could, and be ready to defend our purses and our lives at every moment! In full credence of these reports, we provided ourselves most plentifully with arms, which were carefully loaded, and placed ready for immediate use; for, as we heard that nothing but fighting would carry us through, we determined to put the best face we could upon the matter. It may, however, ease the reader's mind to know, that no occasion to shoot any thing more formidable than a partridge, or a hare, ever presented itself; and that we finished our journey with the full conviction, that traveling in Hungary was just as safe as traveling in England!" The writer subsequently gives us the reason for the circulation of these fearful stories. "The Hungarians *do* sometimes talk about liberty, constitutional rights, and other such terrible things!" Paget's Hungary and Transylvania, vol. i. pp. 13 and 14.

elected to the throne left vacant by the death of the Second Louis on the field of Mohacz. To gain the higher nobles of the kingdom to his cause, he tendered to them a written manifesto, while the fortunes of the day were against him, declaring, that, in the event of his success, "he would preserve inviolate all the rights and liberties of Hungary," with the same fidelity as if he had been a native and lawful prince. Some of the great nobility turned traitors and went over to the usurper. Zapolya was not at once defeated. In 1538, a treaty was concluded between the combatants, styled the Peace of Grosswardein, by which it was agreed, that hostilities should cease between them; that, *ad interim*, Ferdinand should be obeyed in the west, and Zapolya in the east of Hungary; and that, should Zapolya die during the continuance of this armistice, Ferdinand and John Sigismund, Zapolya's son, were to divide the kingdom between them. In 1540, Zapolya died; and, in the same year, the Turks invaded and conquered the country as far west as Buda. Ferdinand died in 1564, after acknowledging the right of Sigismund to eastern Hungary, leaving the western portion to his own son, Maximilian. The death of John Sigismund, in 1571, conferred his right of sovereignty upon Stephen Bathory, one of the greatest of the Hungarian statesmen; but Rhodolph, the successor of Maximilian, not only despised his opponent, but gave existence to that long struggle, now just closed by the butcheries of Haynau, by which the destruction of the Hungarian Constitution was to be effected by the combined instrumentalities of treachery, stratagem and blood. His successors, Matthias and Ferdinand, pursued the same determination; and Leopold the First, by waging a war of extermination against the free princes of Transylvania, by securing the elevation of his cruel instrument, John Kemeny, to the principality thus bereaved, and by the massacre of thousands of the citizens of Hungary, who had risen to defend the constitutional liberties of their native land, not only forced the election of his son, Joseph, to the succession of St. Stephen, but compelled the prostrate Diet to acknowledge and proclaim that son their *hereditary* monarch. The same bloody weapons, therefore, by which the sacred crown had been snatched from its lawful owners and laid upon the brow of a foreign tyrant, now conferred the eternal succession of that ensign of royalty, with all the majesty it confers, upon the *male* offspring of the original usurper.

To illustrate the manner by which this foul work was done, a single example may be taken from the reign of Leopold. Immediately after his accession, he had avowed his purpose, to some of his confidential servants, of "exterminating the Magyar race," as the people that gave the Austrian monarchy all its trouble. He had abolished their Constitution. He had governed them, without calling their Legislature together, by imperial mandates. He had made the crown hereditary in his family. He had made himself an absolute and irresponsible sovereign over a once free, constitutional and independent kingdom. Foreseeing that so spirited a people could not be expected to suffer thus without resistance, he struck out a plan of keeping them in silence, which would do no injustice to the character of an infernal spirit. In the north of Hungary, he erected what has been fitly called the Bloody Theatre of Eperies, headed by the infamous Caraffa, and provided with thirty executioners. It was the duty of this tribunal to examine the opinions of the leading Magyars, and to punish such as were found guilty of harboring any attachment to the prostrate liberties of the nation. The judge of this wicked inquisition used to say, that, "if one of his pulses should beat for Hungary, he would cut it out and burn it." Not only men, but women and children, were haled before this bench, where thousands of them, as innocent as angels, were tried, condemned and executed, if such a farce can be called a trial, without a hearing or a witness. The entire land was searched for patriots. The blood-hounds of the imperial tyrant tracked the footsteps of every citizen. Spies were employed for every city. They were planted in every house. No place was so secret, none so sacred, as to defend its occupants from the most critical inspection. Men were beheaded for lamenting to their wives, in their private chambers, the unhappy condition of their country. Wives were led to a similar fate for listening to the voices of their husbands. Children of tender years, whose only crime was that of having an executed patriot for a parent, were brought before this court, which ordered their brains to be dashed out against the posts of this Austrian guillotine. The ill-fated victims, against whom no witnesses could be brought, were put to the most excrutiating tortures, and compelled to accuse themselves, or to die as obstinate traitors, if they made no confession. Such was the determination, such the temper of these despots. Whoever admires the subsequent success, and power, and grandeur of the despotism of Austria, or whoever dares defend it, let him remember the means by which that despotism was established![6]

The National Assembly, in the year 1620, having become satisfied of the revolutionary intentions of the throne, met and lawfully deposed their king, Ferdinand the Second, who, by breaking his oath and the constitution, had forfeited even his own unjust pretensions to the Hungarian crown. They elevated Gabriel Bethlen to his place. For nine years Bethlen was acknowledged as their legal monarch. On his demise, in 1629, George Rákóczy, whose patriotic spirit was the glory of the people, received the high office by the suffrages of the nation. Thus, according to two perfectly constitutional acts, the line of succession in the Austrian house was broken, annulled, abrogated by the highest authority of the kingdom. These acts have never been reversed. From that day to this, by the fundamental laws of Hungary, the emperors of Austria have been, when constitutionally considered, nothing more than

[6] Coxe's House of Austria, vol. ii. chap. 66, p. 1083.

successful intruders, whom the nation has been compelled to receive under martial force. James the Second, in 1688, was expelled from the throne of England; his crimes were precisely those alleged by the Magyars against the Hapsburgs; he was deposed exactly as the Austrians were deposed; and, therefore, if the descendants of the latter have any legal claims to Hungary, the offspring of the former are, at this moment, by a much stronger title, the rightful monarchs of the British empire.[7]

Right and wrong, however, are nearly synonyms with such a race of tyrants as the imperial kings of Hungary have been. The next three sovereigns, Joseph the First, Charles the Sixth and the celebrated Maria Theresa, changing the instruments but not the policy of their house, undertook to overthrow the Hungarian Constitution, not by arms, but by dissimulation, flattery and persuasion.

In the year 1708, Joseph assembled the Diet at Pressburg, where he made a great many specious and flattering promises to the representatives of the nation. His predecessors had been engaged in bloody wars, the object of which had been to overturn the popular constitution of St. Stephen. He now promised the Hungarians a total cessation of hostilities, and a great many additional blessings, on condition of their yielding to him the free election of one of their most important officers, their demand for the acknowledgment of their constitutional immunities and liberties under the sanction of certain foreign powers, and several other things in which was clearly involved the annihilation of their constitution. The National Assembly could not be moved by the soft speeches of the monarch; and he, to secure a temporary tranquility for the accomplishment of some other purposes, which he had at heart, granted a peace without conditions. He died, however, in 1711, before this last act of his reign, called the Peace of Szathmár, was ratified.

[7] Smith's Parallels of England and Hungary, pp. 40 to 48 inclusive.

Charles the Sixth of Austria, the third of his name in Hungary, inherited the absolutism and intolerance of Leopold, his father. His weapon was flattery. He confirmed the Peace of Szathmár. He always spoke in the highest terms, in the presence of the Hungarians, of his "dear Hungary"—"cara Hungaria"—declaring his Magyar subjects to be the most magnanimous and grateful of all people. His predecessors had governed the kingdom by means of the Hungarian Chancery located at Vienna. He, on the contrary, always expressed the wish of doing the most important portion of his work in person. They, by one excuse after another, had evaded their sacred pledge to spend a part of each year at the Hungarian capital. He, to show his paternal love, made no such excuses, but actually went to Pressburg, at three several times, and took his place in the House of Magnates. The magnanimity and gratitude of the Hungarians were equal to the royal eulogies. The Magyars forgot their grievances. In the nobleness of their nature they forgot, too, their duty to themselves, to their country, and to posterity. Twelve years of artful flattery, supported by a very moderate use of imperial authority, had so far closed the eyes of the whole nation, that, in the year 1723, they not only confirmed the doctrine of *hereditary succession*, but, by the passage of the Pragmatic Sanction, extended the right of the inheritance to the *female* heirs of their Austrian sovereigns. The grant is made, however, on the express condition, so constantly maintained by every generation of the people, that the liberties and integrity of the kingdom be kept inviolate. It is the faithful observance of this condition, placed last in the important document, that it might always in the perusal of it make the last impression upon king and subject, by which the grant is to be preserved in its life and force. As in all other contracts, or covenants, one violation of this essential condition, by any king of Hungary, absolves the people from the obligation of continuing the gift; and it must be particularly noted, that, notwithstanding the fair words of Charles, and the apparent willingness of the National Assembly to bestow it, the gift was made by a nation reduced to despair by a war waged by its kings upon it, and menaced, though not in words, with still bloodier oppressions in case of a refusal.[8]

The Pragmatic Sanction was proposed and passed to open the way for the beautiful and accomplished daughter of Charles the Sixth, Maria Theresa, to the Hungarian throne. Her right to it was at once contested by a male heir of her house, the elector Charles Albrecht, who declared the document just mentioned to be unconstitutional and consequently void. His position, undoubtedly correct, was supported by all the continental governments of Europe. In her last extremity, the young queen fled for safety to her Hungarian subjects, who, struck with her beauty, her accomplishments and her distress, unwittingly or unselfishly pledged to her their support. They might now have easily declared and maintained their independence. They might have recovered, by a single act of pardonable self-respect, every thing they had lost. But their antagonist was an unprotected female. She had trusted to their generosity in confiding to them her cause. With her little Joseph in her arms, she had presented herself before the representatives of the nation, weeping in the anguish and bitterness of her heart. The tears of a distressed woman are always eloquent; and they have a sort of omnipotence with persons of a feeling and generous turn of mind. Such were the Magyars before whom she stood. They could not, they would not, be selfish in an hour like that. The old cavaliers,

[8] The present sovereign, Francis Joseph, repudiates the concessions of his immediate predecessor, on the ground that they were made while under fear and force. Should the Hungarians apply the same argument to all the grants of title ever made by themselves to the emperors, on which alone the rights of these emperors are based, how suddenly the "legitimate sovereignty" of Austria over Hungary would evaporate!

burying the wrongs of their nation in the depths of their magnanimous compassion, rose up and brandished their sharp swords. The commons stamped their feet with an outburst of emotion. Through both chambers, and from the chambers over all the land, the national watchword—"*sanguinem et vitam*"—clamorously went forth. The word of the Magyar was enough.

No sooner had Maria, by the help of her Hungarian supporters, taken possession of the throne of her ancestors, than she discovered the characteristic trait by which her relationship to the Hapsburgs was clearly proved. Having reached her position by force of arms, she resolved to act the part of a conqueror, by uniting all the subjugated kingdoms and provinces into one glorious realm. With a woman's ardor, she proceeded at once with her mighty business, forgetful of the vast difficulties in her way. The independence of several of these parts of her dominion, and the peculiar rights and reservations of them all, had been guaranteed by the oaths of every king before her, as well as by her own. The Hungarians, in particular, by whom she had been raised to power, deserved a special consideration. But, though not an ungrateful woman, as a monarch she had the gratitude only of her house. This, whenever it conflicted with the family ambition, was no gratitude at all. The work of demolition went forward. Centralization was the order of the day. All the kingdoms, provinces and dependencies, over which she ruled, must resign their nationalities, and fall into the great nationality undertaken to be formed. The identities of all these states, and fractions of states, as well as the identities of all the individuals of which they had been composed, must consent to be swallowed up in a new and unknown something, of which no one could draw to himself a very tangible idea. There was to be no longer such a being as a German, or an Italian, or a Bohemian, or a Magyar, or a Sclave. All were to be Austrians from that plastic hour. All were to be equally related to a common throne. That throne, like a sun in the centre of the heavens, was not only to govern the motions of all this complicated system of dependent bodies, but throw out upon them a ceaseless flood of light, and life, and even *liberty*, while all together should fulfil the prophecy or the threat of Frederic, and rule the nations of the globe.

In the execution of this scheme, Maria had only one race to fear. The Germans in Austria were then, as they are yet, few in number. The Sclaves of Bohemia, of Gallicia, of Hungary, were, as they have been described, but little more than slaves. The Italians were too much divided among themselves to give her any serious trouble. The Magyars, however, so soon as they should see her object, were sure to rise in opposition to her plans. The politic and crafty sovereign was determined to silence them, to close their eyes, till her points were gained. She shackled them with her favors and dazzled them with her smiles. Her whole administration was a succession of seeming demonstrations, that, whatever might be the end aimed at by the royal reformer, the Magyar was winning every thing he desired. She committed her person entirely to his keeping. Hungarians were almost the only servants and ministers she employed. She gave them all the eclat and glory of her reign. Their Constitution she always enthusiastically applauded, though, at the same time, she governed them as if there never had been such a constitution in the world. Like a serpent, which, fixing his eye upon a bird, puts forth his gayest colors, his blandest look, his subtlest and most secret charms, concealing the venom of his tooth and the flashing of his fiery tongue, till the poor victim of his lust is lured within the reach of his sudden spring, so the queen captivated the nation by her charms. Before the Hungarians saw their danger, they were caught; and when, in 1770, Maria was carried to her grave, she had laid down and established the precedent of governing a constitutional kingdom without respect to its constitution, the place of which had been supplied by the imperial decrees. When the Magyar, shaking off the spell by which he had been bound for a period of just thirty years, rose to self-consciousness again, he found himself stripped of his liberties, despoiled of his country, robbed of his nationality and independence, acting the part of a favorite footman to that triumphal car, in which Austrian despotism displayed its glory and its power.

Joseph the Second, son and successor of Maria, carried to the throne all the ambition, but no portion of the personal or political suavity of his mother. In the unchanging spirit of a Hapsburg, he resolved to take up the work of Austrian aggrandizement exactly where his predecessor had laid it down. She, at the moment of her death, had just reached the point, where she could have safely avowed the secret policy of her house. She died, in fact, with the declaration of that policy on her lips. Joseph, feeling his situation to be sufficiently secure, threw off the long-worn mask. The anagram of Frederic now came to light. Austria now confessed, that she determined to rule, at least, a large portion of the world. On the day of his coronation, the new king offered an insult to the Hungarian nation, which was to try its spirit and settle the question, whether it was ready to acknowledge itself a slave. He refused to be crowned in Hungary. He spurned the coronation oath, by which all his predecessors had bound themselves to maintain the Hungarian nationality and constitution, and without which he could not be a lawful king. He positively and openly rejected the constitution. He abolished the municipal self-government of the villages and counties. He declared the entire government of the kingdom, legislative, executive and judicial, to be no part of the business of the people, but the inalienable prerogative and property of the crown. That crown was his by hereditary descent; and he needed no election, no coronation, nothing that the Hungarian people could do for him, to make him king. They were his subjects, not his constituents, or his fellow-citizens. The goal, so long aimed at, was now attained. The work of centralization was complete. Despotism had nothing more to do. Austria was all. Hungary was no more! At the death of Francis the First, in 1832, who had followed the brief reign of his immediate predecessor, Leopold the Second, Joseph's successor, with a long course of tyranny, the Hungarian constitution was a thing generally unmentioned. It was not dead, and buried, but, with the world at large, as unthought of as if it had never been!

When the constitution of a people is abolished, the next step toward the total destruction of their nationality is to suppress their religion. It is particularly necessary to do this, if that religion happens to be on the side of freedom. Such was the religion of the Magyars at the time when the House of the Hapsburgs seized the crown of Stephen. The Magyars were then Protestants. The first article of their faith was that of religious liberty. Religious liberty is the certain harbinger, at all times and places, of civil liberty. This was understood by the Austrian tyrants, who, as the champions of absolutism, could not behold, without a struggle, the establishment of a system of free worship. As the avowed defenders of Catholicism in Europe, they were bound to abet the efforts of the Roman pontiffs, in their attempt to exterminate the Reformation. Resolved to eradicate the whole Magyar race from Hungary, they could not fail to make their zeal for Christianity a pretext to cover their malicious purpose. They clearly saw their position and their interest; and they were never known to be slack in any thing involving the great object of their ambition. Their work was undertaken with their characteristic spirit. No charity was to be exercised toward the Magyars. A foul spot was now upon them, which rendered them doubly odious to all the other races, which made it popular to hate them, and which rendered it a piece of piety in the monarchs to oppress them. Their first movement illustrates the depth and breadth of their despotic spirit, as well as the readiness and freedom of its action, when there is no fear of impolicy in the way to check it. It clearly demonstrates what they would always do, could they, at all times, freely act out their nature. The movement was prompt enough to satisfy the temper of any tyrant. An imperial decree, repeating the words of an older one promulgated by one of their predecessors, was proclaimed and published. It was posted, on every thing capable of holding a placard, throughout the kingdom. It was not a lengthy document. Excepting the date, address and signature, two Latin words embraced the whole of it; and, in our tongue, its brevity is almost as startling: "The Lutherans must be burnt!"[9]

It is scarcely necessary to relate with what energy such a decree, under such circumstances, would be executed by such a race of despots. The first act of Rhodolph the Second was a plan for the extermination of the Protestants. He recalled the few Catholic nobles of Hungary, whom the doctrines of Luther had not reached, to resume their places in the National Assembly. He filled all the vacant committees, as well as the subordinate offices of revenue and of justice, with Catholics. He forbade any cure, or benefice, to be conferred upon any person not openly *devoted* to the church. He ordered, that no student should receive an academical degree, and that no scholar should be eligible to a college chair, who had not signed the Catholic formulary of faith. He permitted no town to appoint a secretary, or clerk, without his knowledge and approbation. He admitted no person to the rights of citizenship, whether native or foreign, who had not undergone a religious examination, and taken an oath of perfect and unqualified submission to the priests. He shut up the churches of the Protestants. He took from them their estates without the form even of a trial. That no complaints might trouble him, he caused the Aulic council, another star-chamber, to

[9] Lutherani comburantur! Pulsky's Hist., Introduction, p. 110.

thunder the ban of the empire against every man, who dared to say a word on the side of clemency. He paid no attention to the civil government of the country. He refused to fill the great secular and ecclesiastical offices, or conferred them on his favorites. He suffered the important post of Palatine, which would have stood as a defence of the people against his barbarous and lawless persecutions, to remain vacant. He filled the country with foreign troops, that, while he was proceeding with his persecutions, the population might be awed into a state of quiet. At his instigation, the mercenary soldiers, ready to do any thing for pay, as well as eager to satisfy their lusts, entered the habitations of the Protestants, usurped their best apartments and their tables, expelled the fathers of families from their own houses, and committed the worst of barbarities upon the persons of their wives and daughters. Scores of villages, belonging to Protestant cities, were seized, pillaged and put under military discipline. The peasants of the country were dragged from their ploughs to answer for their opinions. The whole land was left to lie without cultivation. Famine, disease, death filled every neighborhood. In the great capitals of the provinces, Austrian generals and governors, like Belgioso in the city of Kassau, paraded the streets with executioners in their train, devoting every individual, male and female, to instant execution, who ventured to utter the slightest disapprobation of these cruelties.[10]

It is difficult to tell, by which the heart of a liberal and compassionate man is moved the most—the enormities practised by these emperors—or the plaintive murmurs sent up by the nation thus oppressed. The thoughtful reader may decide this question, by pondering upon a single extract of one of the decrees of the Hungarian kingdom:

"Sorely grieved and vexed at heart, the faithful magnates and estates feel impelled—as formerly, so now—to complain

[10] Coxe's House of Austria, vol. ii. chap. 40, *passim*.

to God and the King, that all their entreaties, remonstrances, and representations have never helped them to obtain even the slightest mitigation of their sufferings, horrors and miseries, but that the same have gone on increasing, from day to day, and from year to year. When we are told that the Hungarians are in the habit of coming into parliament with tears and all kinds of wailings and woful lament, and that, when weary of sighs and of words, they proceed to business, we will not, indeed, deny, that such is the case. But who is there that will command the tears of the lacerated and wounded? Who will stop the wailings of children, when they submit their sufferings to their parents?

"Nor are the grievances of Upper Hungary, Sclavonia, and other parts of the kingdom, less and more bearable. In these provinces, the soldiery take possession of the cities, market towns, villages, houses, and noble *curias*, as if they had come to them in the due course of inheritance. They divide the same, and treat the natives of the soil, in their own homes, not as proprietors, but as vagrants or bondsmen. In *many* places, the foreign soldiers attack and plunder the cottages of the peasantry, and the seats and possessions of the noblemen. They, by main force, open churches and graves, rob the corpses and bones of the departed of their funeral dresses, and flagellate, wound and kill the fathers of families. By force and violence, they bear away wives from their husbands, children from their parents, infant daughters from their mothers, chaste virgins from their paternal home, and abduct them to the haunts of infamy and vice, where—may God pity the bitter sufferings of the Hungarian people!—they are sacrificed to beastly violence, and afterwards brought back, if ransomed with large sums of money!

"Large numbers of dwellers within these realms, scions of old and honored families, once happy in befitting affluence—now expelled from all their possessions—wander about, naked, hungry and forlorn, praying for bread at every door!

"Such is the lamentable condition of the rest of the Hungarian people—a condition which even hearts of stone must pity. That people was once eminent in martial honors, wealth and merit; but, at this present time, we are bent with severe affliction, not on account of the *tolerable* dominion of the Turks and Tartars, but on account of the *unrestrained* misdeeds of foreign soldiers!" How terrible must have been the despotism, which could wring from the lips of a courageous and manly people such pitiful lamentations! It was by such means, indeed, that Catholicism was established in Hungary, by a succession of tyrants, as the religion of the state![11]

The civil and religious liberties of the Hungarians being thus abolished, the imperious despots next addressed themselves, with a still more open malice, to the destruction of the beautiful and expressive language of the nation. That, which was a region of darkness to the rulers, was supposed to be the last asylum of Magyar liberty, nationality and independence. The institutions of the free state, they saw, might be overthrown; the rights of conscience and the resources of a free religion might be withdrawn; and yet, so long as the incensed and insulted race could relate their sorrows and consult upon measures of redress, in a language unintelligible to the tyrants, the work of annihilation was not done. Those tyrants, therefore, now determined to make a final end of that strange speech, in which the spirit of democratic liberty had so long been nursed. Edict after edict was thundered from the throne. With all the presumptuousness of folly and despotism united, the German language was declared to be the language of the state. All the laws were to be published in it. The delibera-

[11] This decree (13th Rhodolph, 1602) may be compared with Klapka's History, Introduction, p. 46, and with Coxe's House of Austria, vol. ii. chap. 40, p. 657. For an account of Ferdinand's persecutions, see House of Austria, vol. ii. p. 814–815. The barbarities of Leopold may be found in the House of Austria, vol. ii. p. 1072, *passim*.

tions of the National Assembly were to be had in German. German masters and professors were sent into all the schools and colleges of the land. The Hungarian was entirely excluded. Hungarian books were discouraged or interdicted. Hungarian literature, in all its departments, was denounced. The friends of a native literature were regarded and treated as traitors to the crown. If, in the county assemblies, or in the gatherings of the villagers, a word of the contraband dialect was employed, the unhappy culprit, who, perhaps, could speak no other language, had to pay the severe penalty of his crime. The very peasants, indeed, had to converse about their lands and crops in an unknown speech, or be entirely dumb. The Magyar merchant and mechanic, sailor and soldier, not less than the peasants and professors, had to talk of their business and their books in German, or not talk at all. The mother, deprived of the first privilege of nature, was forbidden to teach her infant to lisp her own words and accents, and compelled to hold all her intercourse with the fruit of her own body in a language, which, as a general thing, she did not understand. No words, indeed, can exceed the intolerance, the severity, the madness of this crusade against the Hungarian tongue. Fines and penalties, such as are usually laid against heinous or capital offences, were fixed for the punishment of those, who persisted in the use of a language taught them by their parents and once spoken by their sainted dead. From the beginning of the Hapsburg sway in Hungary, this hostility had been at work, first, in discouraging the Hungarian for the Latin, and, secondly, by displacing the Hungarian for the German. During the Latin era, the work of extermination was carried on by a thousand artful schemes of a concealed but consistent centralizing policy; but, at the opening of the German period, the Austrians had so gained and grown in power, that they dared to avow their object, and continue their efforts in the light of day. For two-thirds of a generation, from 1770 to 1790, the German war of annihilation lasted. At the conclusion of the struggle, the work was so far accomplished, that the despots began to consider Hungary as a German province. For the space of the next forty years, the language of the Magyar, in all public places, was almost as dead as Latin; and it survived the imperial tyranny only by clinging, in spite of the Austrian decrees, to the farms and firesides of the common people. The magnates had ceased to use, many of them to understand, the noble and patriotic forms of a speech, which carried within itself the liberty, the independence, the nationality of the race that had employed it.[12]

It has been recently imagined, by some popular writers, that the late ordinance of the Austrian government, forbidding the Magyars wearing their collars turned over after the fashion of the Americans, is an unprecedented piece of despotism. This supposition is a mistake. Similar decrees have been sent forth against the Magyars at many periods of their history. The one great object of Austria has been, let it be remembered, to exterminate the Magyar nationality. Not only his liberal constitution, his free religion, his patriotic language, but his national dress, has frequently been put under the imperial ban. More than once has it been made a crime for the Hungarian to be seen wearing his *kalpag*, or native cap.

---

[12] Peter Bod, who wrote, during this German era, the Introduction to his "History of the Church Militant," complains that he could not venture to write the proper names, even, of the Hungarians in their own language, as they would not be recognised by the nation! City of the Magyar, vol. iii. p. 54. The declension of the Hungarian, which almost amounted to a loss, is not only stated but lamented by scores of the more recent Hungarian authors. It is no wonder, therefore, that Hungary has produced so little of native literature of high rank. It is a wonder, however, in her circumstances, that she has been able, I will not only say to produce any literary works at all, but to preserve enough of her interdicted tongue to form for it the beginning of a new existence.

More than once, to wear that ensign of his relationship to the hated race subjected a citizen to as severe a punishment, as if he had robbed his neighbor on the public road. The loose frock coat, that representative of the original elegance and freedom of the still looser oriental robes, was forcibly displaced for a German suit, which, to the eye of the patriot, seemed as ignominious, as for an honorable man, in any other country, to be clad in a bandit's garb or a prisoner's attire. It was the dress of his worst enemy. To wear it, at least willingly, was to cease to be a Magyar, and to become a German. The light sash, or belt, the mark of the universal knightly independence of the nation, was strictly interdicted. Austria, despotic in the smallest particulars, as well as in those of the greatest moment, must not only make the laws, control the pulpits, bind the language, but cut the garments of her Hungarian subjects. The noble-hearted and keenly-sensitive Hungarian must submit to this intolerable oppression. He must consent to be stripped of every thing that made him a Hungarian. Bereft of his civil liberties, of his rights of conscience, and of his native speech, he must next clothe himself in the apparel of his oppressor, and move about among his conquerors as a walking monument of their victory, an object of their laughter. When the Jews had inflicted every other indignity upon the rights and person of our Savior, they stripped him of his own raiment, and compelled him to walk about, in the judgment hall, in the habiliments of his royal persecutor. The cutting keenness of this malice has, perhaps, never been repeated upon any individual, though a real malefactor, by the most brutal of subsequent oppressors. Austria, however, has not only revived it, but multiplied the individual to a nation, whose only crime has been, that it did not wish to sink into absolute and eternal annihilation.

When every thing, in which the Magyar nationality could find a resting-place, had been subjected or overturned, to keep the race in perpetual bondage, the foreign despots perfected their system of subjugation by surrounding them with the links of a military chain. A standing army of foreigners, divided into convenient parts, and commanded by German officers, was ranged all along the western and northern frontiers, under the pretence of guarding the passes of the Carpathians against the Russians and the Poles. The southern and eastern border was defended, professedly against the Turks, by the Military District, a strip of country nearly a thousand miles in length, whose inhabitants were all soldiers, who, though citizens of Hungary, were made amenable to the Austrian government. The interior of the land was occupied, at various points, by strong garrisons, which were ostensibly created as recruiting stations, but which, in fact, were only the folding end of the chain, that wound its involutions around the nation's heart. The other end, of course, was securely fastened to the throne. Thus, hand and foot, body and spirit, the race of Magyars, after being robbed of every thing that made them Magyars, or guaranteed their existence as a nation, were bound down to a hopeless and everlasting bondage. So far as they were concerned, the anagram of Frederic was realized; and, by their subjugation, Austria had taken its position as the arbiter, if not the imperator, of the European world.

It cannot, indeed, be doubted, even by the warmest apologists of Austria, that, from the very beginning of her history, it has been the single aim of her despotic rulers to extend their despotism over all the states acknowledging any connection to their imperial sway. The states were, therefore, by every means, to be reduced to the condition of imperial provinces. Their independence, of course, had first to be destroyed. Their national institutions, and particularly their municipal rights and regulations, had to be overturned. Their religion, if different from the religion of the tyrants, had to be extirpated. Their language, dress, manners and customs, before there could be a complete amalgamation of the conquerors and the conquered, had to be annihilated. All these things were necessary to the accomplishment of the one great end in view. Such, it is certain, have been the purposes of the House of Austria in all her subject principalities and kingdoms. In Bohemia, in Gallicia, as well as in the territories of the original arch-duchy, the work was not very difficult. In Italy, there was no limit to the design but a change of language, which, by reason of its impossibility, has not been attempted. Everywhere, in fact, outside of Hungary, the work of absolutism, of centralization, has been effected without any signal opposition. The people, in all those countries, had been well prepared for despotism. Italy, for two thousand years, had known nothing but despotism. Bohemia had always been in bondage to some imperious monarch. Gallicia, though animated with the thoughts of liberty, while holding a connection with the republic of the Poles, had ever been too weak, or rather too plastic, to offer any serious resistance. In Hungary, however, the question of liberty, or slavery, was a very different question. The kingdom had never been otherwise than free and independent. The nation had always been the champion of popular institutions. The people had enjoyed, from their origin, the blessings of personal and social liberty. Their constitution, laws and civilization were all entirely liberal, if not democratic. The spirit of democracy was their life-spirit. To take away this democracy was to take away their breath, their vitality, their very being. Still, just as far as the work of annihilating Hungary was difficult, just so far it was positively essential to the great object. Austria could not be a safe or a perfect despot, so long as her largest and most powerful dependancy, larger and more powerful than all the rest of her possessions, should remain free, liberal and democratic. The time might come, unless this nation of liberty-loving Magyars should be transformed to a province of abject Austrians, when, in spite of all the mighty despotisms about it, this Hungary might not only reassert her own independence, but proclaim liberty to her sister captives.

The time might come, when, fired by her ancestral spirit, and emulating the bravery of her first inhabitants, she might raise her keen sabre against the heart of this all-encompassing tyranny, and strike the fetters from the hands and feet of central and southern Europe. The time might come, after all their sufferings and reverses, when these unconquered Magyars, rising in their pristine majesty, might resolve to make their country the centre of a new system of nations, whose government, like their own, should be democratic, whose religion should be anti-papal, whose civilization should be liberal and expansive, and whose very beginning should be the end of European slavery.

The possibility of such a period has pressed, for three hundred years, upon the forebodings of the imperial despots, and contributed to make them, what their whole history has proved them to be, the most determined, the most unscrupulous, the most unfeeling and relentless enemies of civil liberty, that Europe has ever seen. Their entire policy has been, so far as they have had to do with Hungary, to overthrow the nationality and break the spirit of the Magyars, who, in that quarter of the globe, have been almost the only consistent and unflinching friends of human freedom, and the absolutely indomitable foes of despotism, on the battle-fields of humanity for more than eleven centuries of time.

CHAPTER VIII.

THE MAGYARS DEFEND THEIR NATIONALITY.

It has been recently reported in the papers of Vienna, that, in the spring of 1850, Haynau, the Austrian butcher, had an interview with the children of the immortal Kossuth. He addressed the younger of them in the German. The reply was in Hungarian. On seeing that the commander-in-chief did not understand him, the boy spoke French, remarking that every general must certainly understand that tongue. Neither of the children could be induced to speak the first word in the language of their father's enemies.[1]

It must not be supposed, indeed, that, at the present moment, or in former ages, in the midst of the terrible oppressions of their imperial rulers, the Magyars have bowed their necks with a Sclavic stupidity to the despots. Far from it. They have always offered resistance to these oppressions. It has been only after the most strenuous opposition, in every instance, that they have finally yielded to the necessities of their position.

They, therefore, who have charged the present generation of Hungarians with a morbid sensitiveness; with a mutinous disposition, unprecedented in the conduct of their brave and patriotic fathers; with having raised up a revolution out of trifles, to which no attention has been paid in former ages, have not studied very carefully, if they have searched at all, the annals of this manly and spirited race of people. The history of Hungary, since its connection with the Germans,

[1] The incident was reported by the Pesth correspondent of Lloyd, and afterwards published in the Vienna Times.

is the history of a constant succession of revolutions. The Magyars have never been contented; and, unless they had been cursed with a servile temper, contentment could never have been so much as possible.

The earliest of the Hungarian insurrections, against the despotism of Austria, was raised by the religious persecutions mentioned in a previous chapter. At the very outbreak of the Lutheran Reformation, the emperor Charles the Fifth called together the imperial Diet, at the city of Worms, "to concert with the princes of the empire effectual measures for checking the progress of those new and dangerous opinions, which threatened to disturb the peace of Germany, and to overturn the religion of their ancestors;" and, while the Diet was in session, he drew up and signed that memorable declaration, which, for thirty years, overwhelmed all Europe with a deluge of blood: "Descended as I am," said the bigot, "from the Christian emperors of Germany, the Catholic kings of Spain, and from the archdukes of Austria and the dukes of Burgundy, all of whom have preserved, to the last moment of their lives, their fidelity to the Church, and have always been the defenders and protectors of the Catholic faith, its decrees, its ceremonies, its usages, I have been, am still, and will ever be devoted to those Christian doctrines, and the constitution of the Church, which they have left to me as a sacred inheritance. And as it is evident, that a simple monk has advanced opinions contrary to the sentiments of all Christians, past and present, I am firmly determined to wipe away the reproach, which a toleration of such errors would cast on Germany, and to employ all my power and resources, my body, my blood, my life, and even my soul, in checking the progress of this sacrilegious doctrine!" It scarcely need be added, that when, in the estimation of a powerful, proud and superstitious monarch, *toleration* is regarded as a *reproach*, which must be wiped off by all the energies of his mind and might, there is little to be hoped for the object of such a threat; and when it is considered, that the power and resources of the rampant emperor were spread from the shores of the Atlantic to the borders of Russia, from the northern limits of modern Germany to the southern borders of ancient Cicily, and into the New World then recently discovered, it will be seen what causes the yet unenslaved and unbending nation of the Magyars were to have for opposition.[2]

Charles the Fifth, however, was too busy with his German persecutions to leave him time for any particular attention to the Hungarian nation; and his brother Ferdinand, who claimed to be king of Hungary from 1527 to 1564, was not able, for nearly thirty years, so far to settle his authority in the kingdom, as to give it any special trouble. In 1556, Ferdinand was elected emperor; and though, after that event, he was a much more powerful monarch than before it, the Magyars maintained their opposition to him with their accustomed spirit. From 1527 to 1540, John Zapolyi, and from 1540 to 1571, John Sigismund, led the Magyar forces against Ferdinand and his successor, Maximilian; but this latter emperor was so wise, so kind, so just a ruler, that, in spite of the illegality of his pretensions, he gradually acquired a high degree of popularity with those over whom he sought to set up his sway. Sigismund, however, still heading a very formidable resistance, kept the philosophic and generous usurper from getting possession of the country; and, when all other means had failed, he followed the example of his opponents, and put himself under the protection of the Turks. On the death of Sigismund, in 1571, the war of succession, which had raged for nearly half a century, ceased; and the west of Hungary, which had found its opposition useless, temporarily submitted to its fate. Thus terminated the first general resistance to the extension of the tyranny of the Hapsburgs into Hungary.

[2] Coxe's House of Austria, vol. i. pp. 410–418

Transylvania, however, which was farther from the scene of action, though prudently acknowledging the supremacy of Austria, soon rose again in arms. In this act of resistance, it was undoubtedly encouraged by the Turks, who, having been invited into Hungary by both parties, and having thus taken possession of the entire course of the Danube, including nearly all the national garrisons and forts, wished now to conquei and hold the whole kingdom for themselves. This they could not, in their own name, do, without rousing the dormant hostility of the European world. Looking through the country for a fit instrument of their ambition, they found another Sigismund, son of Christopher Bathori, whom they elevated to the princely rank, and under whose banner and auspices they professed to fight. This scheme, ingenious as it was, would have had no great success, had not the iron-handed oppressions of Rhodolph the First, then claiming the crown of Stephen, startled every Magyar from his confiding sleep. Those oppressions, to which the reader's attention has before been called, brought the entire nation to its feet. Forgetting, in the moment of their just indignation, that their cause could receive from a Turkish alliance no honor, nor any lasting good, they accepted of the proffered services of the Turks, and rushed to the field of battle to defend their rights. Rhodolph met them with an overwhelming force. Sigismund was defeated. He was compelled to lay down his power, to cede his territories to the emperor, and to go into exile on a small pension allowed him by his foe.

At this event the sultan was violently enraged. Raising an immense army, he marched into the bosom of the ceded territory, and vigorously attacked the German troops, who, in Rhodolph's name, had taken possession of the grant. The Mahometan was everywhere victorious. Sigismund was speedily recalled. For a considerable time, success crowned all his efforts; but subsequently, in a bloody battle with the Austrian army of occupation, he lost so many of his men, that he was forced to retire the second time. Rhodolph, hoping to buy him off, settled on him certain lordships, which, had the Hungarian not been fighting for his country rather than for himself, would have been sufficient to satisfy him for his troubles and his loss. General Basta, the emperor's commander, took martial possession of the country, and reared over the heads of the people a military despotism more onerous, more sanguinary, more brutal than the country had ever known before.

The rest of Hungary, at the same time, stretching from the banks of the Theiss to the western borders of the kingdom, was still more seriously afflicted with the direct, open, galling tyranny of the Hapsburg monarch. He paid no attention whatever to the welfare, internal or external, of the nation. He appointed no magistrates, nominated no pastors, published no laws, nor manifested the least concern for the civil, social, or religious prosperity of the country. The entire management of affairs was left to his military chieftains, who ruled the citizens by the sword, and gratified without restraint every lust of barbarism and brutality on the lives, properties and persons of both sexes. When petitions were sent up to the emperor, such as the one recorded in another place, he is said to have received them with a hearty laugh. They were proof, as he thought, that the nation was about subdued; and it made him merry to look over its pitiful concessions of his success. Historians have also remarked, that, after the reception of these melancholy appeals to his generosity, he was always more cruel, more thoroughly despotic, than before; for, from each new evidence of the probable accomplishment of his purpose, he acquired a renewal of inspiration for the prosecution of his work. It is well known, too, that, instead of restraining the lawlessness of his soldiers, he personally and perpetually encouraged them in their infamous and reckless life. Hundreds of estates, belonging to Hungarians, were claimed and confiscated by the fiscal of the state. Count

Illeshazy, the first of the Magyar magnates, both in honors and in wealth, and a consistent Protestant, had performed great services for his country, not only as a citizen at home, but as a general abroad. For being a Protestant, however, and because he ventured to express compassion for his countrymen in these dark and bloody times, he was deprived of his honors, stripped of his property, and sent to be an irreclaimable exile from the land he had dared to love. Endurance was no longer a virtue. The Magyars rose up in strength. Choosing Stephen Botskay, the first nobleman of Upper Hungary, as their leader, they raised their banners for their country and their faith.

The Transylvanian Magyars, in the mean time, after the defeat and departure of their prince, Sigismund, were industriously searching for another chieftain. Under the terrible administration of Basta, they had been driven to despair; and, unless they could lay their hands upon a man of the first order of abilities, they saw nothing before them but still greater enormities of a licentious, greedy, beastly military power. Fortune at last favored them. There were, at that time, large numbers of Hungarians in Turkey, who, after having struggled nobly against the extension of Austrian despotism over Hungary, had fled for personal safety before the devouring forces of the Germans. It was not cowardice that impelled them to this flight; but, not having succeeded in their opposition, they wished to prolong their lives in a neighboring land, from which they might watch the vicissitudes of liberty and slavery at home, and, upon a favorable opportunity, return to resume the contest against their imperial foes. That opportunity now seemed to have arrived; and among them there was a hero, whose valor, whose abilities, whose patriotism, had been severely tried. That hero was the far-famed Moses Tzekeli, who, at the head of his choice band of exiles, entered Transylvania in spite of all opposition. His countrymen, glorying in their great chief, flocked to his standard from all parts. Others of them, seeing the necessity of dispatch, rushed to the strongholds of the country, took possession of the fortresses, and expelled the Austrian garrisons from their posts. Battle after battle was fought. The Magyars were almost uniformly victorious. Thousands of the enemy were slain; thousands were taken prisoners; and the rest were struck with a panic, from which they recovered only by their usual intrigue. Distressed on every side, in their extremity they begged the help of certain hordes of Turkey, and, as has ever been the custom of Austria when fairly beaten, owed their restoration to the assistance of foreign mercenaries. The bandit Turks, who, in this interference, contradicted the well-known policy of their government, could, nevertheless, give the best of bandit reasons for their conduct. In addition to the yellow florins of their employers, they were promised the "booty and beauty" of the country. Lust and avarice succeeded. Tzekeli, whose bravery would not permit him to fly again from peril, was slain in the hottest of a battle. His followers, regarding him as their only hope, dispersed to the fastnesses of the neighboring mountains. Basta, the lawless despot of the still more lawless and despotic emperor, again spread his forces over the province, again set up his insufferable military sway, again undertook his task of keeping the people in subjection to the house of Austria, by every act that can degrade the character of a tyrant.[3]

The patriots were more successful in the western portion of the kingdom. Botskay, whose age, and rank, and purity of life, and nobleness of character, secured him the veneration of his countrymen, went to the capital of Bohemia in person, that he might there hold a conference with the royal persecutor, and dissuade him, if possible, from farther acts of cruelty and oppression. Proceeding to the palace of the monarch, he sent in his name and the object of his visit, but was not at

[3] Coxe's House of Austria, vol. ii. p. 90.

once admitted, as his position demanded, into the royal presence. Sitting hour after hour in the antechamber of the king's residence, where he was abused by the lowest menials of the emperor, he at length became indignant at the insult. Without farther efforts to get an audience, he left the house, proceeded to his own stopping-place, and immediately returned to his afflicted and now insulted country. When he reached home, he found his friends and neighbors in great excitement, not so much, at that moment, over their own misfortunes, as his losses. In his absence, and probably while sitting as a neglected suppliant in the palace, messengers of the imperial government had been sent to his place of residence, where they had made public proclamation, only a few hours before his own arrival, that his possessions were open to the plunder of his enemies. He found his houses and lands robbed, his family and friends insulted, and all those nameless atrocities committed upon his estates, which, however frequently they may be discovered in the annals of these tyrants, will not bear to be written out in this country, even for the information of the public.[4]

The measures of the great Botskay were taken with becoming spirit. He at once published a manifesto to the Hungarian nation, in which he stated not only this recent outrage, but a summary of the grievances of the country. He told the Magyars, what was very true, that the claim of Austria to the crown of Hungary was unfounded; that the emperors had been nothing better than fortunate usurpers; that their object was to overthrow the constitutional government of the people and to set up an irresponsible tyranny in the place of it; that, if they now succeeded in breaking the spirit of the nation, there might never be a time when it would have courage to raise up an opposition to the oppressors; that that was its chosen opportunity, if it wished to declare and maintain its

[4] Coxe's House of Austria, vol. ii. pp. 91–92

independence, while Transylvania was unsatisfied and unsettled, and while the Turks, the natural opponents of the Germans, held the course of the Danube and its tributary waters. The appeal went home to the hearts of the suffering Hungarians. The voice of patriotism roused them as by magic. Seizing such weapons as they had, some with swords and other martial implements, many with forks, and scythes, and pruning-hooks, they crowded to the head-quarters of their liberator, which rang with the watch-words of liberty and independence. The whole kingdom was filled with similar enthusiasm. The royal army itself, which was posted in convenient stations throughout the country, could not resist the contagious spirit of the populace. Thousands of them deserted from the imperial standards, and joined the ranks of the uprising people.

At this signal, the patriots of Transylvania again mustered. Putting themselves under the command of Gabriel Bethlen, whose name has been before mentioned, and whose courage and military skill were equal to his position, they marched out of their own territory into Upper Hungary, and united their forces to those of Botskay. The beautiful valleys of their fair country were thus deserted to the unrestrained rapacity of Basta. His work of devastation, however, was about completed. He had little more, if any thing more, to do. "All traces of human industry," says the historian, speaking of Transylvania at this period, "were swept away from its once fertile plains and fruitful hills; towns and villages offered nothing but the spectacle of ruin and desolation; corn was bought at the price of gold; horses, and even domestic animals [such as cats and dogs] were used for food; and, at length, the people were driven to the tombs to seek a wretched sustenance from the putrid bodies of their fellow-creatures. The most dreadful disorders were produced by these execrable aliments; and pestilence swept away many of those, who had escaped from famine and the sword!"[5] Leaving such a land behind him, Basta hurried after the fugitives, intending to join his troops to those of Belgioso, who had the command of the king's army in the north and west of Hungary.

The imperialists and patriots soon met. The Austrians were routed and driven completely from the country. Botskay was proclaimed king of Hungary and woiwode of Transylvania. The entire nation supported the proclamation; and the new monarch was readily acknowledged by the Turks. The famous sultan, Achmet, sent him a club, a sabre, and a standard, in honor of his victory, of his bravery, and of his office. The hero, however, refused the crown, wishing only, as he said, to give freedom to his countrymen, and then to enjoy that freedom as a private citizen. His popularity was unbounded. All Hungary stood ready to obey his wishes; and the Protestants of the whole German empire, particularly of Bohemia and Austria, would gladly have marched behind him to the walls of the imperial capital. Such was the end of the second war of opposition to the unjust claim of the Austrians over Hungary.

On the death of Botskay, Sigismond Rakoczy was elevated to the principality of Transylvania; but Hungary, excepting a small portion east of the river Theiss, had been recovered by the emperor. The crown of Hungary was soon after laid on the head of Ferdinand the Second, son of Matthias, who had succeeded to the empire on the demise of the hated Rhodolph. Ferdinand was a cruel prince. Under his auspices commenced one of the bloodiest persecutions, which Protestantism ever suffered from the Catholics. Count Thurn in Bohemia, and Gabriel Bethlen in Transylvania, raised the standard of resistance. The Magyars of Hungary were not to be outdone in patriotic service to their country. With characteristic ardor, they thronged to the field of battle,

[5] Coxe's House of Austria, vol. ii. chap. 42, p. 687.

resolved to defend their religion, as well as their homes and firesides, from destruction. Ferdinand repeated, and even outstripped, the horrors perpetrated by his predecessors. Determined to force Catholicism and absolute monarchy upon his Protestant Hungarian subjects, and totally unscrupulous how he effected his purpose upon such a race of heretics, he sent marauding parties to scour and devastate the rural districts, confiscated the estates of the wealthy gentlemen and nobles, impressed the peaceable citizens to fill up his immense military levies, assassinated, massacred, robbed and pillaged the industrious population, violated the wives and daughters of every Protestant household, and spread the gloom of desolation and despair over the most beautiful of all countries. Such proceedings naturally excited, to the highest pitch, the allied forces under Thurn and Bethlen. The former, coming down with the impetuosity of an eagle upon Vienna, carried every thing before him; and the latter, bursting from the confines of Transylvania into Hungary, captured all the great fortresses, scattered the emperor's forces under the command of Homonai, took Pressburg by assault, swept onward into Austria, and, joining his troops to those of Thurn, waged battle with the imperial commander-in-chief, Buckoy, and drove him from the walls and intrenchments of the city.

Count Thurn returned in peace to his native land; and Bethlen, as soon as he had crossed the frontiers, was proclaimed king by his victorious soldiers. The people, not only of Transylvania, but of all Hungary, ratified the choice of the army, and crowned the successful defender and deliverer of their country.

Ferdinand, fearing a second irruption of the patriots into his patrimonial territory, made the most vigorous exertions to recover by bargaining, by intrigue, by artful diplomacy, what he had lost in battle. Sending a beggarly petition to the king of Spain, he assured his Catholic majesty that he had been fighting only for the honor and extension of the Church, and concluded his appeal by asking a rich subsidy of gold and a loan of troops. The money and the men were granted; but Bethlen had intrenched himself so completely in the affections of his subjects, that Ferdinand was compelled, at last, to acknowledge the new sovereign and conclude with him a truce for twenty years. Nine years afterwards, in 1629, a second truce was signed; and when Bethlen died, he carried with him to his grave the satisfaction of having saved his country from the double curse of political despotism and religious persecution. With him closed the third war of Hungarian independence.

George Rakoczy succeeded, in Transylvania at least, to the throne left vacant by the death of Bethlen; and in Hungary his claims to the succession were generally acknowledged by the magnates. During the progress of the thirty years' war in Germany, from 1618 to 1648, Hungary, including Transylvania, was generally able to maintain its independence; but the peace of Westphalia, which gave to the emperors of Austria the opportunity of recovering their old possessions, renewed the troubles and sufferings of this interesting country. In 1660, George Rakoczy the Second was raised to the woiwodeship of Transylvania. Soon afterwards he died; and he was followed by Kemeny, Barczay and Abaffy, who successively maintained their country's cause against imperial ambition and military rule. The Jesuits of Austria, the worst of all Jesuits, soon began to plot against the Magyar Protestants, and particularly against the great Wesselènyi, at that time Palatine of Hungary. They were "the favorites and the counselors of the emperor; they had wealth, station and power; 'but all this availed them nothing, so long as they saw Mordecai, the Jew, sitting at the king's gate.' On every opportunity, therefore, they influenced the minister to persecute the Protestants in Hungary, and unfortunately with too much success."[6]

[6] The reader will find a good summary of these cruelties in the

The barbarities of other years were repeated. Scaffolds and executioners were again common. Murder, assassination, rape, extortion, and every conceivable crime, spread dismay throughout the country. The patience of the people was at last exhausted. Resistance became necessary, not only to preserve the last shadow of independence, but to maintain the peace and purity of social life. The noble Palatine, whose oath of office bound him to interpose between the oppressor and the oppressed, raised the standard of opposition, and his countrymen flocked to him from every quarter. But Wesselènyi suddenly died; and the patriots, by the neglect of the emperor to appoint a successor, were compelled to choose by suffrage another leader. The choice fell on the unfortunate Francis Rakoczy, son of the second George Rakoczy, and a man of splendid abilities and great influence. The new commander was not successful. The emperor, freed from all his foreign troubles, had nothing to do but carry out the cherished design of his house, of crushing the liberties and exterminating the religion of the Magyars. Rakoczy was forced to acknowledge himself a rebel, in the bad sense of the word, and to sue for pardon. The Magyar spirit, however, the indomitable spirit of an indomitable race of men, was not humbled. It only waited for its opportunity and a new general. In the mean time, the Jesuits urged their policy, and with unlimited success, upon the imperial cabinet. "It was officially announced that the Protestant teachers had fomented the late rebellion; courts were instituted to crush the obnoxious heresy; everywhere Protestant schools and churches were dispersed and pulled down; and a body of two hundred and fifty ministers of that persuasion were sold, at fifty crowns each, to the galleys of Naples."[7]

Encyclopedia Metropolitana; but, if he wishes to examine the horrible picture more minutely, he must consult Coxe, Pfister, and Menzel, but particularly the Histoire des Revolutions de Hongrie.

[7] The sale of two hundred and fifty clergymen, into perpetual

The blood of the Magyars was again boiling. The whole nation arose against its destroyers. It found a worthy chieftain in the person of Emeric Tökölyi, who, from his early, constant, and unsparing hatred toward the house of Austria, has been fitly compared with Hannibal. If not on his father's, yet on his country's sword, he had long before sworn eternal hostility to the Austrians. He was a brave man, a good diplomatist, a skilful manager, and a most impetuous warrior. Repairing to Transylvania, and gaining the favor of Abaffy, whom he had served for several years as a common soldier, he returned to the southern side of the Danube at the age of twenty, to take command of the Magyar army of insurrection. All classes of his countrymen supported him in his measures. Nobles and peasants, men and women, vied with each other in giving him assistance. Victory everywhere perched upon his standard. After expelling the Austrians from every part of Hungary, and garrisoning all the fortresses of Transylvania, he pushed his way through Austria to the very gates of the great capital.

Leopold the First, then emperor, had, on the 21st of March, 1671, claimed his right of sovereignty over Hungary, not by inheritance, not by the free suffrage of the Diet, not by the

---

slavery, the worst slavery, too, of the middle ages, would hardly be credited, had we not received it on the authority of Coxe (vol. ii. chap. 66, p. 1073) and other credible historians. We are told by Sacy, (tom. ii. p. 315,) that these enslaved clergymen were afterwards rescued from bondage by the humanity of the renowned De Ruyter, admiral of the Dutch fleet then stationed in the Mediterranean. After obtaining for them their freedom, by his powerful mediation with the Neapolitan viceroy, Los Velos, "he took them on board his fleet, and treated them with the greatest compassion and beneficence—an act which honors his name no less," continues the historian, Sacy, "than his most splendid exploits." Who shall measure the dishonor, the cruelty, the cowardice of the government that enslaved them!

consent of his Hungarian subjects, but by that divine authority under which kings have so long and so blasphemously asserted the privilege of being tyrants. Never, however, in the history of all despotisms, had any monarch, autocrat or emperor, from the times of the thirty tyrants to those of Nero, so openly and daringly, so needlessly and tauntingly, made public proclamation of their intended tyranny: "Having, by our victorious arms," says Leopold, "suppressed a wicked rebellion, in which the principal members of the crown were implicated, and had seduced the other orders, attacked and killed our soldiers, assumed a part of our prerogatives in raising troops, levying contributions, calling assemblies and seizing our treasures, and even engaged in a conspiracy against our life, which was frustrated by the providence of God—And whereas it is a duty incumbent on us to provide for the safety of the people, who are committed to our charge, and to prevent Hungary and Christendom from being again exposed to similar disorders—We, *by our absolute authority*, have ordered regulations for the quartering of our troops; and we enjoin all persons to submit, without excuse or delay, *to that power which we have received from above*, and are *determined* to maintain *by force of arms.* We require our subjects to give this proof of submission, lest, contrary to our natural clemency, we should be forced to execute *our wrath* against those, who abuse *our indulgence!*"[a]

This military despotism, audaciously set up in the name of God, to be established and perpetuated by the sword, was in a few months leveled to the dust by the arms and energy of Tökölyi, and humbly revoked by the emperor himself. A diet being called at Oedenburg, Leopold abrogated his new style of government, published a general amnesty in favor of the patriots, granted liberty of conscience to the abused Protest-

[a] This terrible document, so characteristic of the Hapsburgs, may be seen in Coxe's House of Austria, vol. ii. chap. 66, pp. 439–440.

ants, and agreed to restore the bereaved magnates of Hungary to all their estates and rights, which had been taken from them. He also annulled his illegal imposts, re-established the national frontier militia, promised ever after to govern the land by the letter and spirit of his oath of coronation, and by the ancient constitution of the kingdom. All, in a word, was gained, so far as any concession can be called a gain, which comes from lips of proverbial treachery and dissimulation.

No sooner, in fact, had the vanquished emperor obtained from Tökölyi a truce of six months, than he sent a secret envoy to the court of Constantinople to get succors from the Turks. The Turks, however, rejected the proposals of the messenger, but resolved to aid the Magyars. Leopold next sent a most cowardly petition to the states of the German empire, calling piteously for help; and, distrusting both his own abilities, and the abilities of his constitutional supporters, he dispatched another ambassador, on the same errand, to the court of Poland, and then fled like a common coward from his own. Tökölyi, supported by an immense army of his fellow-citizens and confederates, and fully advised of the artful but rather unsuccessful intrigues of Leopold, rushed upon the Hungarian places occupied by the Austrians; captured Szathmár, Kassau, Neutra, and many other fortified positions; and compelled the government at Vienna to recall the imperial troops from nearly every part of his hitherto insulted and oppressed, but now victorious, country.

The usual recourse of Austria, however, soon after prevailed against all this bravery. Sobieski, king of Poland, the greatest general of his age, seduced by the falsehoods of Leopold, came to Hungary and partly reconquered it.[9] What could

[9] "My troops," said the emperor, in a letter written by his own hand to Sobieski—"my troops are now assembling; the bridge over the Danube is *already constructed* at Tulsc to afford you a passage"—when every word was as false as a falsehood can be. House of Austria, vol. ii. p. 1077.

not be accomplished, by open and manly warfare, was effected by the ordinary methods of bribery and deception. The Turks were hired to arrest Tökölyi in his career of conquest. He was, consequently, captured by his former friends and sent in chains to Constantinople. There he lived in obscurity and died in want. The peace of Karlowicz was the termination of this contest; and, from the year 1699, the period of its date, it has barred the Turks from meddling in the domestic affairs of Austria, and secured the kingdom of the Huns to the house of Hapsburg as an inalienable and hereditary possession. Despotism again raised its banner, at the close of this fourth and fatal struggle, and waved it in triumph over the lands and liberties of the Magyars.

The last memorable resistance of the Hungarian nation to the illegal claims and intolerable oppressions of the house of Austria is worthy of special record. It was organized in 1703, and headed by the celebrated Francis Leopold Rakoczy. The object of it was to oppose the claim of Leopold the First as a *hereditary* sovereign. The doctrine of hereditary succession was new and strange to the democratic nation. The resentment of the people was still farther roused by the despotic measures taken by the emperor to impose this doctrine upon the kingdom; and when, added to these, he commenced that fierce and furious religious persecution, before mentioned, the patience of the Magyars was exhausted. They rose as one man against the tyrant.

Their leader, Rakoczy, was a character of historical repute, before he had made himself, by the splendor of his deeds, immortal. He belonged to that well-known family of which patriotism seemed to be the natural characteristic. Left an orphan by the death of his noble father, and separated from his mother on the surrender of his native city, lest he should imbibe too much of the spirit of liberty from her instructions, he had been educated under the eye of Austrian tutors, who had done their utmost to bend his mind from the affairs of nations and fix it on the disputations of religion. This artful management had not succeeded. It seemed to be a part of his nature, of his very constitution, to take an interest in political and patriotic questions. While the Jesuits, his teachers, were industriously giving him their lessons in polemical divinity, he was thinking of the wrongs of his country and the deeds of his departed forefathers. After the tasks of the day were done, he might be seen, when the shades of evening were gathering around, sitting pensively by his window, with his eyes towards Hungary, looking with a silent, meditative, mournful aspect on the blue line of Hungarian hills, which, in clear weather, are distinctly visible from Vienna. When he saw those hills refulgent with the soft rays of the setting sun, and thought of the contrast between the placid beauty of those beams and the awful wretchedness to which despotism had reduced the country thus gorgeously and almost tauntingly illuminated, he would think, and look, and then start to his feet with a sudden spring, as if struck by some powerful and irresistible purpose. On seeing his attendants, however, who never left him entirely alone, he would as suddenly compose himself, and resume his quiet posture. Such conduct, nevertheless, could not be overlooked or mistaken. During the rebellion, as it is called, of the great Tökölyi, he was thought to be an unsafe person to live within half a day's journey of the insurgent country. Should he escape to Hungary, as he might possibly do, his name alone, boy as he then was, would avail as much against the Austrians as an army. He was consequently removed into Bohemia and placed under the strictest surveillance of his old tutors. At a suitable age, in spite of the vigilance of his keepers, he fell in love with Charlotte Amelia, princess of Hesse Rheinfeld, a lady of fortune, accomplishments and beauty. The history of their intercourse is itself a romance. Their stolen interviews, effected by methods of almost unparalleled ingenuity, at length prevailed against the intentions of his master and the watchfulness of his guardians. The romantic lovers were privately but lawfully married; and an end was thus put to the plan of making him an ecclesiastic. That he might be still farther removed, however, from the scene of hostilities between the Austrians and his unconquered countrymen, he was encouraged by the monarch to spend a portion of his life in travel. Readily accepting the proposition, he visited the most celebrated capitals of Europe, at each of which he was treated with unusual distinction. Returning, after several years of foreign residence, he found means of making his escape into his native land, where, with his beautiful wife, who had ardently espoused the interests of her husband, he settled down upon the impoverished estates, which had been left him by his father.

There is no peace, however, whether abroad or at home, to a wounded spirit. Rakoczy still brooded, with a melancholy countenance, over the diminished splendor of his family and the ruin of his country. The nation did every thing in its power to revive the natural cheerfulness of his temper. The people loaded him with honors. Wherever he went, though he seldom left his dwelling, he was welcomed as the heir of a great ancestry, and followed by the benedictions of his fellow-citizens. But these personal regards could not soothe the heart, nor satisfy the spirit, of one in whose veins ran the blood of all the Rakoczys. His country was yet in bondage. The chains were weightier than ever upon it. Its constitution had been entirely subverted. A foreigner, by force of arms, had seized a crown, once the property of his ancestors, now his own rightful inheritance. He saw the armed troops of his country's conqueror and oppressor all around him. The cities and the plains, the hills and valleys, of his illustrious land, he saw covered with desolation. Every day, almost every hour, brought to his ears some new outrage of the Austrian tyrant. Now, half a dozen peaceful villages would be burnt to the ground, because their inhabitants were suspected of friendly feelings toward the annihilated constitution. Next, a whole county would be almost depopulated, because the people occupying it dared to worship the God of their fathers in the manner taught them from their cradles. Then, an enormous tax would be laid upon a province, because, in spite of a thousand similar oppressions, the province still seemed able to discharge it. All the time, the brutal soldiery, under the command or connivance of their generals, would enter the houses of the citizens, rob and plunder their possessions, violate the chastity of their wives and daughters, and spread a dismay quite as terrible as death all around them.

In the midst of all this general desolation, the personal recollections of Rakoczy were of a character to aggravate, if possible, his feelings. His grandfather and great-uncle had been unmercifully beheaded—beheaded for supporting the laws and liberties of their country—beheaded because that country had made them its representatives in misfortune. His favorite cousin had been condemned to perpetual imprisonment. His own father had been stripped of all his authority and honor, as a prince, and reduced to a state of comparative beggary. His father-in-law, or stepfather, had been proscribed, his venerable and noble mother driven into banishment, and the estates of nearly all his relatives and friends confiscated. Though a portion of his own patrimony had been restored to him, the tenure was only that of a royal grant, which might be revoked at the royal pleasure. His present and his future were at the mercy of a most cruel and unscrupulous despot.

It was a still more melancholy reflection to the patriot, that, in himself, he saw and felt the condition of every liberal, free-spirited, citizen of ill-fated Hungary. It was evidently the determination of the emperor, independently of his own avowal, so to waste and weaken the whole kingdom, that it would never have the ability, if it could get the courage, to offer any farther resistance to his claim of hereditary sovereignty. A volume would scarcely hold the names of those, from the peasant to the prince, who were thrown into dungeons, despoiled of their possessions, sent into perpetual exile, or murdered in cold blood, because they were guilty of the crime, at all times unpardonable in Austria, of being the advocates of religious freedom and democratic liberty. Leopold had resolved, as he often boasted, to cure the nation of its heresy, both ecclesiastical and political.

Rakoczy, had he been a man of superficial genius, would never have endured so long the cruelties and calamities heaped upon him. During all this time, however, his mind was at work laying the foundations of a future effort. With the sagacity of a philosopher, he was surveying and studying his position. His hour at length came. His country could wait no longer. His countrymen could bear no more. Appealing, in the most emphatic and patriotic language, to his fellow-citizens, he raised the standard of opposition in the name of oppressed and insulted liberty. Betrayed, arrested and imprisoned, he escaped from his keepers and returned with renewed zeal to the rising contest. He called upon the sons of Hungarian freedom to assist him in asserting the original and legal independence of the kingdom. His voice was welcome to the impatient Magyars. They sprang to arms with a boundless ardor. The whole land, on the instant of this appeal, bristled with military weapons, and resounded with martial music. The watchword, at this moment, was "death or liberty."

Rakoczy was a statesman quite as much as he was a soldier. His visit to Paris, at a former period of his life, had been remembered in the revolutionary capital. He had made an impression on the French people. At this juncture, he found no difficulty, such were his talents, of forming an alliance with the French, from which he had reason to expect great assistance. The period of this attempt, however, was not propitious. It was the unfavorable posture of European politics, in fact, which had so long delayed his movements and occupied his profound cogitations. Spain, at that moment, was just breaking off from her subjection to the house of Austria. The most of the Hungarians considered this circumstance as highly advantageous to their undertaking. Rakoczy saw the future with a deeper penetration. He saw that Spain and Austria would not be the only parties to the coming combat. The event justified his foresight. France took the side of Spain; and England, as almost a necessary consequence, espoused the quarrel of the imperial Austrian. While the war between these four powers lasted, the Hungarians were at liberty to pursue their purpose without opposition; and it may be emphatically asserted, that they did not fail to make the most of this brief hour of fortune. An army of one hundred thousand followed the footsteps of the Hungarian general. Everywhere, in Hungary and in Transylvania, he was entirely successful. He routed the king's forces in every battle. He stormed and took the strong-holds and fortresses of the country. He occupied all the cities and towns with patriot garrisons. At last, such was the uniform splendor of his success, he expelled every Austrian from the kingdom, formed a provisional government on the basis of democratic liberty, and sent up the flags of a redeemed nation from every hill-top throughout the country.

The celebrated battle of Blenheim settled the question, for that time, between Spain and Austria. It may be said, also, that it settled the question between Austria and Hungary. The Austrian despot, according to his custom, had employed the troops of a foreign country to defend him in the hour of peril According to that same custom, he now made use of a part of the same mercenary army to secure his authority, and establish his despotism, over the Hungarians. Sending his grateful acknowledgments to Marlborough, the English general by whose abilities he confessed himself saved from impending ruin, he dispatched the German portion of the victorious host against Rakoczy. The end of Leopold, however, was at hand. He died before he had seen the accomplishment of his enterprise.

Joseph the First, nevertheless, continued the policy of his father. Herbeville, his commander-in-chief, with a powerful and well-disciplined force, marched down on the southern bank of the Danube, hiding his movement, as much as possible, from the Hungarians, crossed the river at Buda-Pesth, pushed rapidly forward to the Theiss, forced a passage to Szegedin, raised the blockade of Great Warasdein, deceived the vigilance of the Magyars, pressed his way through the fortified pass of Sibo, and, on the 22d of November, 1705, entered Transylvania with an army flushed with its recent successes and certain of victory before the first blow was given. A few blows, in fact, were sufficient for that distant and therefore unguarded province. After taking Hermanstadt, the capital, he quickly reduced the whole country, and everywhere raised the standard of Austrian domination.

In the west of Hungary, however, the fortune of the day was very different. There the patriots were entirely victorious. Not only did they hold possession of all parts of the country, to the exclusion of every man attached to the emperor, but they made hostile inroads beyond the limits of the kingdom, invaded Austria, Moravia and Styria, and laid the engines of war before the walls of the imperial city. The next moment it was the intention of the Magyars, after securing what they had thus achieved, to recline back upon the Austrians in Transylvania, meet them wherever they could be found, and free that province entirely from their presence.

The emperor saw clearly the tide of fortune turning in favor of the patriots. His soldiers could do nothing with them. Some other weapons must be employed against them. No tyrants ever knew better what weapons to use in such an exigency. Their mode of warfare has been stereotyped for ages. First, they endeavor, as the cheapest means, to do what is necessary by their own military forces. When these no longer avail, they purchase the assistance of some mercenary ally. Lastly, if they have either gold or honors left, they spare no pains to bribe the leaders of the opposition, paying them their own price for their treacherous quiet. Such was the last resource of Joseph. Sending a minister to Rakoczy, he offered the chieftain the Margraviate of Burgau, as an equivalent for Transylvania, the restoration of all his patrimonial estates, and the dignity of a prince of the Austrian empire, if he would desert his countrymen, and deliver them to his mercy. To the patriots, at the same time, he secretly held out the offer of acknowledging the recently-formed Hungarian confederacy, with its democratic basis, the confirmation of the constitutional rights and liberties of the people, and all the blessings of their municipal self-government, if they would desert their leader, or hand him over to imperial clemency.

It is scarcely necessary to tell the result of such base proposals. They were spurned by the general and by the nation. Neither party would treat with the despot unless the other was included in the treaty. Nor was either of them to be satisfied, whatever overtures might be made, until the Austrian government should be willing to acknowledge, in the strongest terms, the absolute independence of their country. They were ready, it is true, to consider Joseph as their lawful monarch, provided he would abandon his claim of hereditary succession and submit to the usual and time-honored custom of election. This, however, was the very point, which Joseph had studiously excluded from his propositions.

The war went forward. Herbeville was replaced by general Heuster. On the 17th of August, 1708, that able general crossed the Waag under cover of the hills and forests, surprised the main body of the patriots under Rakoczy, and gained a decided victory. Six thousand Magyars were left upon the field, and as many more were captured. Rakoczy, stunned by a fall from his horse, made his escape with difficulty from the sabres of his enemies. The defeat was perfect. The routed patriots were dispersed to all parts of the surrounding country. The Austrians again planted the ensign of their oppression.

The loss, however, was only that of an army. The commander-in-chief was saved. The nation was unconquered. Other armies rose up, one after another, all over the kingdom, to fight for the freedom of their country. But it is singular, and worthy the study of a philosopher, how mysteriously every thing is inclined to go against a people, or a cause, however manfully that people or that cause may be defended, after a single disaster like the one just recorded. The loss, in such a case, seems not to be in the numbers killed, nor in the decreasing courage of the defeated, nor in any want of determination to do as valiantly as ever. Generally, after a defeat, the unfortunate party returns to the combat more nerved than before it, resolving to redeem its tarnished honor by some splendid and overwhelming action. Generally, in spite of this resolution, they find it difficult to equal their usual conduct, if they are able to stand at all before a new, unseen, unintelligible force, which their own discomfiture has imparted to their opponents. The moral power of an army is as important as the physical; and it is the first duty, as well as the highest policy, of a general, through all vicissitudes, so to interpret and manage even his misfortunes, as to maintain among his followers the expectation of ultimate success. This, indeed, may be the solution of the mystery; for, it is well known, that, in the affairs of individuals, confidence in one's self is more than half the battle of this mortal life. Nations, too, have always acted, more or less, with a view to this fundamental principle. Before every battle, the ancient Romans used to seek for the sureties of success through the supposed vaticination of their priests; and it is historically certain, that more than one of their ablest commanders never failed to instruct their prophets what signs of victory to find in the entrails of the sacrificial animals, in the flight of birds, and in the visions of the night. It is remarkable, also, that, at the very moment now before us, the emperors of Austria, in addition to the victories of their illustrious general, had much to say of the heavenly revelations of still greater triumphs. Leopold professed to have received a presentiment of the issue of the memorable battle of Blenheim. The prophecy, without doubt, contributed to the fulfilment of itself. In the first days of Joseph, too, the figure of an angel, in the Italian chapel of Loretto, was reported to have moved its wings, as if waving a salutation to the events then approaching, by which the cause of the Catholic emperor was about to gain a concluding victory over the heretic nation of the Huns. Even in England, which was still fighting on the side of Austria, the most wonderful portents were seen. The clashing of arms and the shouts of contending hosts were heard in the upper sky. A singular figure, mounted on a milk-white steed, rode through the fens of Lincolnshire, on the day of Marlborough's Austrian triumph, just as the apparition of Castor and Pollux had intimated to Regillus the fall of the Tarquins and the establishment of the infant liberties of Rome.[10]

Whatever may be the reader's opinion of the question, or of the intrigues and artifice of the imperialists, it is well settled, that, for some reason, the cause of the patriots, from the moment of their first defeat, rapidly and steadily declined. Rakoczy, as bold, as prudent, as sagacious, as patriotic as ever, saw every thing beginning to work against him. A misunderstanding arose among the Magyar commanders. Some of them deserted, with whole regiments of troops, to the invaders of their country. Jealousy, and other evil passions, demoralized the martial character of several others. Despondency, when no one could tell the origin or the reason of it, began

[10] Coxe's House of Austria, vol. ii. pp. 513–514.

to show itself in the hearts and in the countenances of the soldiers. As the courage of his compeers waned, that of Rakoczy waxed stronger, and impelled him into the most prodigious exertions of his great mind and soul. He was willing to do any thing, to suffer any thing, to take any place, which could bring any advantage to his nation. Toil, and travel, and exposure, and danger, were all taken as if they had been the dainties of a princely life. But all his sacrifices, all his exertions, all his sufferings, proved unavailing. The mining districts of the Waag first submitted to the conqueror. All Lower Hungary, excepting a single town, was next reduced. Transylvania soon fell. The last remnant of the patriot army, under the command of Berczeny, which had kept possession of the north-eastern part of Upper Hungary, was defeated on the 22d of January, 1710, by the Austrian forces commanded by general Seckingen. Neuhasel, the single unconquered town just alluded to, surrendered shortly afterwards; and, in the following spring, Rakoczy, the greatest of the Hungarian patriots of that or of any former century, was compelled to shed his tears, in his retreat at the capital of Poland, over the prostrate liberties of the Magyars. The peace of Szathmár fastened the chains, which had been so long forging, on the only truly democratic people of modern Europe.

Such was the mournful termination of the final struggle, till a very recent period, for the recovery of Hungarian independence. Rakoczy, after a short residence among his Polish friends, sailed to England. Thence he proceeded to France, where he was, the second time, received with distinguished honors. But the French, as is too much their custom, had disappointed the cause of liberty in its last extremity. They had done but little, if any thing, after the battle of Blenheim, to support the undertaking of their ally. The great general, therefore, was not easy in the society of Frenchmen. In 1718, he went to Spain, hoping to gain the aid of the Spanish liberals, then led by the famous Alberoni, in a new attempt to conquer the liberation of his country. Last of all, he proceeded to Constantinople, was honorably received by the sultan, who gave him the castle of Rodosto, on the sea of Marmora, where he spent the remainder of his days in writing out the history of the enterprise here recorded. In 1723, while he was yet living, the Magyars used his name once more, in a feeble and fruitless attempt then made to regain their independence. From that period we hear nothing of the hero; nor, until the beginning of the recent struggle, which eclipses every other in the annals of the nation, do we hear any thing, worthy of being stated, of a recovery of its liberty and its glory.

CHAPTER IX.

THE AUSTRIAN REVOLUTION.

THE seeds of all the democratic revolutions of modern ages were sown by the monk of Erfurt. Before his days, the central idea of all human society was, that one man's rights and responsibilities could be held and represented by another. In the earliest form of society, the oldest male ancestor of a family, or of a tribe, was styled the father, or the patriarch, who, it was conceded, had the natural right of governing his offspring. The king was only the high-patriarch of several of such tribes united. The emperor, in his turn, was the acknowledged head of a number of these kings. Such, in its idea, was human government till the days of Luther.

According to this doctrine, all the rights of all the individuals of a family, tribe, kingdom, or empire, centred in the father, patriarch, king, or emperor. Rights and responsibilities, however, always go together. If a person has not the right to govern his own conduct, he is certainly not responsible for that conduct. If his rights can be represented by another individual, so can his personal responsibility be thus represented. Indeed, not only do these two things go together, but they must go together. The one involves the other. Where there is no right, there can be no responsibility. Where there is no responsibility, there can be no right. If, therefore, one man can represent another man, in the sense here supposed, then the representative must possess the rights and responsibilities of the represented. The individuality of the represented is lost in the individuality of the representative. If the represented can choose his representative, then, in making the choice, he is a freeman; but, unless he is at liberty to change his representative at pleasure, he is no longer free. Nature has set bounds, a period of cessation, to the authority of the father, who, during the minority and dependence of his children, justly acts for them; but it is the natural tendency of the patriarchal, regal, or imperial rule to perpetuate itself, independently of all individual rights and responsibilities, and independently of the wishes of the governed.

Although the doctrine, that every individual is personally responsible for his own conduct, because he is free to govern his own conduct, is the fundamental principle of the Christian religion, everywhere inculcated in the Christian Scriptures, it was not very clearly understood in the apostolic age, and was totally subverted by the establishment of the papal system. Popery is the perfection of the old doctrine of representation. Instead of taking up the great idea of individual liberty, revealed to us in the doctrine of individual responsibility, and going forward before the world, as Christianity was intended to do, as the champion of personal and universal freedom, it espoused the ancient, obsolete, monarchical idea, that, even in the most private matters, the mass of mankind are not capable of acting for themselves, and of bearing their own responsibilities, but must be represented by persons appointed for the purpose. The idea is carried out with the most rigid and tyrannical exactness. The priest represents the laymen; the bishop represents the priests; the archbishop represents the bishops; the cardinal represents the archbishop; the pope represents the cardinals. The pontiff is the connecting link between society and God. All the transactions, between men and their Maker, must take this road. When the common man has deposited his sin with the priest, by what is called auricular confession, the depositor has no farther responsibility about it; but, as the Roman theory is, it goes before the Judge as an act to be forgiven, or already forgiven, through the personal authority of the representative. If, on the other hand,

20

the layman wishes any grant, blessing, or favor from the Creator and Ruler of the universe, his only recourse is, as before, to make application to him, whose right it is to receive from heaven and to dispense on earth the benefactions of the Almighty.

Protestantism is emphatically a denial of this whole theory of representation. It is a recovery of the original doctrine of Christianity. It makes every man, in every act, and under every circumstance, responsible for himself. It involves, as a necessary consequence, the immediate assertion of personal liberty for every human being; because men are not slow to see, that, if they must answer for what they do, they must be let to do what they please. Catholicism, therefore, in the very nature of it, is the religion of irresponsibility and of despotism. Protestantism, on the other hand, is the religion of responsibility and of freedom. The right of private judgment, the hinge of Luther's movements, has ever been the terror of both priests and kings.

This grand principle of the Reformation spread rapidly through the world from the hour of its announcement; but the first open and practical declaration of it, as a rule of social action, was made by the Pilgrim Fathers. These were Englishmen, who, while being taught, by the English kings themselves, the doctrine of the right of private judgment, which includes the most absolute liberty of conscience and of worship, were not permitted to enjoy what was thus theoretically allowed them. Indeed, in their day, the Reformation in Great Britain was but little better than a favorite abstraction. The country at large looked upon it as a beautiful speculation. With the Puritans, however, it was a real substance. They saw in it the germ of a new dispensation. They made it their own by giving their whole life, and thought, and being to it. They resolved to make it, for themselves and for posterity, a tangible and living reality. It was for this resolution that they were obliged to leave their country, and, in the heart of

Germany, to undergo the pains of exile. It was for this resolution, that, while in their place of banishment, where the native people were not yet entirely emancipated from the papal theory of society, they had to suffer a thousand intolerable inconveniences. It was for this resolution, that, after their patience was exhausted, and they had nothing more to hope in Germany, or in Europe, they breasted the billows of the Atlantic, braved the dangers of an unknown region, and made for themselves a settlement and a home within the depths of the American wilderness. It was for this resolution, that, after a century and a half of oppression by the mother country, which still followed them to their last retreat with her practical denial of her speculative instructions, they raised and supported the standard of American Independence. Here, on this soil of ours, for the first time since the world was made, the doctrine of individual responsibility and liberty became the avowed and fundamental principle of human society and government.

In the great struggle of our Revolution, France was our chief ally, to whose assistance we are eminently indebted for our national existence. The leading motive with the French government, in granting us its friendship, it cannot be denied, was derived from its settled and historical animosity toward England. Still, when the work of the allies was completed, when the independence of this country had been achieved, France became directly and personally interested in the cause, to which she had generously given her support. She beheld with admiration the image of a free government, which had risen into being upon our shores, working with a harmony, a beneficence, and a promise never realized by any government before. Her sons, who had been pupils in the bloody school of our Revolution, went home to tell their countrymen of the first fruits of civil freedom. The French nation, in the progress of more than two centuries since the days of Luther, had had time to drink deeply at the fountain opened by that reformer. It received, with a very general sympathy, the reports of those heralds of human liberty from the fields of Monmouth and Saratoga. Lafayette, the leading disciple of our Washington, became the great apostle of French emancipation. Catholicism, of course, opposed him; but the infidels, as they were called, paralyzed for the time the arm of popery; and thus the French sprang up as the first consequence of the American Revolution.

It is an acknowledged fact, as generally confessed in France as in any other country, that the French Revolution, begun for the sake of liberty, grew up to be at last the very worst of tyrannies. Such, also, is the geographical position of the nation, and such is the disposition of its possessions, that, more emphatically than can be said of any other country, it can never move without imparting its motion to the states about it. When, therefore, out of the ruins of the democratic revolution, the Man of Destiny arose to be a commanding spirit, he had only to stamp his foot to make Europe tremble all around him.

The result of the French Revolution was seen in the great Congress of Vienna, where, by their diplomatic representatives, the crowned heads of the nations, after long and mature deliberation, brought to light their celebrated Settlement of Europe. The primary object of this Settlement was to organize the leading European monarchies against the democratic spirit of their respective populations, and particularly against the French, who had stepped forward as the champion of republican institutions.

To accomplish this work, it was necessary to reconstruct the nations, adding to one by taking as much from the others, and uniting governments, which had always been separate and independent. Thus, in the first place, Austria and Prussia, the two leading Powers, must be regarded as the center of the new system, and they must receive, also, the chief benefits of the arrangement. All Europe must be so disposed of as to maintain their ascendency, and make them secure in it, without prejudice to the more distant and less interested nations. France, as the sinning nation, which had caused all the expense and hubbub, must give up to the two central Powers a large tract of her fine country west of the Rhine. Holland and Belgium must be united in order to form a northern barrier to it. Poland must be partitioned for the satisfaction of the great Russian autocrat, whose influence was predominant in the congress. Sardinia must be aggrandized at the expense of the minor and less royal of the Italian States. Saxony must be confiscated for the gratification of German claimants. Hanover must be confirmed in its English leanings to win the support of Britain; and every thing else must be done to make Austro-Prussian Germany the center of central Europe, and to guard that center by a barrier of friendly nations.

But the obstacles to this arrangement were very great. Old national land-marks were to be taken down and new ones erected. No respect was to be paid to blood, or race, but people of different and hostile descents were to be united. The three religions of Europe, the Greek, the Catholic, and the Protestant, were to be entirely overlooked, and their votaries crowded together, and made to live in amity.

These were formidable objections to the new Settlement; but the Settlement must be made, right or wrong, wise or unwise, for the present safety of European monarchy against the growing democracy, and particularly against that of the French nation. It was made; and the result was what a prudent man, or a philosopher, should have expected.

In the first place, France was more mad than ever. She had lost her "line of the Rhine," and with it some of her richest provinces. Next, Holland and Belgium began to quarrel; and the struggle between them terminated in the independence of the latter country. Then Poland raised her voice against her own destruction, but was soon lost in the grasp of Russian ambition. Italy, too, had been unsettled by this

Settlement, and began to agitate herself in behalf of her own nationality and independence. Neither she, nor the kingdom of the Netherlands, wished to be merely the sentinels to this Austro-Prussian domination. Spain was dissatisfied, as her hereditary claim to Holland had been virtually confiscated by her superiors; and even Russia was unsatisfied, having received nothing from this great bargain worthy of her acknowledged greatness.

Next, the monarchs of these several nations, feeling themselves more than ever secure against domestic popular commotions, began to bear down upon their subjects with an oppressive tyranny. Though their people might rebel, when they could no longer endure, the kings had agreed to help each other against all such democratic struggles. Disturbances, however, did arise; the people were disappointed; some of the kings themselves, who had not gained all that had been expected, or who had lost something by the Settlement, were uneasy; and a second meeting of the Allied Powers was held at Aix la Chapelle, in 1818, to resettle the Settlement of Europe.

Prior to this second Congress, in spite of the general treaty between the Powers represented in it, several of them had made private arrangements among themselves, and with their nearest neighbors, which had given great dissatisfaction to the Alliance. But the meeting at Aix la Chapelle could not remedy the evil, nor even prevent its continuance and growth. No sooner had the representatives gone home the second time, than those brotherly monarchs began their private intrigues again, bargaining and re-bargaining, plotting and counterplotting, as if no general understanding had been made.

France, mad from the very first, and resolved some day to have her revenge for her lost "line of the Rhine," and her fair provinces on that natural border, started several theories to effect this object. First, she began to agitate what her political writers called the *Alliance Russe*, namely, the conclusion of a treaty, offensive and defensive, with Russia, against the rest of Europe. The idea was a natural one. It was easy for the *dis*satisfied and the *un*satisfied to form a league. But it was never formed. France feared the overbearing absolutism of Russian politics; and Russia was as fearful of the mercurial spirit of democratic France. The bait, however, on both sides, was tempting. France offered Turkey to her colleague; and Russia was to re-establish France in her Rhenish provinces. But fear ruled. There was no love, or confidence, or even common faith, between them.

The next idea of France was to form a grand alliance between herself and those minor nations of Europe not represented in the Congresses of Vienna and Aix la Chapelle, of which she, of course, was to take the lead. This was not a new idea. It was the idea of the old Federative System of France, which sprang from the fertile brain of Richelieu, and which had been the support and glory of the Capets. From the death of Henry the Fourth to the French Revolution, a period of about two hundred years, this policy had made France the most powerful of the European kingdoms. It was now to be revived. The second-rate nations, which had had no hand in the Congresses, were naturally jealous of their haughty and powerful superiors, by whom they had been overlooked; and France was fully able, with their co-operation, to make head against the world. Every thing was ripe for this great measure, when, in July, 1830, the Revolution of the Three Days broke out, which overturned all prior calculations by setting Louis Philippe upon the throne of France.

Now, a third idea arose from the selfish and conservative mind of Louis, and spread by degrees through the kingdom. It was the idea of the *Alliance Anglaise*, by which England and France were to become friends for their common good. The navy of the one, and the army of the other, could together sweep both sea and land. They were both constitutional monarchies, and hence had a common interest at stake;

and the commerce and manufactures of the one, and the agriculture of the other, would cause them to harmonize at every point. Thus, Louis established the English policy in France, and, by the support of it, intrenched himself in an almost despotic power. He surrounded Paris with high walls. He fortified the city, not so much to defend it against a foreign power, as against the citizens themselves. When thus strengthened, he began more daringly to show his hand; and he seemed determined to kill, before his death, that democratic temper which the people of France have so long possessed. But he was unequal to the task. The old mania, the "line of the Rhine," still survived. The lost provinces were not forgotten. The passion for popular freedom and republican institutions was yet alive. New doctrines, too, totally hostile to monarchies, of socialism and its cognates, had risen from obscurity to power. The Pope had been strangely setting to all Catholic nations the example of reform. His first act, after his elevation, had been to recal all persons exiled for political offences, who, in general, were the leading republicans of his dominions. He had next liberated the Jews from their social imprisonment in the Ghetto, giving them the right of choosing their residences in any portions of the city. He had made himself the friend of the poor and the advocate of universal progress. By nominating the democratic Mamiami and his associates to the ministry, after the assassination of Rossi, he had converted his government into a democracy, which instantly took the lead of reform in Europe. France, more susceptible than any other European state, was the first to feel the significancy of this Italian movement. Her people were in raptures over the liberality of the new pontiff. Her monarch, however, remained what he had been. His policy was yet monarchical and British. He was thus separated, more than ever, from the national feeling and common sympathies of his people. His English leanings, at a time of popular agitation, covered him with suspicion. The eternal antipathy to England, and to every thing English, was still rankling in every French artery. Meetings of the citizens began to be called. They were so numerously attended as to excite the apprehensions of the monarch. The monarch forbade them; and, lo! the torch was set to the train, so long prepared, and so ready to take fire, when all Paris exploded like a mine!

Berlin was ready for the match. For more than thirty years, the Prussian monarchs had been promising their subjects a regular constitution; and for thirty years they had been deluding them with fair promises and no fulfilment of their pledges. At last, when the patience of the slowest race of men on earth was utterly exhausted, and they began to demand some tangible acknowledgment of their liberties, the king called the representatives of the nation together, only a little time before the events of Paris, and gave them an *oral* constitution, declaring that it should never be written, as he would have no mere piece of paper forming a barrier between him and the people given him of God! The representatives were astounded. They retired in amazement mingled with revenge. They made a supper of brilliant lights and empty dishes, as an emblem of the bright promises and worthless performances of their king. Being the first men of Prussia, and not a few of them princes, they found no difficulty in spreading their discontent among the people; so that, as soon as the first news of Paris reached them, the masses of the population, headed by leading minds, were ready for their work.

Austria, too, was not less ripe for a revolution. The tyranny of the Hapsburgs had not spent itself against the Hungarians alone. It had long been felt at home. It had been acknowledged as well as felt. From the earliest times, it had been too open, too daring, too sweeping, to be overlooked. In the first years of the Reformation, a large proportion of the Austrian people, if not a majority of them, were Protestants.

Under the reign of Maximilian, a secret friend to Luther, they were protected from Catholic persecutions; and they came very near getting into their hands their domestic government. The state of things, however, changed. The successors of Maximilian were all rank Catholics. Still, after all the harsh measures of all the selfish and unfeeling sovereigns of that imperial house, the political influences of the Lutheran doctrine had been preserved from utter annihilation among the middle classes of the papal dukedom. While the very rich, by reason of their ambition, and the very poor, by virtue of their ignorance, had long since followed the court in its religious intolerance, a highly respectable portion of the independent and enlightened commonalty, by far the most valuable part of every monarchical country, had retained no little of the spirit, if not the letter, of the Reformation.[1]

The schools of Germany, also, had done much to perpetuate, and even to increase, the democratic spirit. Austria had enjoyed nearly her full share of this tendency of the higher education. The imperial University of Vienna has long been one of the first in Europe. Its faculties have been numerous, large, learned, and generally patriotic. Its students, always immense in number, have been extensively from the wealthiest, proudest, noblest houses of the whole empire; and the remainder of them have been the representatives of the leading merchants, bankers, manufacturers and mechanics. This body of young men, the flower of the first families of Austria, by the time their course of educational discipline is completed, are carried quite above the narrow, bigoted, selfish policy of their rulers. It is a singular fact, worthy of observation and recollection, that a truly liberal education seldom fails to make a man liberal in his feelings. In all countries, since the cause of education has had a history, the graduates of the world's

[1] Coxe's House of Austria, vol. i. chap. 25, p. 387, and many other places in the same volume.

great schools have generally been, at the time of graduation, stanch republicans. Personal ambition, lured by the corrupting influences of society around them, has too often bought them off, in monarchical countries, from liberty to despotism; but many of them, in spite of all the temptations of their position, have remained, in every land, the friends and advocates of human freedom. It has been so in Austria. The thousands of young gentlemen, who, for many generations, have been pouring out from her higher seminaries of learning, and particularly from the University of Vienna, have been annually filling the empire with enlightened democrats. To whatever post they might afterwards be raised, or into whatever circumstances of honor or of influence they might chance to fall, they were sure to remember, with a lively interest, though they might seldom mention, the bright visions of universal happiness and freedom vouchsafed to them by the Attic goddess, and the indelible pictures of social liberty drawn upon their young hearts, while they were perusing the democratic pages of the Greek and Roman classics.[a]

It must be remembered, too, that the capital of Austria lies less than thirty miles from the lines of Hungary, where democracy is the life and spirit of the dominant population. Between the two countries, there has always been an open and general intercourse. While many of the Magyar magnates, who have made their residence at Vienna, have sold themselves to their country's tyrants, so far, at least, as to remain silent at the sight of that country's wrongs, thousands of the Austrians, on the other hand, have learned to admire the people, and to pity the nation, thus cruelly oppressed. Between the Austrian and Hungarian democrats, there has always been, since the death of Francis the First, quite a general sympathy,

[a] Since the late revolution, Austria has inserted several of the more liberal of the Greek and Roman writers in her Index Expurgatorius!

which needed only some common purpose to render it positive and strong.

That common purpose was destined to take its origin from the Magyar land. The Hungarian Diet of 1832, the year in which Francis died, was a Diet of reform. Though, by the constitution, it is the source of all law to Hungary, the National Assembly had not been convoked for full seven years.[a] While the French war lasted, the emperor called it frequently together, because he could not otherwise resist the French. The Magyars were his chief reliance in the hour of need. The session of 1807, however, after making an appropriation, complained severely of the profligacy of the ministers of the crown, and threatened to withhold further supplies, unless a prudent expenditure of the revenues should be promised and maintained. It made a declaration, also, in favor of free trade. In 1812, as had been foreseen by the Magyar Assembly, Austria declared herself a bankrupt. The Hungarian diet of that year refused to give its sanction to such an act. It boldly told the emperor, that, to preserve the honor of the whole country, he ought to pay his debts. It told him, that if he would secure a frugal use of the moneys granted, the Magyars would pay their full share of his liabilities. Such language could not be pardoned by such a king. The National Assembly was prorogued; and it was not called again, till, in the very last year of a long and eventful reign, the aged and dying monarch saw the sceptre about dropping from his hand. He wished, of course, to settle such questions as related to the succession before his death.

When called together, however, in a legal manner, after so long a dispersion, the Assembly resolved to do its duty to the nation. The first of its bold undertakings was the emancipa-

---

[a] Paget (Hungary and Transylvania, vol. i. p. 129) says *twenty-five* years; but the traveler is in a mistake. There were diets in 1807, 1812, and 1825. See Pulsky's Hist., Introduction, pp. 131–132.

tion of the peasants. The peasants of Hungary, as we have seen, were originally placed in as eligible a condition as they had any reason to expect. During the two native dynasties, male and female, their position was not greatly changed. In the beginning of the sixteenth century, after Hungary and Austria had been united, they were reduced to the state of serfs. They remained in this condition, with several unimportant fluctuations between the years 1547 and 1556, till the publication of Maria Theresa's celebrated code of serf-laws, styled the Urbarium, more than two centuries from this latter date. For two hundred years, they were but little better than common slaves. In one respect, the lot of the slave is decidedly preferable to that of the Hungarian serf, as held by the Austrian rulers of that land. The serf was bound to live and die upon the spot that gave him birth. He belonged to the soil, by the Austrian law, as much as the trees that stood in his master's field. With it he was bought and sold. If his landlord was a cruel man, there was scarcely the hope of any remedy, such as is common in a land of slavery, because his release involved the sale of the entire estate of which he made a part. In 1764, by the publication of her peasant-code, Maria Theresa conferred a new condition, almost a new existence, upon this class. Such was the romantic character of her despotism, that she published her code without waiting for the consent of the representatives; but, after the death of Joseph the First, it was formally sanctioned, "till another and more liberal one could be prepared." By this body of laws, the peasant was forever emancipated from the soil. He could leave his landlord at pleasure, by giving him due notice, and by the payment of his own debts. While remaining with him, a fixed quantity of land was assigned to his personal use, which, so long as he performed certain duties, he could hold by law. The burdens upon him, nevertheless, were very great. For a full portion of land, he had to labor for the owner one hundred and four days of every year. Every four peasants had to furnish a man and a horse, at the bidding of a landlord, for a two-days' journey. Of all the productions of the earth, with a few trifling exceptions, in addition to these duties, every peasant had to deliver up one-ninth to his master as his lawful rent. Besides all this, the peasants had to make all the roads, bridges, canals, and other internal improvements of the country. They had to feed the army, both in peace and war, and pay all the expenses of the government of their country, though they could not act directly in the creation and execution of the laws. Should they complain, or prove refractory in any case, the master could inflict corporal punishment, though the lashes allowed him were restricted to twenty-five. Such were the leading provisions of this code. The single fact, that the landlord could whip his tenant, as often as he thought proper, is a sufficient proof, that the peasant was legally regarded, not as a citizen, even in the lowest signification, but as a slave.

The diet of 1832, acting upon the long-neglected provision laid down at the adoption of this code, that it should exist only until a better one could be made, declared, that the time for that better one had come. This was the beginning of the Hungarian democratic party. It was a beginning, however, to a rapid progress and a glorious result. It was a noble sight, a sight never seen before, to behold the parliament of a great nation, in which chiefly the land-holding classes were represented, debating the propriety and duty of relinquishing a set of lucrative claims, over a prostrate race, when those claims were fully guaranteed by the sanctions of custom and of law. But the democratic spirit had taken such hold of the Hungarian mind, that nothing less than the personal emancipation of every peasant would satisfy its high demands. Hungary resolved to be a land of citizens, not of serfs, of freedom, not of slavery. After determining to make every male inhabitant of mature age a voter, thus basing the liberties of the country on the equality of its people, the National Assembly proceeded to lay down a course of action, for the Magyar nation, which, if carried out, would make it indeed a nation, and not a province of a neighboring and tyrannic realm. It restored the language of the country by new and strong enactments. It prepared the way for the revival of the native literature, by incorporating a national literary institution, to which the democrats subscribed the most liberal sums. It commenced a series of internal improvements, of which the great suspension-bridge at Pesth is a memorable result, by which the depressed country was to be elevated to the condition of a modern state. For four years, without interruption, this body of patriotic legislators went forward with their work, ever keeping the renovation and glory of the Magyar land in view.

All these measures were steadily opposed by the Austrian government. It would not do to have a democratic country, as large and powerful as Hungary, in the heart of a despotic empire. Every thing was to be done rather than see so dangerous a result. Every thing was done, that could be done, to quench the democratic spirit of the Hungarians. When the ordinary means of opposition had been exhausted, means the most extraordinary in other countries, but common enough in this, were at once adopted. It seems that the baron Wésselényi, at that time the leader of the patriots in the upper Chamber, during the debates, made use of some very strong but very appropriate epithets of reproach against the course, which, for centuries, Austria had been taking. He told the Magyars, that, in their new efforts to benefit and bless their country, they should not be troubled by what the Hapsburgs might do, or say, or think; that it had always been the intention of those monarchs to reduce Hungary from the condition of an independent kingdom to that of a royal province; that they had ever pursued a policy by which they hoped so to weaken the Hungarian nation as to render it incapable of making resistance to the imperial despots; that, among the steps taken to secure this end, they had always been opposed to the political and social elevation of the Hungarian peasants; and that their abettors were those Magyar magnates, who, bribed by the royal favor, under the pretence of maintaining the privileges of their class, were acting a part in opposition to their country.[4]

Such freedom in telling an unwelcome truth was not to be let pass in silence. It might stand as a precedent for the re-establishment of the liberty of speech in Hungary. That would be sure to work the downfall of Austrian domination. Wésselényi was impeached for treason. The cause, of course, went against him. In both the courts, before whose tribunals he was successively arraigned, the judges were the creatures and the tools of Ferdinand. The baron was sentenced to a three years' imprisonment, in some strong-hold or castle, for what he had uttered in debate, in an open parliament, on a question legitimately up for discussion!

At the same time, and before the same tribunals, several young men were tried for treason, against whom the charge was laid of having held certain political meetings during the sessions of the diet. By what mode of reasoning the imperial government pretended to make such an act a crime, and especially a crime of the highest grade, I am not informed. The probability is, that no reasoning was made use of, or required. The act of impeachment was merely an exercise of power. The young gentlemen were friends of their country; and that, in the eyes of a Hapsburg, is at all times crime enough. According to the laws of their land, they could not be imprisoned for such a cause, as there was a statute positively forbidding it. But laws are no obstacles to a tyrant, when he has the might. As the civil code could not punish them, it was expressly suspended in their case; and they were

[4] The language of the baron, respecting one item, was terribly severe. He said Austria was "sucking the marrow of the Hungarian peasantry." City of the Magyar, vol. i. p. 232.

sentenced, by military law, to a close confinement for three years in some convenient prison.[5]

Finally, in the presence of the same judges, and by a similar process, another individual was brought up, at the time spoken of, for treason. He was a young man, in the prime of early manhood, whose appearance at once arrested the attention of spectators. He had been lying for several months in prison, contrary to the statutes. Of middling size, but of a most noble bearing, he gave evidence to every beholder, that he was no common culprit. In color, his countenance was a lively brunette; his face was round and full; his forehead, high and open; his hair, black, rather long, glossy, and falling in natural ringlets; his eyes, blue, very prominent, and full of soul and meaning; his eye-brows, large and black, overhanging the parts they shaded; his teeth, full in numbers, evenly set, and as white as ivory; his mouth, small but neatly formed, the very paragon of this organ; his movement, easy, dignified, and remarkably prepossessing. An immense concourse of his countrymen, who surrounded the hall of justice, proved the interest that his previous career had raised for him. From the evidence and pleadings in the suit, it appeared, that he was the son of a poor but respectable Hungarian, who resided in one of the northern counties; that, by the energy of his own character, without the help of any of his kindred, he had acquired a liberal education, and graduated with the highest honors of his college; that, still helping himself, he had completed the study of the law, and made himself a master in the profession; that, pushing his inquiries forward, he had acquired a deep and extensive knowledge of public matters, and, while yet a youth, had gained the reputation of being a profound statesman; and that, in consideration of his marked talents, though still very youthful, he had been selected to appear in the current session of the diet as the representa-

[5] City of the Magyar, vol. i. p. 233.

tive of an absent magnate. Not being allowed, in that capacity, to take that part in the proceedings of the Assembly, which his great abilities demanded, he had occupied his spare time in furnishing the Hungarian people with a full and correct account of the transactions of their servants. Prior to his day, such a thing had never been attempted, as there was an Austrian law against it. To effect his purpose, he had condescended to learn the art of short-hand writing, and had given himself up to the task of writing out the votes and speeches of the members. To avoid the law, which forbade the "printing and publishing" of what was transacted in the diet, he had gone to the expense of *lithographing* the matter thus prepared by him. In this way, he had started a public journal, at the seat of government, and had gained for it a prodigious circulation. Soon after its commencement, however, the new journal had been interdicted. The young patriot had been forbidden to lithograph, as well as to print and publish, a political newspaper for the benefit of the Hungarian people. Not yet daunted, and not to be foiled in his patriotic undertaking, he had next devised and executed the plan of publishing a manuscript paper, against which no law could be leveled, that would not equally abridge the necessary practice of writing letters. The new edition of the journal, indeed, was nothing but an open letter, containing the proceedings of the National Assembly written out in a perfectly legible handwriting. At first, the copies of it had been folded and sent by post; but, on discovering that they were not delivered to his subscribers, but destroyed by order of the government, the editor, still determined to outdo the machinations of the despot, had organized a system of private expresses, which ramified to every town, village and hamlet of the country. Such had been the demand for his publication, in this form, that he had circulated an edition of ten thousand, every line of which had been copied by young scribes employed by him for the purpose. Thus, in spite of the censorship of the press in spite of the tyranny of the post-office, in spite of all the power of a most powerful and stringent government, a free paper had been prepared, published, read and felt everywhere, by the fertile and indomitable spirit, by the energy and courage, of that beautiful young man, who now stood up to answer for his conduct. Foiled in every attempt to master him, the Austrian tyrant had sent his ministers to apprehend him, and to stop the paper by throwing its proprietor into prison. In the dead of the night, while walking for meditation on the shore of the Danube, he had been snatched up by the myrmidons of the imperial court, blindfolded, and conveyed to a dungeon of which he knew not the name. After a long confinement, during which the Hungarian people were entirely ignorant of his condition, he had been released for trial. It was to defend himself against the accusations of such an enemy, that he was now permitted once more to appear in public. It was to witness the issue of this strange proceeding, that so vast a multitude of his countrymen had assembled. Every movement of the young patriot was watched with eagerness. As a lawyer, profoundly learned in his profession, he knew well enough how to manage his own business. He was highly intellectual, and could meet the ablest of his antagonists, and annihilate the strongest of their reasons. He was eloquent; and, when his learning and his logic had obtained the victory, he could raise the enthusiasm of the spectators, and turn to a deathly paleness the cheeks of his imperial judges. Until that day, Hungary had never witnessed so magnificent a struggle for life and liberty. All the efforts of the young man, however, proved fruitless. He had been condemned before his trial; and the judges only sought pretexts by which to give his punishment a show of legality. He was sentenced to a protracted and solitary imprisonment. He was at once conveyed off and let down into a deep, damp, unwholesome dungeon within the castle-fortress of old Buda. On his way to prison, he leaned his head upon his hands, as if lost in meditation. Some one asked him how he felt. "I feel something *nameless* in me," was his only answer. What was then nameless, however, has since been turned to history. That young man was Louis Kossuth.[6]

The news of these tyrannical proceedings flashed with the speed of lightning to the Austrian capital. The people of Vienna were by this time fully prepared for action. The revolution of opinion had become visible among them. Not only those called democrats, but the body of the population, were beginning to be excited. The bond of sympathy between the German and the Hungarian patriots was now perfected. They both saw, with no little clearness, a common interest, and a common object. From that moment, till the breaking-out of the European revolutions, they had acted very much in concert.[7]

In the year 1834, an association was formed in Vienna, consisting at first of only twelve members, who held secret sessions for political and revolutionary purposes. The society was organized within the walls of the Austrian university; and the twelve original members were professors and students of the Institution. The merchants of the metropolis, together with the better class of artizans and mechanics, had been so long and so grievously oppressed, by the imperial system of taxation, that they had generally become quite hostile to a

[6] City of the Magyar, vol. i. p. 233. The description of Kossuth's person is given on the authority of the Hue and Cry sent out after him by Austria at a subsequent period. There is, therefore, no flattery in it; and I shall make it a rule, in all that I have yet to say of that hero, to confirm my language by the statements of his enemies. See, for example, Louis Kossuth and Hungary, by an anonymous, but evidently an Austrian writer, from the press of John Rodwell, London, chap. iii. pp. 17–32.

[7] "Thus it appears," says the Austrian tory, "that the more intelligent among the Hungarians acted in concert with the reformed party in Germany; and they had a mind to establish themselves as a revolutionary party." Louis Kossuth and Hungary, p. 51.

monarchy, and had even begun to theorize privately about the establishment of a republic. The students knew the wishes of the citizens; but the citizens did not, at that period, fully comprehend the democratic temper of the students.

Kossuth, it was acknowledged, nevertheless, had been sacrificed to the Austrian doctrine of the censorship of the press. There was no difference of opinion respecting that point. In Austria, and in Hungary, he was regarded as a martyr. The liberty of the press, therefore, became at once the salient point of his increasing party. For the three years that he was lying in the lower walls of the castle-fortress, the patriots of the imperial capital, in conjunction with their Hungarian associates, were hard at work infusing into the public mind correct ideas concerning this fundamental subject. In 1841, the martyr was restored to liberty. His first act was to look about him for his companions in misfortune. Soon afterwards they appeared from the cells in which they had been separately incarcerated. But they came not back from prison as they had entered it. The cruel treatment they had received had been nearly fatal to all of them. The great Wésselényi was entirely blind. Lovassi, one of the young gentlemen, had become a maniac. The three others had contracted mortal diseases and were about ready for their burial. Kossuth, possessed of a firmer constitution and of a stronger will than his associates, by which to resist the natural effects of suffering, came out without the loss of any faculty, bodily or mental, but with broken health. From the hour of his release he was never well. He went immediately to the watering-place of Parad, among the Matra mountains, for the restoration of his attenuated and damaged frame. His name, his spirit, his high purpose, went to Vienna, while they enjoyed the power of an omnipresence in his native country.

In the year 1846, a petition to the emperor, for the abolition of the censorship, was signed by the members of the association, and then circulated among the principal inhabitants of the Austrian capital; and when it reached the hands of the monarch, only a few days after its appearance, it carried with it the weight of more than two thousand well-known names.

The next two years did the work of a century against the absolutism of the Hapsburg house. In Hungary, the democrats achieved prodigies of labor for the cause of the people; and the people began to know their friends, and to reward them for the risks they ran and the deeds they performed. In Austria, the tyranny of Metternich began to be talked of openly by the populace; and their secret conversations took the form of charges against his administration. They complained, and very justly, that he had hindered the empire from making a development of its resources, lest it should become strong enough to resist the despotism of his master; that, still farther to weaken it, he had established the habit of fanning the jealousy of the races, maintaining the ascendency of the king in Austria by setting the Sclavic Bohemians in opposition to their German countrymen, and preserving the submission of Hungary by pitting the Sclavonians and Croats against the Magyars; that he had kept the subject realms and provinces in a state of absolute paralysis, by an interchange of standing armies, cunningly employing Italian and Swiss troops in Hungary, Hungarian troops in Italy and in Switzerland, and a mixture of these foreign troops in Austria, thus holding each people down by such soldiers as would not hesitate, from any feelings of kindred or of country, to use the most bloody methods against any popular demonstrations; that, not satisfied with binding the hands and the feet of his several victims, he had laid his shackles upon the mental and moral capacities of the empire, by forbidding the pen to write, the press to publish, or the tongue to speak the first syllable of remonstrance against this system of oppression, or the first letter in favor of the slightest freedom of opinion; and that, as a necessary and fatal consequence, the world around them was careering onward in the paths of prosperity and of glory, leaving Austria entirely behind, a standing but decaying monument of her own stubbornness and folly. Every word of these respective charges was as true as the words of a revelation. They expressed, in the briefest manner, the long-continued policy of the Hapsburgs. It was the policv, by which they had maintained their position, as the representatives of an insignificant dukedom at the head of a large empire, for several ages. The Austrians themselves, the most favored of the imperial subjects, could bear that policy no longer. Metternich, the able and unscrupulous supporter of the weak but equally unscrupulous emperor, had become an acknowledged reproach to the party by which his administration had been upheld. Not only the untitled gentry, but many of the highest nobles, worn out by his unpatriotic measures, or tired of his unpopularity, had deserted his standard and left him to his doom. The great barons, Dobblehof and Stifft, together with the counts Breuner and Montecuculli, had joined the ranks of the liberals, then headed by professors Hye and Endlicher, whose influence in the university was supreme. It had even been circulated, but with very little credit, that the arch-duchess Sophia, the most influential member of the famous Camarilla, or kitchen cabinet, was secretly favorable to the opposition. Nothing, however, derogatory to the monarch was at that time uttered by responsible individuals, while a thoroughly revolutionary politics was rising into a most active though noiseless life, and silently spreading among the people. The hearts of a majority of the citizens had been perfectly converted to a revolution; from the heart the revolution had gradually ventured to the lips; but, as yet, the lips had confessed the general faith only in the softest and most secret whispers. When, at the opening of the great revolutionary year, Ferdinand the First used to ride, unconscious of his danger, through the wooded parks and delightful pleasure-grounds of Shönbrunn, the vast empire, of which he was chief, was tottering to its dissolution. It was held together by the fears of the many and the hopes of an ambitious few. These bands were destined to be broken in a day.

The Hungarian patriots, during the two years now under consideration, had been heartily at work. No language can describe the popularity of Kossuth and Wésselényi after their liberation. Wésselényi, in other years, had been the great champion of Transylvania; and the Transylvanians now carried the old patriot in their arms. Kossuth, though the champion of the whole kingdom, was a Magyar; and the Magyars now repaid him for his sufferings by every mark of honor in their power. Before his imprisonment, he had supported his mother and his three sisters at the expense of hard labor and many personal sacrifices; and when, in consequence of his confinement, he could protect them no longer, they were maintained by the voluntary and abundant contributions of the people. No sooner was he out of prison, than all men sought his company, and his name was blessed from one border of the country to the other. Such was his fame, that an engraver at the Hungarian capital established himself in the single business of taking impressions of his portrait, and selling them at wholesale in all parts of Hungary. As the two patriots had been one in misfortune, so, when restored to liberty, they resolved to be one in their patriotic labors. Kossuth, whose talents as a writer were surpassed only by his sagacity as a statesman, undertook the publication of the Pesti Hirlap, a political newspaper, the sole object of which was the advocacy of Hungarian independence. Wésselényi, blind and feeble as he was, commenced a series of pilgrimages over Hungary, as an apostle of liberty, to preach the doctrine of Hungarian freedom to his countrymen. The venerable martyr was everywhere welcomed with enthusiasm; the cause of the country received a new impulse; and, in 1847, while the two friends were still at work, in spite of the power and gold of

Austria, Kossuth was returned to the National Assembly as the leading representative for Pesth.

Before going to his place in the parliament of his country, the young statesman spent a portion of his time, crowded with occupations as he was, in establishing a political society, called the Association of Protection. It was the object of this association to defend the Hungarians against the iniquitous tariff of duties, laid upon all imports and exports, by which the business and industry of Hungary had been annihilated. The members bound themselves to wear no garment manufactured from foreign cloth, to use no raw materials in their occupations derived from Austria, and to give no encouragement to importations of any kind, or for any purpose, until the duties should be reasonably reduced. From among the members, a company was organized to start several manufacturing establishments for the production, at home, of the most necessary commodities. A severe blow was thus struck at the despotism of the imperial government; and Hungary was opportunely encouraged to repudiate her financial dependence on a foreign country, and to enter the business world on her own account.

Hardly had the new representative become accustomed to his seat, in the National Assembly, before he was acknowledged by all parties, and by all people, as the greatest orator that had ever stood there to speak. "The parliamentary speeches of Kossuth," says an enemy, "were, even at that time, like burning arrows, which he hurled into kindred minds, thereby urging them to a fanatic enthusiasm." "His oratory," says the same writer, in another place, "was like a large battery with heavy pieces of ordnance, whose discharge did the most fearful execution. The poisonous sting of his interpolations, his despotic power in the house, and his intrigues out of doors, formed in themselves a power—so to say, an army—against the stand-still policy of Metternich." At another time the young member is more graphically presented, by this historian, as the orator "with the flaming tongue," who stood behind his great friend, Louis Batthiány, "hurling his fiery projectiles" at the heads of his quailing adversaries, and reveling in his power to kill and make alive. There can be no doubt, that, at this period of his life, Kossuth was the most formidable debater of modern times. There he stood, planted in the very presence of his Austrian opponents, advocating the cause of popular liberty for his country, meeting every objector that ventured to rise up against him, and scathing and blasting all unmanly opposition, with a resistless sweep of eloquence, which rendered dumb whom it did not convince. Such had been his career during the first year of his incumbency. The Paris revolution found him at his post.[8]

The news from France ran to Vienna with telegraphic speed. On the 2d day of March, the naked announcement of a French revolution reached Pressburg, where the Hungarian Diet was in session, but the details were still to come. The next day, before those details were known, Kossuth arose in his place and pronounced the most memorable speech, though not the most eloquent, of his life. Its sagacity, and its boldness, have never been surpassed. From the first words of the introduction, it was manly, decisive and independent: "I am happy and grateful," said the orator, "in seconding the motion of the honorable member for Raab, although I am firmly convinced, that the extraordinary features of the present time compel us to take our leave of private bills. I second his motion, because I think it a fit opportunity to entreat you to be alive to the enormous responsibility of the moment, and to raise the policy of the parliament to a level with the times. The local question in relation to the bank I will not now discuss. It is true, Magyars, Austria has embarrassed us enough. But this is a secondary matter. What we ought to ask for is the budget of the Hungarian receipts and expenditure, which have hitherto

[8] Louis Kossuth and Hungary, pp. 98–102.

been mixed up with those of our neighbors. We ought to ask for the constitutional administration of our finances. We ought to ask for a separate and independent financial board for Hungary; for, unless we have this, the foreign government, which rules us without our advice, is likely to embarrass our finances almost to hopelessness. In a recent speech, touching the relations of Austria to this country, I expressed my conviction, that the constitutional future of our nation will not be secure, till the king is surrounded by constitutional forms in all the relations of his government. I expressed my conviction, that our country was not sure of the reforms it desired at home; that we could not be sure of the constitutional tendencies of those reforms, and of their results, so long as the system of the monarchy, which has the same prince that we have, remains in direct opposition to constitutionalism, and so long as that privy council, which conducts the general administration of the monarchy, and which has an illegal and powerful influence on the internal affairs of the country, remains anti-constitutional in its elements, its composition, and its tendency. I expressed my conviction, that, whenever our interests conflict with the allied interests of the monarchy, the differences thus created can be removed without danger to our liberty and welfare only on the basis of a common constituency. I cast a sorrowful look on the origin and the development of the bureaucratical system of Vienna. I remind you, that it reared the fabric of its marvelous power on the ruins of the liberty of our neighbors; and, recounting the consequences of this fatal mechanism, and perusing the Book of Life, I prophesy it in the feeling of my truthful and faithful loyalty to the royal house, that that man will be the second founder of the House of Hapsburg, who will reform the system of government on a constitutional basis, and re-establish the throne of his house on the liberty of his people."[9]

[9] Louis Kossuth and Hungary, pp. 102–118.

These sentiments, which every Hungarian felt, but which no other Hungarian had dared to utter, came upon the National Assembly like an electric shock. They constituted the first open, positive, responsible utterance of a revolution. The revolution was to be, not of one race against the other races, as the enemies of the Hungarians have vainly said, but of all the races, of all the nationalities, of all the integral portions of the empire, rising up in behalf of a government, which was to be at once liberal, constitutional and universal. The words of Kossuth, carried by the wings of lightning to Vienna, were adopted as the confession of faith of the Austrian patriots. Two days afterwards, the particulars of the French revolution, confirming entirely the first telegraphic announcement, were published at the Austrian capital, and read with general enthusiasm by a majority of the populace. The government, however, was apparently not alarmed. Some of its officials, like Pulsky, a Hungarian nobleman, foresaw the future and began at once to speak of it; but their admonitions were derided, at least they were disregarded, by nearly all the members of the imperial cabinet.[10]

Kossuth's demand, however, for a constitutional government, which was to acknowledge the equality and independence of all the nationalities, and unite them all in the formation of one great country, continued to resound all over the Austrian empire. It was particularly accepted and seconded at the royal university. Clearly seeing, that the work before them was not to be entirely a bloodless work, the society of the students organized a military company, styled the *Legio Academica*, to which the citizens secretly furnished arms. The cause of the revolutionists now went forward with accelerating speed. Every man's heart and mind seemed to be enfranchized. Every man began to feel and to think for himself. The tongue next resolved to speak without restraint.

[10] Pulsky's Memoirs of a Hungarian Lady, vol. i. p. 108.

The press soon followed on, in the same spirit, and asserted for itself the right of putting into general circulation what had been freely uttered in the smaller but equally responsible circles of private conversation. Fetter after fetter was thus broken, till, before the slightest alteration had been effected in the laws of the land, statutory or fundamental, the people had asserted and achieved a constitution, as real as if it had been written with the point of a diamond, or recorded on a plate of brass.

The Austrians, however, were not satisfied, because they were not yet safe. They had claimed their rights as human beings; but their claims had not been ratified by the still existing though nearly nominal authority of the state. They wished to secure the public assent of the emperor to the freedom thus obtained. Unless they could thus entrench themselves behind the forms of law, the imperial government might afterwards restore its despotic power, and support the restoration by force of arms. The possibility of such a result, however, was immediately cut off for the current time. On the 13th of March, in less than two weeks after the first rumor of the revolution at Paris had taken wind among them, the Academic Legion, supported by a vast concourse of Viennese, marched out of the city in a solid body to the imperial palace, to echo the demand of Kossuth for a constitution, for a liberal monarchy, for the immediate abolition of the irresponsible monocracy. The imbecile and unmanly emperor, a much weaker man than he was generally supposed to be, is reported to have fled to an under-ground passage-way behind the royal residence, which he and his cowardly predecessors are said to have constructed for their personal security against popular outbreaks, toward which they were conscious a despotic government is incessantly contributing. Nothing could induce the feeble old monarch to leave his subterranean strong-hold. All the assurances offered him, that no one wished to harm his person, that a hair of his head should not be violated, that his royal sanction to certain political measures was the only object of this visit, were not enough to recal him from his place of burrowing. Like a frightened denizen of the ground, he considered it the safer part not to return to the light of day, until the game should be given up and the chase abandoned. The chase, however, was not in sport. While the people meditated no indignity to their absconded prince, they were determined he should not thus evade them. No sooner was their resolution known, than the king capitulated, surrendering his power, but not his person, at discretion. He treated with his subjects and granted them every thing they wanted. From his unknown retreat, with the tramp of his people heavy on the ground above him, he sent forth to them those self-humiliating but glorious concessions, by which the liberty of the press, the publicity of law-courts, trial by jury, the instantaneous dismissal of prince Metternich, and the promise of a representative and free constitution, according to the idea before laid down by Kossuth, were secured, one after the other, to the victorious patriots. At the close of this eventful day, in which Austria had been legitimately revolutionized and emancipated without the shedding of one drop of blood, all the citizens went home to tell their wives and children, that the tyranny of the House of Hapsburg was no more to haunt them. The centre and the south of Europe were that day redeemed from bondage.

No man of modern history has been more generally or justly celebrated, for the exact appreciation and improvement of his time, than Louis Kossuth. His plan of a constitutional empire required, that each country, according to its historical limits, should become an independent member of the imperial confederation. He asserted this doctrine for Hungary, with a distinct emphasis, because she would thus be recovering what actually belonged to her. She had been an independent and sovereign country from the days of Arpad. She had never resigned that independent sovereignty; and Austria, during the whole period of its domination, had been compelled to make a theoretical acknowledgment, that Hungary was not an Austrian province, but a separate kingdom. This acknowledgment had been made in the most important particulars. Among the Magyars, the emperor of Austria was never known as emperor, but as king. His title was entirely different in the different portions of his dominions. The imperial Charles the Sixth of Austria, for example, was simply the royal Charles the Third of Hungary. In the same way, Ferdinand the Fifth, as the Austrians styled their recent monarch, was known as Ferdinand the First among his Hungarian subjects. The laws of Hungary have always recognised this necessary distinction. The governments of the two countries, too, in the first years of their connection, were entirely separate, each having its own cabinet of ministers. All the officials of the Hungarian kingdom, the vice-royal Palatine, the lords-lieutenant of the counties, and the judges of the royal courts, were always regarded, not as the representatives of the House of Hapsburg, but of the House of Almos, or of Arpad. Joseph the Second, so late as 1770, by refusing to be crowned king of Hungary, though he was confessedly the emperor of Austria, was never acknowledged by the Hungarians, but his name has been scrupulously denied a place on their list of sovereigns. Leopold, his successor, before he was allowed to perform the first act of sovereignty, was compelled to submit to the ordinary practice of being crowned, and to take the customary coronation oath, by which he bound himself to administer the laws of Hungary, as if he were simply the monarch of that country, without another foot of dominion in any other quarter of the globe.[11]

All this, however, at the time now under notice, though still constituting the theoretical government of the kingdom, was practically null. It was merely a concession in form,

[11] Leopold. Secund. Decret. Art. x. 1790.

without the least actual validity. The emperor of Austria, though he changed his title upon crossing the Hungarian border, was the emperor still. The officers, judicial and executive, appointed to represent the king, really represented the imperial will. The cabinet of native ministers, who, in the first ages, had always resided at the Magyar capital, and attended to Hungarian questions, had been reduced to a little bureau of clerks, called a Chancery, which formed an attachment of the Austrian court at Shönbrunn. While the name of independence was thus kept up, the substance had long before passed away. Kossuth resolved that that substance should now be restored. This, as he justly thought, should be the first step toward the creation of a constitutional empire, because, the moment that Hungary could recover her independence, more than one-half of that empire became subject to a regular constitution. It would be the first step, also, toward the instauration of liberty in the center and the south of Europe, because the Magyar constitution was not only liberal, but democratic. The course of such a man as Kossuth, under such circumstances, could not be doubtful. The revolutions all around him were only the outward expressions of the popular demand, for the restoration of rights once exercised, or for the realization of concessions often made. The Austrians, too, had just obtained the promise of a general and liberal constitution. The next thing, as Kossuth thought, was for each element of the empire, for each distinct country, to assert its own independence. In this way, when arranged under one general constitution, they would form a confederation of united states, like that of our own free country. This was Kossuth's original idea. At all events, whatever might be the doctrine or the destiny of the other provinces and kingdoms, he was positive, that the period had come for the Hungarians to claim and recover their own separate integrity, which had been so long and so violently withheld from them. The claim was made. Like the other, it came from the lips of Kossuth. By the first rumor of the revolution at Vienna, he was startled from his seat in the Hungarian diet. With a promptness, a sagacity, a courage, an eloquence, scarcely ever found united in the same person, he arose before the assembled legislators, when all others sat confounded, and openly proposed to send a deputation of their body to the emperor, demanding the immediate dissolution of the Hungarian Chancery, and the restoration of the original and constitutional cabinet, which should at once take its place in the legislative assembly of the nation. With a manner equal to the dignity of the occasion, and with tones of almost superhuman eloquence, pointing to the ministerial seats so long left vacant, he exclaimed:—"For six hundred years, Magyars, we formed a constitutional state. We will, therefore, that, from this moment, ministers again sit upon these benches, to hear and answer our questions. From this day forth, Magyars, we wish to have a Hungarian ministry!"

The speaker sat down. A short period of the most perfect silence followed. It was a sublime moment. A nation was considering whether it would assert, or yield up, its existence. It was Hungary in the act of deciding, whether it would continue as the virtual province of a foreign power, or again be itself a country. The struggle of thought was not protracted. The words of the eloquent statesman had gone to the hearts of his noble auditors. The call, suddenly as it had fallen upon the diet, was almost unanimously supported. A committee was at once raised, with the originator of the movement at its head, which was to repair at once to the residence of the emperor, and ask for the creation of a new cabinet of ministers, composed of native and resident Hungarians, whose sole business should be to attend to Hungarian affairs. Kossuth, with his deputation, reached Vienna on the 15th of March, where his voice was decidedly more powerful than that of Ferdinand. The poor young man, who had made his own fortunes, and who had just been the victim of the imperial government, had become more mighty than that government. Wherever he appeared, his footsteps were followed by vast throngs of Viennese, who covered him with the glory of their eulogies.[12]

Personal glory, however, was not the aim of Kossuth. Proceeding directly to the palace, and avoiding as much as possible all ostentation, he met the ministry of the trembling monarch, and the monarch himself, face to face. Ferdinand must have remembered the prisoner of Buda. It would have been an enviable sight, could the walls of the royal residence have been rendered transparent for the moment, to have beheld the majestic bearing of the Hungarian patriot, in the presence of his abashed king, and heard him giving utterance to his country's high determination, in that magnificent and overpowering eloquence so peculiar to himself. Though the scene of that great hour is left to some future poet or painter, who shall be found worthy of the task, the results of the strange interview have been given to the world. The king yielded at every point. Count Louis Batthiányi received the royal command for the immediate formation of the proposed cabinet. That cabinet was created almost upon the spot. It was composed of men whom Hungary will have reason to remember to her latest day: Louis Batthiányi was Prime-Minister; Louis Kossuth was Minister of Finance, the most responsible position in the government; Bertalan Szemere was Minister of Home Affairs; Francis Deak, of Justice; General Lazar Meszaros, of War; Gabor Klauzal, of Trade; Count

[12] Baron Pillersdorf, late Austrian Prime-Minister, and now the apologist of the emperor, is forced to acknowledge the popularity of the delegation: "In this conflict, in which every spring was put in motion, in order to weaken and exhaust the vital powers of the empire, inflicting, at the same time, the deepest wounds on the commerce and industry of the capital, *the majority of the people inclined toward the Hungarian leaders.*" Political Movement in Austria, by Baron Pillersdorf, London, 1850, p. 55.

Stephen Széchényi, of Public Works; Baron Joseph Eötvös, of Public Instruction; and prince Paul Esterhazy was appointed to be a sort of Mediator between the Austrian emperor and the Hungarian king! The style of his office was that of Minister of *Foreign Affairs*, as if Hungary, in her future dealings with the House of Hapsburg, in its imperial character, had already resolved to treat it as the head of a foreign government!

The revolution of Hungary was now practically complete. The constitution of St. Stephen was restored. The patriots, after giving their blessing to their democratic brethren of Vienna, returned in high spirits to their expectant country; and that country, from the walls of Pressburg to the turrets of Belgrade, applauded the noble and successful daring of the diet, and particularly the foresight, the courage, the energy, the persevering and triumphant patriotism of its leading man. By his personal sacrifices at home, and by the magic of his name abroad, he had begun and completed the revolution of the empire, including both Austria and Hungary, within the compass of just twelve days, and that without the expenditure of the first drop of blood. Well might the name of Kossuth, from that glorious moment, be echoed and re-echoed over many lands!

The success of the great Hungarian was not lost on the patriots of the imperial metropolis. The emperor, it is true, had pledged his word to them in favor of the measures, which they had pressed upon his attention on the 13th of March. But the sight of the Magyars, if not the advice of Kossuth, reminded them that no confidence could be placed in the royal word. The history of the imperial house was a sufficient justification of this distrust; and Ferdinand, in particular, was evidently too weak, too craven, to be firm. The revolutionists demanded a written document, signed by the imperial hand, publicly confirming what had been only privately granted in an hour of dread. On the 16th of March, with the readiest compliance, Ferdinand proclaimed a constitution, which, after a full acknowledgment and satisfactory sanction of all his verbal concessions, gave authority to the citizens, not only to provide themselves with arms, but to organize a national guard, whose duty should be to maintain a just execution of the laws. The army, so long the bulwark of Austrian despotism, was now more than counter-balanced by the imperial grant. The people, in a word, had won the day. Their will, for ages stifled, was not only perfectly enfranchised, but armed with the decisive authority of the sword. The revolution was legally confirmed; and, on that evening, till a late hour at night, every house in the Austrian capital blazed with a sudden illumination, excepting only the palace of the twice-fallen king. This was shrouded with perpetual darkness, as if emblematic of the fact, that the glory of royalty had departed from its halls, and found a more fit resting-place in the habitations of the people.

Until the 21st of March, though Metternich and his ministry had been dismissed, a ministerial interregnum occurred, on which day count Ficquelmont was placed at the head of the first reform cabinet. All his associates, excepting only general Zanini, Minister of War, were noblemen, so ready were the people to leave to the monarch the enjoyment of every non-essential gratification, if he would only allow them the benefit of wholesome laws and a liberal constitution. Although the new charter was not universally satisfactory, with a due amount of caution, and with a wise condescension to the wishes of the better classes, the government might have proceeded, without farther revolution, to a gradual and final settlement of the state. But the new ministry seemed bent on their own destruction. In direct contradiction to the *octroyed* constitution, and in open violation of the public faith, they published, on the 21st of March, their famous Regulations of the Press, denying to the citizens the free use of the pen, when they had wrenched from the fallen monarchy the authority of the sword. The public had conquered the right of doing what they pleased; but they could give no full and free account of their own proceedings, not even to themselves. Such a contradiction could not last long. The citizens again rose; the government again yielded; and the first reform ministry, with the exception of a single member, were hurried into private life.

The second cabinet, with baron Pillersdorf as President and Minister of the Interior, had no sooner taken its position, than another error, more flagrant than any of its predecessors, shook every corner of the realm. In the *octroyed* or imperial constitution, the immediate convocation of a Constituent Assembly had been promised. This body was to be authorized, by the joint consent of the people and of the government, to prepare a new and more perfect constitution. The best policy of the ministers, therefore, evidently was, to call that assembly into existence as soon as possible, that the excited populace might have occasion to take their eyes from the king and his cabinet, and throw the responsibility of meeting the emergency upon a body to be created by themselves. Thus, several months of quiet would have been easily secured, during which the passions of the masses would have had time to cool. But wisdom had departed from the imperial halls. The Constituent Assembly was deferred by every petty pretext within the reach of ministerial ingenuity and power. The President of the ministry, in the mean time, was daily closeted with the political theorist and speculator, Hok, drawing up a second constitution, which was to be foisted upon the country before the assembly should be convened. On the 25th of April, this cabinet document, which was merely an expansion of the well-known Belgic Fundamental Laws, was published to the world. All classes of the citizens were astonished. The patriots felt themselves insulted. The National Guard arose in arms. The Academic Legion, always first in the cause of liberty, tore up every copy of it, on which they could lay their hands, and scattered the flying fragments to the winds.

The folly of the government was still unable, or unwilling, to receive instruction from these facts. By a third movement, it perfected the annihilation of its credit with the people, whom it professed to serve. The National Guard was now fully organized; and, in its transactions with the throne, it was represented by a Committee of Public Safety, elected from its own body by itself. This Committee, necessarily large to give it proper weight, was too unwieldy to meet the daily emergencies of the public with suitable dispatch. Out of this larger body, therefore, a smaller one was chosen, styled the Central Club, whose duty it was to attend to sudden wants. The Club held daily sessions, in which the conduct of the ministers, and the condition of the country, were discussed. As the cabinet sank lower and lower in the confidence of the public, this small delegation of the most able and prudent citizens was compelled to accept of more important duties, until they became the virtual rulers of the state. The pride of the ministry was now piqued. They resolved to put this new power out of their path. The mode of executing their resolution was very blundering. In the first place, Baron Pillersdorf called on several members of the Committee of Public Safety, and inquired into the transactions of the Club. These gentlemen could very truly say, that they knew little of what the Club was doing, as the larger body was not called together, whenever the smaller one could meet the exigencies that arose. The President of the ministry, therefore, very rashly and foolishly concluded, that the Club was an unauthorized body, because some members of the parent Committee were not conversant with its acts. An edict of abolition next thundered from the imperial press. Vanity of vanities! Little did the people care, at this time, what edicts, or interdicts, issued from the palace of a cowardly, obsolete and imbecile king. The very next morning after the publication of this decree, the Academic Legion, supported by a large escort of the Civic Guards, and followed by crowds of the enraged populace, marched out of the city to the pleasure-palace of Schönbrunn, filled all the courts and corridors with armed men, and clamorously demanded the withdrawal of the interdict upon the Club. The ministers refused. The agitation thus excited no language can describe. The citizen-soldiers surrounded the royal residence with a wall of arms. A deputation was sent in to make the requisition, in behalf of Austria, not only of an instantaneous recantation of the hated interdict, but for the revocation of the April constitution, the immediate calling of the Constituent Assembly, and a considerable expansion of the new law of suffrage, by which the elections were to be governed. "In this dilemma," says Pillersdorf, speaking for himself, "conscious of having lost the confidence of the people, the ministry, *in order to preserve the inviolable prerogative of the throne*—[that is, to save the king from making the concessions asked for by an outraged people]—tendered their resignation, and thus transmitted to their successors the decision of the pending demands!" Cured, at last, of their madness, by the sure results of their impotent attempts at despotic domination, when the people had become the ruling power, they were unwilling to meet the storm raised by their own agency, and, therefore, resigned. Two days afterwards, on the 17th of May, the poor old emperor, fearing that his subterranean burrowing-place might not now protect him, without giving the slightest notice of his intentions to his ministers, whose resignation he had refused, fled from Vienna to Innspruck, the chief city of the Tyrol, leaving his cabinet and his capital to their fate.

The work of revolution was now done. The old monarchy had passed away. The citizens had caught the robe of empire as it fell. The Club, and the Committee of Safety, now took command. Ferdinand was not only gone; but he might not be able to come back. Hid among the mountains of the Tyrol, which nature has made almost inaccessible to troops, he looked out upon the agitated world, and was glad, amid the universal wreck of monarchy and of monarchs, that he could call his own life his own. Wherever he turned his eye, he saw nothing but the signs of annihilation to his house. Not only was his great capital in arms against him, but, also, nearly every department of his widely-extended empire. Hungary had led the way. Bohemia had risen for a nationality of her own. The Croatians and Sclavonians, whom he had excited to rise in rebellion against the Magyars, had given him much reason to doubt, whether they would ultimately join with their brethren of Bohemia, or with him. His Italian provinces, prepared by thirty-three years of gross oppression, had raised the standard of independence, and defeated all his armies in the bloodiest of fields. The Tyrol itself, to which he had confided both his fortunes and his life, might catch the sparks of the Italian conflagration, through the passes or over the summits of the Julian Alps, and surround his last retreat with the flames of a devouring fire.

If he looked to foreign countries, he could see no hope of succor, but a similar ruin prostrating or threatening the monarchies of the European world. All Prussia was, by this time, rocking with the heaviest throes of her revolution. The smaller kingdoms and principalities of Germany had hurled their petty tyrants from their positions. There was no longer a king in France. Norway, Sweden and Denmark were supposed to be on the brink of a civil outbreak. Ireland had demanded an instantaneous repeal of her union with Great Britain. Great Britain, which, in the beginning of this universal trouble, had dispatched Sir Stratford Canning to carry her consolations to her Austrian confederate, was now pale with the impending horrors of a united Chartist and Hibernian rebellion. Rumors of a republic had come from the capital of the Russias, promising to give the Czar so much occupation, that he would not be able to lend a helping hand to his Austrian cousin. The people of the Roman States had nearly achieved a liberal constitution. Sicily had declared her independence of the Bourbon sovereignty of Naples. Naples was trembling at the voice of an outraged population; and even the valiant queen of Spain, the invincible Christina, on hearing of all this trouble, had sunk in a swoon in the midst of her warlike attendants. The fearful old emperor of Austria, concealed among the impregnable crags on the south-western border of his dominions, beheld nothing, in the day of his own humiliation, but the rubbish of prostrate thrones, and the upraised banners of popular revolution, all around him!

NOTE.—It is with pain that I have stated the conduct of Great Britain in relation to the Hungarian movement; but the statement is made on authority, which cannot be disputed: "The English government," says Baron Pillersdorf, in the work heretofore quoted, "during the ominous period of Austria's embarrassment and distress, *never withheld warm manifestations of sympathy, and assurances of its spontaneous support!*" Political Movement, p. 40. The people of England were the friends of Hungary. The government was the ally of her oppressor. After the war was over, the government was compelled, by the voice of the people, to show its sympathy for the Hungarian refugees; but, soon afterwards, Lord Lyndhurst and Earl Graham proposed the reënaction of the infamous alien act, that the freedom granted to these champions of civil liberty might be suppressed! Pillersdorf is a competent witness; for he was all the time a minister, and part of the time prime-minister, at the period to which he refers; and the proposition of the two British lords is reported among the published proceedings of the upper house of parliament for the 28th of March, 1851. *Proh pudor!* Such is my respect toward England, that it is mortifying to be obliged to record such a fact!

CHAPTER X.

THE REBELLION OF THE SCLAVES.

According to the laws and customs of the kingdom, the new ministry, which the Hungarians had at last obtained from Austria, could not go into actual service, until the close of the existing Diet. The Palatine, therefore, who had been clothed with regal authority in the absence of the monarch, appointed a Provisional Commission, to which he gave civil and military power, to conduct the administration of the government, till the ministers could be qualified in due form. This Commission consisted of four gentlemen—Gabriel Klauzál, Bertalan Szemere, Francis Pulsky, and Paul Nyáry—whose names have since become familiar in other lands.[1]

Kossuth and his colleagues, in the mean time, returned to their places in the National Assembly; and, in connection with the patriotic party, they resumed the task of redeeming their country from the condition to which the oppression of three centuries had sunk it. As they had not, in consequence of the disturbances of the world around them, raised their demands on Austria, so, when their long-standing requests had been granted, they took no advantage whatever of their new position, but went directly forward to carry out those measures, and those measures only, which had ever been the object of their patriotic efforts.

In 1832, but more distinctly in 1847, when Kossuth became a candidate for election to the lower House, they had published a programme of their principles to the nation. Touching their relations to Austria, they emphatically de-

[1] Memoirs of a Hungarian Lady, vol. i. p. 112.

clared, that they asked nothing new. All they wanted, they said, was what every Austrian king of Hungary had sworn to, with a single exception, since the two countries had been united. They wished simply, that the constitution should remain as it had been for more than eight hundred years; that the independence and integrity of the kingdom should be maintained; and that the king should administer the laws, not through foreigners, but by the hands of native Hungarians, who could be made to feel their responsibility to the people over whom they ruled.

Such were the international politics of this party. Their internal, or national, policy was equally liberal and patriotic. They set down that policy in a series of brief but explicit propositions:

1. That all the peasants of the kingdom, whatever might be their religion or their race, should be at once emancipated from all urbarial dues and obligations to their landlords, for which the landlords were to receive a just indemnification from the state.

2. That, without exception of religion or of race, all the inhabitants of the country, noble and non-noble, should be declared equal before the law.

3. That every inhabitant, whose income amounted to ten pounds a year, which would include all persons not vagabonds or state-paupers, should be clothed with the elective franchise, and thus help make the laws under which they lived.

4. That every inhabitant, who should have this elective franchise, should bear his equal proportion of the expenses of the government, by being taxed according to the value of his income.

5. That the National Assembly, and not the Hungarian Chancery at Vienna, should decide on the employment of the public revenue.

6. That the revenue, and other national interests, should be put into the hands of a cabinet of native ministers, who

should be responsible, not to Austria, but to Hungary, the country to which those interests pertained.

7. That the right of heirs to recover property once sold, by what was called *aviticite,* which was the Hungarian law of entail, should be abolished, thus securing the business and internal credit of the country against the great land-holders, who, under the old laws, could prevent their estates from passing out of their families, whatever might be their liabilities, or however fairly they might have once parted with their possessions in payment of their debts.[2]

Such, indeed, had been the politics of the patriotic party, from 1832 to 1847; and the intervening period had been spent in preparing the nation to receive them. These were the doctrines preached by the blind old Wésselényi in his ceaseless pilgrimages. These were the doctrines which Kossuth had published and defended in the Pesti Hirlap. These were the principles which the two leaders of the Hungarian patriots had breathed into the breasts of a majority of their countrymen. On these the newly-appointed ministers, while still holding their places in the National Assembly, again planted their feet, resolving to see them enacted into laws, before they should be obliged to leave the halls of legislation to accept of their respective positions in the cabinet.

Though, as has just been asserted, a majority of the nation was clearly on the side of these democratic measures, they met with some opposition in the Diet. Besides the patriots, there were two other parties in that body, as well as in the kingdom. The magnates, headed by Count Stephen Széchényi, with all their patriotism, were excessively conservative, wishing to keep all things exactly as they were, and decidedly unwilling to declare for a ministerial separation from Austria, as well as still more decidedly opposed to the internal policy of

[2] Blackwood's Magazine, vol. lxv. p. 628, as well as all the leading political periodicals of America and Europe for 1848–1849.

the patriots. There was, also, a radical party, in the lead of which was the powerful and accomplished Baron Eötvös, who was imbued with the leveling doctrines of the French Socialists. They regarded their country as a *tabula rasa*—a new-born country—whose future was to be made, not from the precedents and institutions of the past, but from the ideas and aspirations of the present. The patriots, on the other hand, under the guidance of Louis Kossuth, seeing that things as they were, at that moment, were only the perversion of things as they had once been, resolved to recover what was lost, and so build up the future, according to present light, on the tried and venerated foundations of the past. The struggle between these parties, at the time now under consideration, was very brief. The eloquence of Kossuth carried every thing before him. Not only the Conservatives, but the Radicals, yielded to his logic, and declared themselves convinced. Since the days of Demosthenes, there has probably not been such a triumph. Every one of his measures, international and national, was sustained in both branches of the Diet. "By unanimous votes of both houses, the diet not only established perfect equality of civil rights and public burdens among all classes, denominations and races in Hungary and its provinces, and perfect toleration for every form of religious worship, but, with a generosity perhaps unparalleled in the history of nations, and which must extort the admiration even of those, who may question the wisdom of the measure, the nobles of Hungary abolished their own right to exact either labor or produce in return for the lands held by urbarial tenure, and thus transferred to the peasants the absolute ownership, free and forever, of nearly half the cultivated land in the kingdom, reserving to the original proprietors of the soil such compensation as the government might award from the public funds of Hungary. More than five hundred thousand peasant families were thus invested with the absolute ownership of from thirty to sixty acres of land each, or about twenty millions of acres amongst them. The elective franchise was extended to every man possessed of capital or property of the value of thirty pounds, or an annual income of ten pounds; to every man who had received a diploma from a university; and to every artizan who employed an apprentice. With the concurrence of both countries, Hungary and Transylvania were united, and their diets, hitherto separate, were incorporated."[3] It was enacted, also, that all real estate should be held responsible for its owner's debts; that the whole tithing system, by which the poor had been so long oppressed, should exist no longer; that the nobles, though they had thus generously given away nearly half of all their possessions, should pay taxes to the government, according to what remained to them after this gift was made; that the Jewish and all other foreign inhabitants should no longer be subject to special legislation, but hold the rank and enjoy the rights of other citizens; and that eight millions of the public money should be at once expended in making such internal improvements as the condition of the whole country at that time required.

[3] Blackwood's Magazine, vol. lxv. p. 629. Blackwood, whose political articles are written chiefly by Mr. Alison, would be regarded as the best of authority on such a question, whatever might be the circumstances under which its testimony should be given; no journal in the world is more careful, or more laborious, in collecting and collating the *facts* on which its *opinions* are founded; but, in this instance, it declares itself to have been in possession of the laws themselves, translated from the Hungarian, as they passed the Diet of the nation. Blackwood, however, is not alone in this particular. Nearly all the other great journals of Europe and America have made the same statements on the same authority; but I have thought it best to quote the words of Blackwood, because, in addition to its high character, its politics give its declarations a peculiar weight in the Hungarian question. No one can accuse it of leaning too far toward the popular movements of any country; and, at the very time, when these concessions were made to Hungary, it was pouring out its indignation on the general revolutionary spirit of Europe in a series of most able and effective articles.

It ought to be particularly remarked, that these blessings were not restricted to any district, or to any nationality, of the Magyar kingdom, but were freely given to all its inhabitants of every race, sect and section. They were given, too, without requiring any thing to be yielded on the part of any of the nationalities. All the nationalities remained exactly as they had been. At their capital of Agram, the Sclavic representatives of Sclavonia and Croatia were to continue to assemble, and to transact their provincial business according to their old customs. They were still to be represented in the National Assembly by their own delegates; and these, only three in number before this period, were not only increased to eighteen, by the magnanimity of this most magnanimous of all nations, but clothed with powers never enjoyed by them since their connection with the kingdom.[4]

On the eleventh day of April, after the National Assembly had closed its session, all the new enactments of the kingdom were laid before his majesty, king Ferdinand. To make them laws, they required his royal signature. That signature was promptly and emphatically given: "Having graciously listened to, and graciously granted the prayers of, our beloved and faithful dignitaries of the church and of the state, magnates and nobles of Hungary and its dependencies, *we* ordain, that the before-mentioned laws be registered in these presents, word for word; and, as we consider these laws and their entire contents, both separately and collectively, fitting and suitable, we give them our consent and approbation. In exercise of our royal will, we have accepted, adopted, approved and sanctioned them, assuring, at the same time, our faithful states, that we will respect the said laws, and cause them to be respected by our faithful subjects." Such were the words of Ferdinand, signed by his own hand, and countersigned by Batthiányi, the Hungarian Prime-Minister just appointed by himself, in

[4] Blackwood's Magazine, vol. lxv. p. 629.

the presence of the arch-dukes Francis Charles, Stephen, Francis Joseph, the present emperor, and of the Hungarian deputation, on the eleventh day of April, 1848. The work was now done. Kossuth had carried out the patriotic measures of his party; and that party, now including nearly every inhabitant of the kingdom, could hardly find words by which to celebrate the glory of their great leader.

Never, perhaps, in the progress of sixty centuries, was there ever so disinterested a step taken by any nation. The Magyars, the dominant people of a country, at a time when they could have increased instead of relinquishing their hold upon their tenants and subject-tribes, gave them all their freedom, gave them a perfect equality with themselves, and gave them about half of their own possessions in order to render them, not only free, but independent. Well might the nation, the whole nation, rejoice over such a consummation. The nation did rejoice, the whole of it, from Belgrade to Pressburg. There was a perfect jubilee throughout the kingdom. All the religions, all the tribes, rejoiced together. The Magyars rejoiced, as all benefactors do, because they had done such an act, and filled so many bosoms with such an unexpected happiness. The other tribes rejoiced, Sclaves, Germans, Jews and Gipsies, as men always do, when they receive great and unlooked-for blessings. It was, undoubtedly, a real satisfaction to these tribes, who had always entertained so unworthy opinions of the Magyars, to be now compelled to do them justice. "Is it possible," said the Sclavonian, the Sclavack, the Croat, the Serb, "that we have so long misunderstood the character, and misrepresented the intentions, of our Magyar countrymen? Let us repay them for the wrong with interest!" The rich and the poor had their mutual congratulations and rejoicings. The landlord went home to his tenants, and told them that they were no longer slaves; that they were his equals; and that, to make their equality worth something to them, the land they then cultivated was no longer his, but theirs, which they could own, occupy, and then transmit to their descendants. The peasants, on hearing this strange news, leaped for joy, and, in a transport of gratitude, kissed the hands and necks of their former masters. There was joy in Hungary; and the Magyars, who had before reigned as the superior race, in mental and military qualities, now reigned in the hearts of their countrymen by virtue of a moral superiority. The individual Magyar, wherever he appeared, was sure to hear his praise from the lips of all the other peoples; and the Sclaves of the south of Hungary, in particular, sent a numerous delegation of their tribe to thank the Magyar nation for its unbounded and unparalleled magnanimity. Such had Hungary become under the legislative management of Kossuth.

No sooner, however, were these things done, while the acclamations of the people were still echoing from the Drave to the Carpathians, than the old and wicked policy of Austria was again set in motion. Metternich, as has been shown, had kept the empire in subjection to the imperial despot, by rousing the mutual jealousies of the races, thus rendering it impossible for them to unite against their common tyrant. The same instrument of distraction was again employed. Amidst all the commotion of the Austrian revolution, in which Bohemia and Italy had heartily united, while the citizens were revolutionary and democratic, the soldiers had generally remained conservative and monarchical. The army, therefore, served as the basis for the re-establishment of the old policy; and a great part of the Austrian standing forces were the soldier-citizens of the Military District, lying along the entire south of Hungary, peopled by the Sclavonians, Croats, Serbs and Wallachians, whose ignorance is unbounded, and whose national prejudices are the most easily excited. The Sclavic delegation, who had expressed the gratitude of the Sclavic tribes to their Magyar benefactors, had scarcely returned to their places of residence, when the emissaries of the Austrian party began to swarm through Sclavonia and Croatia, busily

24

engaged, like so many fiends from the world of darkness, in reviving the dissensions of the races. "Do not be deceived," they said, "with these fair pretences. The Magyars are your old enemies. They conquered you in battle. They look upon you as a subject people. This great act, which you now blindly celebrate, is nothing but a trick against you. It is the beginning of a work of centralization, by which they intend to unite all the races of Hungary, it is true, but only for their own advantage. They wish you to give up your nationality, to forget it altogether, that they may the more easily establish their own. They intend to blot you from existence. If you want proof of this, whatever they have done in other respects, you have the evidence in their decrees about your language. Your mother tongue has been abolished. You are all of you compelled to become Magyars, by forgetting the dialect of your fathers, and learning and employing the speech of your so-called benefactors. Singular benefactors! They wish to effect your annihilation; and you, Croats, Sclavonians, Serbs, are so blind as to be led willingly and even thankfully to the sacrifice!"

Such were the wily falsehoods scattered all over the southern provinces by the party of the imperial court. That very man, who had just "accepted, adopted, approved and sanctioned" the late laws, pronouncing them "fitting and suitable," and promising to respect them himself and to "cause them to be respected," was now secretly engaged in crushing those laws by the most malicious, dangerous, and wicked of all methods. The only truth, on which all these aggravating complaints were founded, was a former law respecting the use of the Hungarian language; and, to make that of any service in the hands of the imperial agitators, its true character had to be misrepresented. The tribes of the south had not been forbidden to use their vernacular tongue. They were expressly allowed and encouraged to use it. Not only in their schools and families, and in all business transactions, but in their provincial legislature, the Sclavic was to be the legal language. It was to be the medium of their private legislation. The laws of the National Assembly, also, when published within their borders, were always to be accompanied by a Sclavic translation for their special benefit. The only restriction was, that, in a court of justice, or when used in a judicial manner, the Hungarian original of the laws should be the legal standard of their meaning. This legal authority had to be conferred upon the original, or upon the translation, as there could not be two standards; and whether the original, or a copy, of any public or private document, is best entitled to this pre-eminence, can never be made a question.

Another old regulation, however, respecting the legal language, was prominently set forth on this occasion. In 1832 a law had been enacted, making the Hungarian the only language to be employed in the future sessions of the National Assembly. Before that time, the Diet had been a babel, where Latin, German, Sclavic and Magyar were mingled with the most embarrassing confusion. The speeches, it is true, had been generally delivered in the Latin, or in German. The one was a dead language. The other was the language of another nation. The Diet of 1832 resolved to correct this anomaly. In doing so, could the Magyars be expected to choose, as the language of their own legislature, one of the dialects of their Sclavic countrymen? The Magyar was spoken by twice as many people as used either of those other dialects; for, it must be remembered, that the Sclavacks of the north, the Serbs of the east, and the Sclavonians and Croats of the south of Hungary, speak their respective *patois*, which differ essentially from each other. The Magyar language, therefore, was judiciously and justly established as the legal and legislative language of the Magyar nation. But the agents of Austria fastened upon this provision as another text from which to preach dissension. Their success was the first source of a fierce and bloody insurrection.

The Serbs, so lately full of gratitude to the Hungarians, and ever before the allies of the patriotic party in the National Assembly, were thus separated from their Magyar protectors. They began to manifest unpleasant feelings about the first days of June. By the middle of the month, they had assembled in great numbers, at the call of their archbishop, Rajachich, at their capital of Karlowicz, at Perlász, and at several other towns. The seat of the excitement was in the Banat, where the Austrian emperor held large landed possessions, and where his personal influence was consequently great. From the Banat, it spread into the Bacs county, and into the eastern parts of Sclavonia. The archbishop assembled the leading members of the Servian aristocracy at Karlowicz, whom he formed into what he called the Central Committee of the Servian Nation, which undertook to manage the tempest raised between the Serbs and Magyars. They drew up a paper, entitled the Demands of the Servian People, which they forwarded to Pesth by an angry delegation. The Hungarians, and particularly the patriotic party, were overwhelmed with astonishment. They might easily have crushed this budding rebellion; but they soon perceived the origin of these new feelings. They saw that a common enemy had been sowing discord. They pitied, much more than they blamed, their Servian countrymen. They hoped that a little delay, giving time for mutual intercourse and explanations, would open the eyes and cool the passions of the Serbs. They were mistaken. There were influences at work of which they little dreamed. The Serbs went forward with their unnatural hostilities to their friends. Joined by bands of Servian Turks, they rose in all their villages upon their Magyar fellow-citizens, rushed into the neighboring Magyar country, burnt the Magyar towns, massacred the Magyar inhabitants, and committed such cruelties as had not been seen in Hungary for many generations. As they advanced in their horrid work, their barbarities became more and more atrocious. Old men, tottering with age, were murdered in cold blood. Matrons, while quietly engaged in their domestic duties, were cut down by the side of their infant children. Children, snatched from their little beds, where they were softly sleeping, were dashed to pieces and thrown in piles upon the dead bodies of their parents. Pregnant women were ripped open with the Turkish knife; and the unripe fruit of their wombs were trampled beneath the coarse feet of the brutal murderers. The wife and daughters of thousands of families, after being compelled to receive the revolting embraces of a whole company of savages, were hacked and mangled by the swords of the soldiers, then cast upon the heap of their immolated kindred. Not only the villages, but the fields and flocks of the unprepared and unresisting inhabitants, were destroyed by these infatuated rebels. The voice of lamentation was spread over many districts. A cold shudder convulsed the Magyar nation.

While these scenes were being enacted in the east, the southern portion of the kingdom was undergoing a change, and putting itself into a hostile attitude. The Sclaves of Croatia and Sclavonia had always been, as before stated, the dupes of Metternich. He had made them his special instruments, for a whole generation, against the dreaded consolidation of the kingdom; and the thousand suspicions of Magyar superiority, which he had lodged in their bosoms, still remained there, after all that the Hungarians had done to disabuse them. In a period of general distraction, when the most liberal and enlightened scarcely knew their interest, or their duty, these people, so long corrupted and misled, were ready to be an easy prey to some artful and ambitious leader. Such a leader was now among them. The Baron Joseph Jellachich, the personage referred to, a Croatian by birth, had been the colonel of a Croat regiment in the army of Italy. Possessed by nature of an honest-looking face, and remarkable for the dignity of his deportment and the insinuating style of his address, he had been chosen by the friends of the fallen monarchy as a fit person to raise disturbances in the south of Hungary to the injury of the emancipated nation. The emperor, at the advice of the Austrian party at home, who were in constant communication with their countrymen in Italy, appointed the colonel to be Ban, or Lord, of his native land. This office gave him supreme command within the limits of his province. His first act was to forbid the magistrates of Croatia from having any intercourse with the Hungarian ministry, saying, that his countrymen ought to resist the new state of things in Hungary; that, as soon as they should become fully aware of the intentions of the Magyars, there would be resistance; and that an open revolt would be, nay was then, encouraged by the king. This doctrine he circulated, by letters and by personal conversation, all over Croatia and Sclavonia. The people began to believe what he said. But there were other things, which the Ban now openly avowed, but which he had not been employed to say. Though acting ostensibly with the imperial party, who were doing every thing in their power to bring on a reaction in favor of the old monarchy, he was secretly working in concert with the Bohemian rebellion, the object of which was to set up a Sclavic government in that ancient and once independent kingdom. While the cause of the Bohemians was in its most promising condition, they had proclaimed to the world their intention of reorganizing the empire, so soon as they should become victorious, on a Sclavic basis; and they had sent forth a warm invitation to all the Sclaves of Southern Europe, to all of their tribe, indeed, not included in the Russian empire, to join in one grand and universal movement for the establishment of a Sclavic nationality and independence. This was one of the influences, which had acted so powerfully upon the Serbs, and which the Hungarians at first did not fully understand. The Serbs had not blindly lifted up the banner of the universal Sclavic nationality. Jellachich, from the beginning of their rebellion, had privately encouraged them to proceed. He wished to prove, at their expense, at least by their instrumentality, whether the Sclavic mind was ready for the great work proposed. His own course was to be shaped by the result. In a letter dated the 4th of June, and addressed to the frontier regiments stationed in Italy, he declared, that the imperial family, though he does not mention the emperor by name, encouraged the Servian revolt. The Serbs themselves professed to be fighting the battles of their king.

The Hungarian ministers, before the insurrection of the Serbs broke out, had been watching the movements of the Ban. They were fully aware of his ambition, of his duplicity, and of his real leanings, whatever might be his present bearing toward the imperial cause. They knew him to be, in heart and in life, a Sclave. They knew him to be, at that time, as at all times, opposed to the German as well as to the Hungarian party. They knew that, should he ever see his opportunity, he would break with the imperialists and desert to the standard of his Bohemian friends. The true character and position of the Ban was, therefore, correctly reported to the emperor. The emperor was convinced, that, in this treacherous movement in his own behalf, he was placing too much confidence, and lodging too much power, in the hands of one, who might turn out to be as double as himself. On the 29th of May, just as the Serbs were beginning to assemble, Ferdinand dispatched an autograph letter to Jellachich, summoning him to appear at Innspruck to answer to his monarch for his recent conduct. He was to answer, indeed, for that very course of action, which he had been commissioned to pursue; but, though his acts had been clearly within the letter of his instructions, his motives, his ulterior designs, were the subjects of complaint. A man's motives, however, when his actions cannot be objected to, can be positively appreciated only by himself; and the Ban, in the case before us, had only to deny the charge of Pansclavism, as the enterprise of Bohemia was denominated, to free himself from the anger of his monarch. It is easy enough to imagine what sort of a conference would have been held, had the Ban obeyed the call, between Jellachich and Ferdinand. "Have you done any thing more, my dear Ban, than to raise the old jealousies of the Serbs against the Magyars?" "Nothing." "But the Serbs have been too much excited, and may carry their part too far, which will be likely to rouse the sympathies of other nations in favor of the Hungarians?" "This they will do, then, on their own responsibility, without my instructions." "And you are now raising a rebellion in Croatia and Sclavonia, on the Sclavic basis." "Well, may it please your majesty, this was the only basis, on which a rebellion could be raised, at this particular time, when the fortunes of the monarchy are so low." "But they tell me you are doing it in aid of your brethren of Bohemia, who have elevated the Pansclavic standard, and invited their race throughout Europe to join them in their attempt." "May it please your imperial majesty, the insinuation against my honor is entirely groundless; and so long as my outward acts correspond exactly with my secret instructions, my motives ought to be considered good." Such, undoubtedly, would have been the substance of the conversation at that time to have been held between the double-minded monarch and his equally double-minded man. Both were traitors; and each knew the other to be acting false. There could have been, therefore, no certain confidence between them. The Ban would have left the king, determined not to break with the crown, so long as there was a doubt, whether, in the reconstruction of the empire, the Germans or the Sclaves would rule. The king would have dismissed his servant, resolved to watch him narrowly, and settle his own future course by what his eyes should see.

A few days were enough, though the conference was not then held, to point out to the monarch, or to his familiar advisers, what policy he should outwardly pursue. He was still the nominal king of Hungary. It would not then do for him to encourage one portion of his kingdom to carry on a civil war against another portion. This would be the king rebelling against the king. Nor would it then do for the emperor of Austria to make war upon his Magyar crown. Such a proceeding would not only excite the Hungarians to rebellion, but so compromise his imperial character, that he might endanger the recovery of the empire, on any basis, whatever might be the success of the particular duplicity in which he was then engaged. An open opposition to the movements of the Ban was called for, as much by his present interests, as by the appeals of the Hungarian ministers. The call was made and answered. He denounced Jellachich as a traitor, removed him from all his dignities and offices, and forbade the people of Croatia and Sclavonia from paying any obedience to his commands.

The imperial manifesto was issued on the 10th of June. Every word of it is a clear and unanswerable defence of the Magyars against the rebellious Sclaves: "You, Croatians and Sclavonians! who, united to the crown of Hungary for eight centuries, have shared all the fates of this country; you, Croatians and Sclavonians! who owe to this very union the constitutional freedom, which alone, amongst all Sclavonic nations, you have been enabled to preserve; you have disappointed our hopes—*you*, who not only have shared in all the rights and liberties of the Hungarian constitution, but who besides—in just recompense of your loyalty, until now stainlessly preserved—were lawfully endowed with peculiar rights, privileges and liberties, by the grace of our illustrious ancestors, and who, therefore, *possess greater privileges than any of the subjects of our sacred Hungarian crown.*

"You have disappointed our hopes, to whom the last Diet of the kingdom of Hungary and its dependencies, according to our sovereign will, *granted full part in all the benefits of the enlarged constitutional liberties and equality of rights.* The legislation of the crown of Hungary has abolished feudal servitude in Croatia as well as in Hungary; and those amongst you, who were subject to *robot*, have, *without any sacrifice on their part, become free proprietors.* The landed proprietors receive for their loss an indemnification, which your own means could never have provided. That indemnification will be entailed on our Hungarian crown estates, with our sovereign ratification, and without any charge to you.

"The right also of constitutional representation was extended to the people in your case no less than in Hungary; in consequence of which no longer the nobility alone, but likewise the other inhabitants and the Military Frontier, take part by their representatives in the legislation common to all, as much as in the municipal congregations. Thus, you may improve your welfare by your immediate co-operation. Until now, the nobility contributed but little to the public expenses; henceforward, the proportional repartition of the taxes amongst all inhabitants is lawfully established, whereby you have been delivered from a great burden. Your nationality and municipal rights, relative to which vain and malicious reports have been spread, with the aim of exciting your distrust, are by no means in danger. On the contrary, *both your nationality and your municipal rights are enlarged and secured against all encroachments;* not only is the use of *your native language lawfully guaranteed to you for ever in your schools and churches*, but it is likewise introduced into the *public assemblies*, where the Latin language has been until now in use."

The royal document proceeds to demonstrate the magnanimity of the Hungarians respecting the nationality of the Croatians and Sclavonians, by citing the acts of the National Assembly for eight hundred years, and then advances to another topic: "Formerly, in Hungary and its dependencies, we administered the executive powers by our Hungarian Chancery and Home Office, and, in military concerns, by our Council of War. To the orders issued in this way, the Bans of Croatia, Dalmatia and Sclavonia were obedient, just as they were bound, in more remote times, to obey the orders of our Hungarian authorities, issued in a different manner and in different forms, according to the mode of administering our executive power." The king then goes on to say, that, with the advice of Hungary, he had appointed the Palatine as his lord-lieutenant, clothed with regal authority, to whom the kingdom was to pay the same obedience as to the king's person. Jellachich, however, had not done this; for, in being summoned to Pesth to answer for his conduct to Ferdinand's representative, he had refused to obey the mandate. He had refused, also, to appear before the emperor himself. This, of course, was open and avowed rebellion. The position of the Ban could be disguised no longer. The monarch, therefore, as a public vindication of himself, was compelled to close his manifesto with a renunciation of all the late acts of Jellachich, besides removing him from his lordship: "No other means was left, to protect our royal authority against the injury of such conduct, and to uphold the laws, than to send our faithful Privy-Councillor, Lieutenant Field-Marshal Hrabowszky, as our royal commissioner, to inquire into those unlawful proceedings, and to indict the Baron Jellachich and his accomplices; and, lastly, to deprive the Baron Jellachich of his dignity as Ban, and of all his military offices."[5]

The Ban, thus legally deposed, continued to hold his power, though the Croatians and Sclavonians, his subjects, had ever been renowned for their servility to the king. They were now, however, no longer Austrians, as they dreamed, but Sclaves. A new empire, as they thought, on a Sclavic foundation, was about to be raised on the ruins of the German. The old German emperor, therefore, to whom they had always before been so obedient, was now of less consequence to them, than the great military leader, Jellachich, who, without doubt, was soon to hold a high place in the nationality about to be

[5] Klapka's War in Hungary, vol. ii. pp. 227–237.

constructed. The Germans, even in the German empire, were few in number, a majority of whom, at that time, were in strong opposition to the German throne. The Magyars, however, were still loyal. They were, also, firm in their princi ples, strong in their attachments, and absolutely unyielding to their enemies. They must be put out of the way. There were Sclaves enough about them, could they be induced to rise, to annihilate the race and blot it from the world. They were surrounded, even in their own country, on all sides by Sclaves. Beyond the limits of the kingdom, the Bohemian Sclaves on the west, the Russian Sclaves on the north, the Servian Sclaves on the east, and the Croatian and other Sclaves on the south and south-west, could all be relied on, it was supposed, to aid their kindred in Hungary the moment they should appear in arms. A constant correspondence, with this unity of movement all the while in view, was kept up between the Sclavic revolutionists of every land. Messengers were sent into every part of Hungary, who were secretly to inform the various Sclavic tribes of the general plan, and to induce them, on a given signal, to revolt. This signal was to be, as we now know, the invasion of the Magyars by the Croatian Ban.

The Hungarians, however, began to see their danger. So little are they inclined to suspicion, so open and manly are they in their own conduct, that they were slow to attribute all this treachery and ingratitude to a people, whom they had always treated well. That the king had any connection with the original rebellion of the Ban they would not believe; and the false-hearted monarch was careful to take every course to make them, and to keep them, blind. His manifesto against Jellachich, which was a part of his double game, was soon followed by a pro-royal speech, in which the duplicity of the sovereign is studiously maintained. It was the speech delivered by the great Palatine, whose sentiments were dictated by Ferdinand, as the document itself declares. It was pronounced before the new National Assembly, which, on the basis of universal suffrage, had been called together by the king to take into consideration the revolt of the Serbs, the rebellious attitude of Croatia and Sclavonia, and the threatening aspect of the times: "In the name, and as the representative, of our glorious king, Ferdinand the Fifth, I hereby open this parliament. The extraordinary circumstances, in which the country has been placed, make it necessary to summon at once a meeting of the estates, without waiting for the completion in detail of all the propositions and administrative measures, which the responsible ministers of the crown were charged and directed by the last parliament to prepare and complete. Croatia has risen in undisguised sedition. In the districts of the lower Danube, bands of armed rebels have broken the peace of the country; and while it is the *sincere* wish of his majesty *to avoid a civil war*, his majesty is, on the other hand, convinced, that the assembled representatives of the nation will regard it as their *first and chief duty* to provide all the means required *for restoring the troubled tranquillity of the country*, preserving the *integrity of the Hungarian realm*, and maintaining *the sacred inviolability of the law.* The *defence* of the country and the *state of the finances* will, therefore, form the *chief* subject to which, under these extraordinary circumstances, I call the attention of the assembled representatives. His majesty's responsible ministers will submit to you propositions relating to these points. His majesty trusts, that the representatives of the nation will adopt *speedy and appropriate* decisions upon all matters connected with the *safety and welfare* of the country. His majesty has learned, with deep feelings of regret and displeasure—although he, in his hearty paternal desire for the happiness of this country, following solely the impulse of his own desire, sanctioned during the last parliament, by giving to them his royal assent, those laws which were necessary to the progress of the country to prosperity—yet that, especially in Croatia and on the lower Danube, evil-minded rebellious agitators have excited the inhabitants of those countries, speaking different languages and holding different creeds, with false reports and terrorism to mutual hostility, and have driven them, under the calumnious representation that those laws were not then sanctioned by his majesty's own free will, to oppose the said laws and the legal authorities—that some have even gone so far in rebellion as to announce that their violent resistance to the said decrees is for the good of the royal house, and that his majesty is privy to their intentions. For the tranquillization of the inhabitants of those districts, of all tongues and creeds, I therefore hereby declare, *under the special commission* of his most gracious majesty, our lord the king, *in his name and as his representative,* that his majesty is firmly resolved to exert his royal power for the maintenance of the integrity and inviolability of his crown against all attacks from abroad, and against all discord within the realm, and to assert and enforce, at all times, the laws he shall have sanctioned. And as his majesty will allow no one to curtail the freedom, assured by the said laws, to the inhabitants of the kingdom, his majesty *expresses his displeasure* with the daring conduct of those, who venture to assert, that *any illegal act,* or *disobedience to the law,* can have taken place *with his majesty's knowledge,* or in the interest of his royal house."[6]

Such was the language of the fallen despot, when he had reason to suppose, that his own agent had turned a traitor to his cause. The National Assembly, not yet prepared to charge their monarch with such deep duplicity, took him at his word. An adequate recruitment was at once voted. A heavy appropriation was made to defray the civil and military expenses about to be incurred. As the royal commissioner, Hrabowszky, himself a Serb, had not been able to convince his countrymen of their mistake, there was no alternative but to put down war with war. It was hoped, however, that, after a few de-

[6] Klapka's War in Hungary, vol. ii. pp. 237–241.

feats, the misguided rebels would be more susceptible of being brought to terms. It was with the utmost reluctance that Hungary, so recently emancipated from a foreign tyranny, and so heartily and enthusiastically occupied with her popular reforms, could be compelled to shed the first drop of blood. She had hoped, that, by giving equal rights to all her inhabitants, she would infallibly satisfy them all. She had hoped, that, instead of the calamities of war, her people would now rise up and go forward in a united career of peace, prosperity and joy. She had hoped to see, in the place of armies, schools and churches springing up over all the land, and, instead of hostile vessels, fleets of commercial steam-ships ascending and descending all her streams. Instead of the tramp and neighing of the war-horse, she had hoped to behold the rail-road locomotive, harnessed to its train of carriages and guided by the hand of man, rushing around every hill and over every valley, rampant only with the lofty duties of its mission, and shouting the advent of a new and peaceful dispensation to the capitals of every province and to the people of every tribe. But she was lamentably deceived. The Sclavic excitement was growing every hour of her delay. Jellachich, the double agent of the Austrians and Sclaves, was perplexing the southern provinces more and more. At length, when a longer endurance would have been the worst of cruelty to all concerned, the soldiers of the nation were sent down toward the seat of the rebellion to quench its flames. They found a large district of country, occupied jointly, by Magyars and Serbs, suffering from cruelties scarcely paralleled in the annals of the world. The fields were entirely devastated. The homes of the people were leveled to the ground. A thousand fires, not yet extinguished, were sending their columns of smoke, from every plain, hill-side and valley, into the over-loaded air. The most awful and revolting spectacles, of barbarities executed upon the Magyar citizens, met them to whatever part they turned. The Serbs, exceeding all that is known of the worst of savages, had "bored out the eyes of men, cut off their flesh in strips, roasted them alive on spits, buried them up to their necks, and so left them to be eaten up by crows and swine!" But history need not blot itself with the record of such things. What is omitted is too horrible for the most indulgent page.[7]

The Hungarian soldiers, though fearfully excited by what they saw, were under instructions, emanating from the cabinet, of which Kossuth was now more than ever chief, to proceed with moderation in their treatment of the Serbs. The rebels were still regarded by the ministers, as well as by the National Assembly, as a misguided people, whom, it was hoped, a due mixture of clemency with the necessary punishment might yet restore to their former friendliness and faith. Numerous battles were fought, before the autumn had expired, in which the Servians were almost uniformly put to rout. Several of the ablest military leaders then in Hungary, among whom were Meszáros, Vetter, Kiss, Damjanics and Perczel, were employed against the insurgents. The victories of Szöreg, Verbasz, Törökecse, Ernestháza, Tomásovácz, Temerin, Perlasz, Foldvár, Kikinda, Turia and Tittel, should have taught a useful lesson to the Serbs. But they were not prepared to learn. Their prompter professed to know the designs of the Pansclavic party in all parts of Europe; and he was liberal of his promises of an ultimate and powerful support. Hurban, and the apostate Hungarian magnate, Count Moritz Pálffy, aided by such men as Hodsha and Stur, a priest and a schoolmaster, were in the north of Hungary, exciting the Sclavacks against their Magyar countrymen, and preaching the doctrines of the great Sclavic nationality. The Sclavacks, however,

[7] Pragay (in his Hungarian Struggle for Freedom, p. 11,) affirms, "on his conscience," that such scenes occurred; but he need not have made the *affirmation;* for the newspapers of that date (July and August, 1848) were full of worse barbarities than he has seen fit to mention in his work.

could not be seduced. "The Magyars," they said, "have done every thing that could be done, by voluntarily resigning their hereditary rights and power into the hands of all the people, without distinctions of sect or race, for the general good. No purposes whatever could induce them to abuse such unprecedented generosity; and, though Sclaves, they were particularly opposed to any Sclavic establishment, under the shadow of the Russian empire, at whose despotic nod such an establishment would have to cower and be a slave. No. The Magyars have laid the foundation of all the freedom that any tribe, or any religion, can maintain. Upon this foundation, as brothers and friends, let us together build, thankful to that noble race by whose magnanimity we have the opportunity to be free." Still, though this ill success was discouraging to the Sclavic party, and particularly to Jellachich and the deluded Serbs, the rebellion in the Banat spread both east and west, till the Wallachians of Transylvania and the inhabitants of Croatia and Sclavonia, at the instigation of the party of the Ban, rose in arms.[8]

By the beginning of September, 1848, the time for the double-minded Jellachich had fairly come. The question had been decided, whether, in the reconstruction of the empire, the Sclaves or the Germans were to be in the ascendant. A wonderful reaction, or series of reactions, in opposition to democracy, had everywhere taken place. Taking its origin in Italy, where the revolutions themselves began, it had spread like a crystalization from one country to another, till all Europe was governed by its influence. The flight of the pope had weakened the power of the patriots, by rousing that respect toward the head of the Church, which, with all its democratic enthusiasm, is found at last to have been laid, by habit and education, at the bottom of every Roman breast. In France, the cowardly insurrection of the Socialists, and the

[8] Memoirs of a Hungarian Lady, vol. i. pp. 145–147.

horrible butcheries of Paris, had taught the nation to fear, that the deeds of Robespierre and of Danton might soon be repeated, should the so-called republicanism of the times be allowed to have its way. In England, the masterly dispositions of the Duke of Wellington, for the defence of the kingdom, whatever occasion for military interposition might arise, had taken the color from the cheek of every Chartist, and given poor Ireland a warning which she was sure to heed. In Prussia, under the wing of Russian protection, the troops of the king had marched into Berlin playing the old airs of the monarchy, formed a circle around the forces of the insurgents, and coolly loaded their arms within thirty paces of their opponents, thus deciding the fate of the Prussian revolution by one bold and successful step. In Austria, the ministry of June, of which Bach was the leading spirit, by coining a few popular maxims, such as "the equality of the rights of all nationalities," and "the democratic empire on the largest basis," had not only recovered the ground lost by the good-natured despotism of the cabinet of Pillersdorf, but broken the unity of the Sclavic party, and captivated many of the revolutionary Germans. The quarrel in the Constituent Assembly, at Vienna, between the high and the low democrats, had greatly demoralized the republican movement. The high democrats, who were chiefly Sclaves from Bohemia, Gallicia and Moravia, denounced the idea of a senate in the projected republic, asserting, that such a body would only be a nest of aristocrats, but really apprehensive of falling in the scale of political influence, because they were conscious of having but few men capable of commanding a place in a house, where great talents and some respectability of rank would be held in consideration. The low democrats, who were almost entirely Germans, while they advocated the establishment of free institutions with great ardor, were more moderate in their ambition, and were willing to set up such a government as would offer some encouragement to intellectual and moral pre-eminence, and some chance of consolation to fallen greatness. The Sclaves, however, had finally been humbled. Windischgräts, by his memorable achievements in Bohemia, had revived the hope of the imperialists, that the old order of the government would ultimately be restored. In Lombardy, where the revolutionists had been triumphant for several months, under the banners of Charles Albert, the veteran Radetsky, by the splendid victory of Custozza, had laid down a solid and reliable foundation on which again to raise the dynasty of the Hapsburgs. That dynasty, from all these turns of fortune, had resumed so much courage, that, on the 7th of August, the timid and imbecile Ferdinand had ventured back to his imperial capital, and once more taken possession of his palace.

On the 4th of September the emperor dispatched a letter to the Ban, written by his own hand, in which he repudiated the edict of deposition. The letter was immediately printed in the Sclavic and German papers and published to the world. The Magyars would not credit what seemed plain enough to all other men. They would not believe that Ferdinand could be so glaringly double, as to command them to raise an army against Jellachich, and, at the same time, support Jellachich against themselves. They regarded this imperial letter as a forgery, got up by the Ban to gain him influence at home, and to weaken the opposition to him abroad. That they might be certain, however, of the mind of their royal master, they sent, on the 8th of September, a large and weighty delegation to him, desiring him to make to them such explanations as the contradictory character of his attitude required. The king was taciturn, evasive, and perplexed. The deputies were unsatisfied. They were, indeed, dissatisfied. Their report threw the new ministry into confusion. The cabinet seemed to have lost the confidence of their monarch. All but two of them resigned at once. Kossuth and Szemere, not daunted by this strange posture of affairs, resolved, at the request of the National Assembly, to remain in power. Kossuth was more popular than ever. Every thing was coming out exactly as he had all the while predicted. From the very beginning, he had told the nation, that the weak but wily Hapsburg would betray them when he could. His conservative colleagues, and the court-party in the kingdom, had disbelieved him. The radicals had believed, but their faith had made them only the more insane against all monarchy, and particularly against all connection with the king. Kossuth, standing upon his moderate and middle ground, declared his resolution of adhering to the sovereign in all his legal acts, and of abandoning him only when it should become absolutely impossible at the same time to acknowledge his allegiance and to serve his native land. He was at once commissioned by the National Assembly, in conjunction with Szemere, to exercise the power and transact the business of the nation.[9]

Jellachich could no longer be undecided. Ready, from the first, to espouse the cause of either party, so soon as he should be assured whether the Germans or the Sclaves would probably be victorious, he now saw, that the Sclavic movement was forever lost, and that, if he was to have any place in the government about to be restored, he must do something, and that speedily, worthy of his ambition. His measures were at once taken. Still holding the personal command, in spite of his deposition, of about forty thousand Serbs, Croats and Sclavonians, whom he continued to delude with his theory of a Sclavic empire, he had begun to make active preparations, about the last of August, for some sudden undertaking. No one knew exactly what feat he meditated. The eyes of all Austria were upon him. The Hungarians watched him with intense interest. The mystery was soon settled. On the 9th

[9] Klapka's War in Hungary, vol. i. Hist. Intr. pp. 66–68. Madam Pulsky (Mem. Hung. Lady, vol. i. pp. 130–140) gives a detailed account of the audience between the emperor and the deputation. She was an eye-witness.

of September, at the head of his own forces, and newly commissioned by his monarch, he crossed the Drave and planted his hostile foot upon that portion of Hungary, which, by universal consent, has ever been the peculiar territory of the Magyar nation. He was here reinforced by six divisions of Austrian regulars from the Styrian garrisons. The Rubicon was now passed. The banner of the Sclavonic and Croatian rebellion was at last raised. The rebel chief, finding the Hungarians unprepared, with fifteen thousand of his troops, marched from town to town, without meeting with opposition, burning, murdering and destroying, till he had approached within a few miles of Pesth. Another corps, under the Austrian general, Hartmann, according to instructions received from Vienna, proceeded by Jháros, Berény and Kaposvár, and joined the Ban at Engeny. A third corps, commanded by general Rott, another Austrian, remained as a reserve in Sclavonia, to maintain the rebellious attitude of the province, but were expected to follow the *gros* of the army, should their services be required.

To meet this insurrection, to defend their houses and their hearths, the Hungarians had only about five thousand men. The main body of their gallant little army were acting against the Serbs. No sooner, however, was it proclaimed through the country, that the traitor, Jellachich, had invaded the soil of Hungary, than the nation showed a readiness to rise. The Ban had asserted, that, on the day when a Sclavic army should unfurl its standard in the kingdom, three-fifths of the inhabitants would fly to it for protection against their domestic foe. Presumptuous and vain remark! Not a Sclave, beyond the direct influence of the invading force, deserted from his country's cause. The constitutional liberties of the nation, restored by Kossuth and his party to their pristine purity, and the establishment of universal suffrage and personal freedom, by which every inhabitant had become a citizen and a man, had given general satisfaction.

Whether with large or small forces, however, it was with great embarrassment that the Hungarians proceeded to defend their country against the Ban. Several of their own generals, of German origin or connection, proved traitors. Oettinger, the commander-in-chief against Jellachich, deserted and joined the rebel. Teleki, a Magyar in name but corrupted by German blood, had no sooner risen to the command, by Oettinger's defection, than he followed the example of his predecessor. The Palatine himself next took the field, but, at a moment when victory was certain, he abandoned the army and fled in all haste to Vienna. Three generals in succession, by the wickedest and worst of all villanies, showed the extent to which the reaction had now advanced in favor of the monarchy. They were alarmed by the declarations of the Ban, that, so soon as the soldiers of the empire should have re-established the power and tranquillity of the throne, every man, who had been found fighting against it, would receive his deserts; that, as every one knew, the Hapsburgs were not the men to make no distinctions between their enemies and their friends; and that the course, which he was himself pursuing, whatever the Magyars might pretend, had been dictated from the beginning by the crown, and would be ultimately acknowledged as the work of the imperial will. The three generals were convinced. General Moga, who succeeded to the command upon the flight of the Palatine, was also convinced. He saw that Jellachich was acting for the king. He saw that the king only waited his opportunity to avow, more openly than he dared then do, the services of the Croat chief. But this insight into the true state of the case only enraged his patriotic heart the more. A Wallachian by birth, but conquered by the recent magnanimity of the Magyar nation, he espoused the cause of the democratic country, with an ardor and with a power of will, which soon conferred a lasting honor upon his name. The duplicity of Ferdinand had stung him to the heart. Retreating from Weissenburg to Velemcze, a position of great strength, he awaited the approach of the invading host.

The Magyars now saw, that, to avoid an open rupture with the king and a bloody civil war, an explanation of the present contradiction, brought about by Ferdinand's double dealing, must be had. One deputation, however, sent expressly for this purpose, having been repulsed by the emperor, the Hungarians now sent an equally respectable delegation to the Constituent Assembly, which seemed to be assuming, more and more each day, the management of Austrian affairs. Here, also, they were disappointed. The German patriots received them gladly; but the Sclaves, as was natural, still dreaming of their Sclavic empire, in which there was to be no chance for any German, or Magyar, or Italian aristocracy, as they said, denied the Hungarians a hearing. Greatly outnumbering the Germans in the Assembly, their will was conclusive. The delegation returned to Pesth. They brought no sign, no hope, of a reconciliation. The National Assembly was again thrown into disorder. They clearly saw, that, if the king had commissioned Jellachich to invade the kingdom, and if the invasion should prove successful, those who might oppose his progress would be treated by Ferdinand as so many rebels to his authority. If, in this first struggle, they should themselves be victorious, the king would probably send other armies to invade and conquer them. It was a period of general doubt, hesitation and embarrassment. There was only one man in Hungary, whose mind seemed to have positive ideas, and to be clear in its sense of duty. That man was Kossuth. He was emphatically the man for the crisis. He told the Assembly, that, whether the letter to Jellachich was a forgery or not, one thing was certain. The manifesto of the 10th of June, and the royal address of the 8th of July, in both of which the kingdom was called upon to defend itself against the Ban, were genuine. He told the nation to go on and do what they had been twice commanded by the king to do; and if there should turn out to be any duplicity, or contradiction, in the conduct of that king, it would be a matter for him to clear up, in his own time, but was not then a subject for their consideration. The words of the minister cut the knot. Every one now saw through the difficulty. The resolution of the Assembly was at once taken. They voted to follow the orders of their sovereign and drive the invader from their territory.

No one, however, could expect, that, with a force not exceeding fifteen thousand men, most of whom had been rallied at the moment, general Moga could stand long in the path of the victorious Ban. The only hope was, that he might retard the march of the rebels, till a larger force could be mustered and the capital put in an attitude of defence. The ministry and the National Assembly, both of which were but the representatives of the mind of Kossuth, resumed their tranquillity; but the population of Pesth, and of the adjacent country, was alarmed. They expected to see their streets and their villages in flames, before the government would have time to draw the sword. They expected to behold the flag of the insurgents streaming from the towers of Buda, and the standard of rebellion planted on the field of Rakosz, before the people would have the opportunity to arm. Still, with all their apprehensions, they manifested no cowardice. Courage, on the contrary, was the mark of every countenance, the feeling of every breast. Every man resolved, against all this inequality, to keep his position, to defend his home, and rise or fall according to the will of God.

Jellachich, in the mean time, laughing at the weakness of the government and flushed with the most ambitious hopes, advanced through the country, confident of being able, in a few days, to silence all opposition by getting possession of the capital. His path, broad as it was, was marked by devastation and death. Though professing to be the friend of the nation, acting only for the restoration of that order of things, which had been overthrown by the demagogues of Pesth, he supported his adherents by robbery and pillage; and, when the inhabitants defended their possessions from the rapacity of the soldiers, he left nothing but the ashes of the houses, and the mangled carcases of their occupants, to define the limits and progress of his camp.

On the 29th of September the two armies met. Thousands of the citizens of Pesth, and of the people of the neighboring country, had flocked to the scene of action, some to witness the expected battle, others to fight, if necessary, in the patriotic ranks. They had begun to realize, that, by a sudden and decided stroke, Jellachich might determine the fate of the country. He might rush from Valemcze to Buda without a halt. If, however, the little band under Moga could keep him occupied, till his troops should become too weary to follow up their expected fortune without a rest, there might be sufficient time thus gained to put the avenues to the capital in defence. The whole future of the nation, therefore, was probably suspended on the chances of a day. Both parties saw the importance of success. Both understood the ruin of defeat. When the rebel general led his forces out, each man was told, that a little energy for an hour or two would open them a road to the metropolis, where every one of them should be gratified with the annihilation of his enemies, loaded with the booty of the public and private buildings, and satiated with the beauty of the fair inhabitants. As the patriots went out to meet them, each individual felt, that his house, his home, his kindred and his country perished or survived in him. The bosoms of the spectators beat with a faltering hope—a hope against hope—and from every heart went up a prayer. Deeds of bravery were done that hour. Deeds worthy of Spartan valor, of Attic eloquence, were done. The first onset, as was to have been expected, nearly decided the question between the combatants. This over, however, the handful of Magyars had earned a single chance of existence against a thousand of instantaneous destruction. But this one chance became the nucleus of success. Around it all hearts rallied. The roar of the cannon, the clatter of the smaller arms, the clash of hostile swords, the confusion and the noise of battle, waxed louder and louder, as the issue of it became more and more doubtful. The culminating period at last came. The uproar began to decrease. Every moment it became less and less. It seemed, also, to incline southward, as if the hereditary bravery of the Magyars were proving too much for the Sclavic host, and the insurgents were bending to the blast. When the firing was done, and the thick sulphur-cloud had risen up and rolled off from the field of blood, the hopes of the spectators were confirmed. The work of victory was complete. There stood the heroic band, in the midst of the field, with the banner of their country flying in the breeze. Heaps of the enemy surrounded them on every side. The invading army had retired from the scene of battle, leaving behind them a bloody proof, that the Magyar, when fully roused, whatever be the odds against him, is never to be beaten by the Sclave.

The fate of the rebellion was now sealed. Jellachich, asking and obtaining a cessation of hostilities, broke the conditions of the armistice, and fled toward the Austrian line. When the Magyar cavalry, which pursued him with all speed, obtained their first sight of him, he had crossed the Laytha, and taken up a position on the special territory of his ally in treachery, the king. His rear-guard, however, which he had left at Weissenburg to cover his intentions, was captured without a blow. His reserves, commanded by General Rott, who had entered the kingdom on the east, were met by Görgey and Perczel, to whom the rebels surrendered without a word. Thus, in about twenty days, this remarkable people, in a manner entirely characteristic of them, at a time when they were totally unprepared, annihilated a most formidable invasion, which had been gathering, and growing, and boasting of its easy work, for about half as many months. The invaders only learned, what their ancestors had been taught a hundred times, that, with the advantage of a full preparation and a choice of time, the treachery of three or four Sclaves is not enough for the ever-ready valor of one Arpadian Hun.

Jellachich, however, is now in Austria. He is now within reach of that monarch, who, on the 10th of June, declared him to be the enemy of his betrayed and indignant king. Now, if that king was sincere in what he said, is the time for vengeance. Now is the time to cut the insufferable rebel down. Now the reaction in behalf of the monarchy has become so complete, that the emperor can again safely act, openly and avowedly, according to his real will. Now he can not only carry out his edict of deposition against the Ban, but hang him, or shoot him, if he chooses, in an hour. If the Croat has actually been rebelling against the Hapsburg, judging from all the past, death will certainly be his fate. Perhaps, indeed, that royal courier, who, on the 3d of October, comes riding in gayety across the plain, alighting at the rebel's tent, is the messenger of the yet angry Ferdinand, whose imperial summons commands the presence of the culprit at the fatal bar. A package is actually handed to the traitor-chief. He opens it and reads: "We, Ferdinand I., Constitutional Emperor of Austria, King of Hungary, Croatia, Sclavonia, Dalmatia, the Fifth of this name, to the Barons, to the High Dignitaries of the Church and State, to the Magnates and Representatives of Hungary, its Dependencies, and the Grand Duchy of Transylvania, in parliament assembled, in our free and royal city of Pesth, Our greeting:—1. We dissolve the parliament by this our decree; so that, after the publication of these presents, the parliament has immediately to close its session. 2. We declare as illegal, void, and invalid, all the resolutions, and the measures of the parliament, which we have not sanctioned. 3. All troops, and armed bodies of every kind, whether national guards, or volunteers, which are stationed *in Hungary* and its dependencies, as well as in Transylvania, are placed, by this Our Decree, *under the chief command of* OUR *Ban of Croatia, Sclavonia and Dalmatia, Lieutenant Field-Marshal Baron Joseph Jellachich!* 4. Until peace and order shall be restored in the country, the kingdom of Hungary shall be subjected to *martial law;* in consequence of which, the respective authorities are meanwhile to abstain from holding congregations of the counties, as well as of the municipalities, and of the districts. 5. Our Ban of Croatia, Sclavonia and Dalmatia, Baron Joseph Jellachich, is hereby invested and impowered as Commissioner of our royal majesty; and we give him *full power and force,* that he may, in the sphere of *Executive Minister,* exercise the authority with which, as *Lieutenant of our royal majesty,* we have invested him in the present extraordinary circumstances! In consequence of these our sovereign letters patent, we declare that, *whatsoever the Ban of Croatia shall order, regulate, determine and command,* is to be considered as ordered, regulated, determined and commanded *by our royal authority!*"[10]

The Ban was by no means startled by what he read. Had he not expected this reception, had he not been certain of it, how would he have dared to come, with a broken army of only eighteen thousand men, and put himself within reach of the imperial hand? Every thing is plain, and perfectly consistent, when the Croat and the king are regarded as confederates in crime. On any other supposition, their motives are as unintelligible, as their deeds were black. Their crime is treason. History pronounces the verdict; and it is confirmed by the universal opinion of mankind. Each wears his mask as long as concealment is essential to success. When this point is passed, the very man, who, but a little time before, has been

[10] The whole document can be seen in nearly every late work on Hungary. It is very correctly translated and printed in Klapka, vol. ii. pp. 241–245.

discarded and denounced, is loaded with honors and approbation, though he has done nothing, which he had not been doing from the very first. By ceasing to act as a Sclave, and espousing openly the German cause, he has only convinced the hesitating monarch, that he has been all the while fulfilling his treasonable engagements to the crown. This being rendered clear, that crown reinstates him in all his former offices, and adds to them the absolute dictatorship of the country, which the king, against the arms of the rebel, has been professing to defend. The imperial veil is now removed. Ferdinand is himself, a Hapsburg, again. Hungary, invaded by one of her own subjects, and betrayed by that false despot, who has twice summoned her to this act of self-defence, at last opens her eyes and stands forth in astonishment before the world. Amidst this maze of double-dealing, she has, however, the single satisfaction, that, with the now unimportant exception of the Banat, she has vanquished all her enemies and driven them triumphantly from her soil!

CHAPTER XI.

THE AUSTRIAN INVASION.

THE appointment of Jellachich to the dictatorship of Hungary, after the disgraceful issue of an invasion, which the king had officially condemned as an act of treason to himself, was an open declaration of war against the Hungarians. Such, at home and abroad, by the enemies and the friends of Hungary, it was unanimously regarded; but the act was looked upon with various sentiments, as the spectators held toward it different relations.

The party of the reaction, including both Sclaves and Germans, considered it a most auspicious movement. The Hungarians, they knew, while as yet perfectly loyal in their principles and conduct, would be the most unyielding enemies to the leading doctrine of the imperialists, that, in the reorganization of the empire, all the nationalities should be melted into one, of which Austria was to be the head. Hungary, which equaled in size and importance all the remainder of the old empire, would not consent, they knew, to this annihilation, for the sake of a little dukedom about as large as one of her own counties. For eight hundred years, it was known, she had been ardently attached to those democratic institutions, by which she had ever been distinguished. For eight hundred years, she had contended against all attempts to overthrow her peculiar liberties. For three hundred years, in particular, she had raised her voice, and frequently her hand, against that very dynasty, which now hoped to effect its long-cherished purpose of breaking down the independence of her people, that Austria might be a perfect despot. For about twenty years, more particularly still, she had been magnanimously struggling within herself, liberalizing her form of government, emancipating her inhabitants, at the expense of the few breaking off the fetters of the many, and converting fifteen millions of masters and servants into a commonwealth of free and equal citizens. For the half of one year, in spite of two insurrections, she had been rejoicing over the blessings of universal liberty. Before the work of annihilation could be effected, such a nation, of course, was to be humbled, or blotted from existence. Despotic Austria had become weary of democratic Hungary. Now was the favorable moment, for the execution of this Austrian measure; and every imperialist was glad of the opportunity of employing such a facile and yet powerful instrument as the Ban, in the accomplishment of the never-forgotten undertaking.

During the summer, while Hungary was acting against the insurrection of the Banat, the Sclavic portion of the Austrian democratic party could not help sympathising, to some extent, with their brethren by blood, the Serbs. It was through their influence, it will be remembered, that the second delegation from Pesth, after the rebellion of the Croats had broken out, were denied an audience before the Constituent Assembly. The events of a few days, however, satisfied them of the true character of the Ban. They saw, almost as soon as he had pitched his tents in the neighborhood of Vienna, that he was playing a double game. They saw that he could not be depended on by them. By the 4th of October they were ready to unite with any party in putting the traitor, as they then loudly called him, down. When they beheld him in his new appointment, as Dictator of Hungary, actively and openly espousing the old imperial cause, their resentment exceeded all bounds. They would have crushed him, had they known how to do it, with a hearty will. From this cause they became the friends of insulted Hungary, against which, as they were now bold to say, the king had declared an unprovoked, a groundless, and an unnatural war.

The German portion of this party, who had allowed their ardor to cool a little, while the Servian and Magyar movement was going on, now returned to their former state of earnestness toward the Hungarian democrats. They had never allowed themselves to be forgetful of their instructors and predecessors in the democratic cause. Much less had they shown any hostility to it. They had only ceased to think of it as much as formerly, occupied, as they were, with their affairs at home. Whenever appealed to by the Hungarians, however, the German patriots had ever been true to their plighted faith; and now, when they saw the reaction rolling up against the patriotic cause like another deluge, and the king resolved to turn the billows over Hungary, as the source and centre of the democratic spirit, the Germans rose at once, and again offered their heart and hand to the hated and oppressed.

In Austria, therefore, and particularly at Vienna, the Hungarians had many supporters. In nearly all other parts of Europe, the majority of the people were their friends. Every where, the policy of the Hapsburgs was well known. Everywhere, the long struggle of the Magyars, the champions of constitutional liberty, against imperial despotism, was the theme of conversation. Everywhere, curses were pronounced against that monarch, who could profess one thing and do another, like the meanest villain of his realms. From every quarter, benedictions upon the heads of the Hungarian patriots, and prayers for their success, were wafted on every breeze to the Magyar land. The friends of freedom, throughout the civilized world, charged the emperor, not only with having been double in his conduct, but with having needlessly insulted the nation the second time, by making the avowed enemy of Hungary its absolute Dictator, clothed with the most unlimited authority over the laws and liberties of the kingdom, and over the persons and properties of that very people, to whom he was legally responsible for a most glaring crime. The man, who, by the statutes of every land, was a malefactor and a murderer, as well as a traitor to his country, was made the irresponsible arbitrator of life and death over those, whose right it was to arraign him as a culprit at their bar. Their state criminal, indeed, who had committed the highest offence known in law, was made the chief magistrate, the maker and executor of all law, to that very nation against which he had done the deed. As king of Hungary, Ferdinand had twice called upon the Hungarians to march out against the rebel, and crush him, if possible, before he could fairly plant himself on Hungarian soil. As emperor of Austria, that same Ferdinand, with the duplicity of a despot, had espoused the interests of that rebel, and, using him as an instrument, declared war against the same Hungarians for doing what he had commanded and exhorted them to do![1]

Such a course sometimes meets with a merited reward. No sooner had Jellachich pitched his wretched camp at Schwendorf, than the Academic Legion, and the democratic portion of the National Guards, asked permission to go out and fight him. The Sclaves in the Constitutional Assembly defeated the proposition, but sent a delegate to the rebel's camp to test his spirit, and to endeavor to buy him back again to the Sclavic party. The measure was unsuccessful. While this negotiation was going forward, Windischgräts was hurrying his troops down from Prague, where he had been perfectly triumphant against the Pansclavic movement, to unite with Jellachich in forming the contemplated blockade of the imperial capital. General Auersperg, who commanded the garrison of Vienna, like nearly all the high officers of the regular army, was a rank imperialist, and watched his opportunity to raise the standard of the reaction. So long as he remained within the city, the people considered him as at least neutral, because he was evidently at their mercy. At five o'clock, on

[1] Pulsky's Mem. Hung. Lady, vol. i. pp. 175–184, and Klapka's War in Hungary, vol. i. pp. 64–65.

the 5th of October, an order was issued, that, on the next morning, the garrison should leave their former quarters, and recede to a position beyond the limits of the city. No one could misunderstand the object of this movement. It was the first overt act of the reaction within the capital. The troops were to go out, of course, in order to join the forces of Windischgräts and Jellachich. Words would fail to picture the popular excitement of that evening. The Constituent Assembly, foreseeing a war and fearing its expenses, was thrown into a position of open hostility to the government. It denounced the measure without mercy. On that very day, the celebrated Dr. Tausenau, the orator of the people, had pronounced a splendid and powerful oration in the Odeon, to ten thousand of the citizens, against the rebel, Jellachich. His words were still burning in the hearts of his auditors. No sooner was the military order made generally current, than all Vienna was broken up into knots, which earnestly and angrily discussed the common topic. The night passed away, however, without tumult. At an early hour on the following morning, a part of the garrison issued from their barracks, and proceeded across the city toward the depôt of the rail-road, on which they were to be carried near the camp of the treacherous Croat. They complied with the command to march with manifest unwillingness. "The Hungarians," said they, "are our brothers, not our foes." They were accompanied by a numerous escort of National Guards, armed and unarmed, whose feelings were still more patriotic. The populace rushed from all quarters to the embankment of the railway. Determined that the troops should not leave the town, they broke down an arch of one of the bridges of the road. A student of the university, and a member of the Academic Legion, arose above the heads of the vast crowd, and made an effective speech, appealing to General Bredi, the immediate commander of the soldiers. He implored the general to signify to Count Latour, then the Austrian Minister of War, that the garrison was not willing to march out against the Hungarians, or to the support of the Croat Ban. The appeal appeared to be successful. The commander promised to notify the minister of the unwelcome fact. While gone to execute this new and singular commission, given him by a young man, whose name was scarcely known, but who had spoken the sentiments of the people, the throng increased; and, on returning with a fresh order to advance in spite of all opposition, he found the masses of citizens so dense, that he could not leave his position, unless the populace should willingly disperse, without cutting a passage by the sword. The populace would not disperse. They crowded before the troops and bound them fast. The general commanded the citizens to retire. They told him to beware of the length to which he pushed the mandates of a fallen power. The warning was proudly scorned. The officer informed his opponents, that he was only executing the order of his sovereign, which had been twice sanctioned by the imperial ministry. The citizens replied, that, whatever might be the authority under which the step was covered, it was looked upon as an open avowal of the Croatian insurrection, an actual declaration of war against Hungary, and an audacious defiance of the popular cause throughout the empire. They declared, that, in spite of all orders so glaringly revolutionary and illegal, not a soldier should leave the city. The issue was now perfect. The Austrian commander, blind to the consequences of his conduct, and determined to obey the emperor by going out to the support of Jellachich, pronounced the fatal word to fire. One or two companies, raised among the peasantry of Gallicia, discharged their pieces. Several of the National Guards, with some well-known citizens, fell. The shot was returned. General Bredi tumbled from his horse. The crowd rushed upon the troops and overwhelmed them. The bruit of the battle spread on every side. The whole city was shortly in a state of general convulsion. The great alarm-bell was rung. Barricades rose, as by magic, in every quarter.

The whole garrison proceeded to the streets. The people, armed in haste, flew to the improvisated breastworks. The carnage on both sides was dreadful. Before the sun went down, however, the cause of the citizens was triumphant. Count Latour had been captured in the War Office, on the Hof, where he was hung as an accomplice of the treacherous Ferdinand; Ferdinand himself, not daring to trust the second time to his subterranean strong-hold, had fled to Olmütz; the soldiers, overpowered at every point, had surrendered to their antagonists; the Constituent Assembly, flying into session on the first rumor of the outbreak, and feeling its responsibility after the departure of the monarch, had declared itself *en permanence*, as the only legal government; and the banners of freedom, of popular liberty, had been again unfurled from every height, tower, and steeple.[a]

Now was the time to seal the fate of the Austrian reaction. Hungary was in the undisputed possession of its own people. Vienna was in the hands of its patriotic citizens. The Constituent Assembly, legally created and now vested with supreme authority, had committed itself fully on the side of the revolution. The garrison of the city had been subdued and driven to their quarters. The forces of Jellachich had been reduced and humbled; and Windischgräts himself, though at the head of a brave and victorious army, could have been cut to pieces, as he was concentrating his scattered regiments upon the capital. At this moment, the Constituent Assembly should have taken the most efficient measures. It should have organized an army for the occasion. It should have called in the militia, who, in all parts of the country, were ready to march at a moment's warning. It should have summoned the help of Upper Austria, where the patriotic cause had long been triumphant. If in any doubt of its success, with all these

[a] Pulsky's Mem. Hung. Lady, pp. 175–191, and Klapka's War in Hungary, vol. i. pp. 71–73. The arsenal was not taken till after dark.

arrangements, it should have sent an invitation to General Moga, who still commanded the Magyar forces, and who had pursued the Ban to the line of Hungary. The Hungarians, too cautious of maintaining a perfectly legal course, even after all law had been annihilated by the despotic measures of the emperor, would not cross the frontier without an express invitation. They knew, of course, that Ferdinand had declared war upon them; but they did not wish to take any step, which could be construed into hostility to the king, until all men should see, that they were not the authors of the civil war then evidently impending. All men have seen what they wished to demonstrate; they have seen, that, at every step, Hungary acted entirely in self-defence against the aggressions of a despot; but they have been led, while admiring the forbearance of the nation, to condemn the policy of its scruples. By one bold and energetic movement, perfectly justified by the recent proceedings of the monarch, the Hungarians might have saved to their land, and to the world, many a brave and noble-hearted citizen, a vast amount of treasure, and perhaps the liberties they had just established. On their march from Valemcze to Pressburg, they should have collected thirty or forty thousand volunteers; they should have rushed upon the Croat and stopped his further progress; they should have pushed forward to Vienna, intercepted the approaches of Windischgräts, counteracted the designs of Auersperg, formed an alliance with the people, held the king as a prisoner in his palace, and thus, without the shedding of much blood, consummated the most auspicious and glorious of modern revolutions.

Such, however, was not the order of events. Kossuth, it is said, privately suggested these successive steps; but, having previously planted himself on the letter of the law, he could not consistently force the country, had he been ever so clear in his convictions, from the basis established by himself. He saw, too, that the National Assembly, in which the conservatives had still some power, would resist the new policy, till its eyes should be a little more opened by the developments, which, he clearly perceived, would soon be made. Keeping his own eyes, therefore, fixed on Vienna, he contented himself with privately urging upon the members a summary course, hoping, in this way, to gain his purpose before the great opportunity for it should pass away. All he could obtain, however, was the passage of a bill authorizing General Moga to demand of Auersperg to disarm the retreating Jellachich, and, only in case of a refusal, to cross the frontier of Hungary in pursuit of the fugitive. A fatal delay was thus occasioned; the Ban reached the neighborhood of Vienna without meeting with opposition; the forces of Windischgräts and Jellachich were united; and the insurrection of the capital, though it temporarily confined the movements of the intra-mural soldiers, did not long prevent them from evacuating the city and joining the troops of the imperial party.

There never was a more singular revolution. Though in open hostility to each other, the soldiers and citizens, when not fighting, met and exchanged civilities with their usual freedom. No attempt was made, on either side, to derange the ordinary course of business. Shops were still open as in the most quiet seasons. Stages were still running without molestation. The telegraph was left undisturbed in its operations. Trains of cars were yet constantly going and returning. Citizens, taking with them what they wished, proceeded to the country at their pleasure. Countrymen, bringing what they chose, were admitted into the city without a question. A revolution had been completed; but there was no hand, no power, to control, to guide, to use it. The people submitted their condition to the Constituent Assembly; and the Constituent Assembly, which the Sclavic members had abandoned, were waiting to be directed, or pushed forward, by the spirit and impulses of the people. The Assembly finally resigned the defence of the city, and of the revolution, to the Common

Council. The Common Council, not accustomed to such bloody business, looked to the National Guards, not only for protection, but for the initiation of all necessary measures. The National Guards could not depend upon their commanders. They changed them three times in five days. General Messenhauser, the last one appointed, though true to the popular cause, was a man of no military genius. He satisfied his ambition, or appeased his conscience, with useless proclamations to the citizens. The citizens, full of animation and as brave as Spartans, wasted their time and their ammunition in firing long shots from the *glacis*, which separates the inner from the outer town, upon the distant camps of their antagonists. The Austrians and the Hungarians, having exactly the same ends in view, were both paralyzed by the same, and a very needless, scruple. They were both vainly endeavoring to carry on a revolution in a perfectly legal manner, until one or the other party should set the example of illegality, by taking some step not authorized by law and custom. The Viennese were waiting for the Hungarians to get impatient and cross the frontier of Hungary. The Hungarians, on their part, were waiting for the Viennese to become weary of this tardiness, and to send a request for their presence at the capital.

While the revolution was in this condition, the Hungarians sent Francis Pulsky as a messenger to Vienna, to make an inquiry into the true state of things, and particularly to learn the wishes of the patriots. He arrived at the capital on the 13th of October. He first went to the Permanent Committee of the Assembly, which was then holding its sessions in the imperial palace. The Committee sent him to the Council. The Council sent him to the Guards. The Guards, partly in the hands of imperialists, and liable to be betrayed at any moment, would scarcely make an answer to his interrogations, and gave him no satisfaction. He returned in disappointment to the camp of the Hungarians.[3]

[3] Pulsky's Mem. Hung. Lady, vol. i. pp. 197–200.

At this crisis the world-renowned Bem reached Vienna on his way to Hungary. He was a Pole of noble blood, of a commanding and pleasing appearance, and with the marks of benevolence and genius on every feature. A patriot from his birth, and a soldier by trade, he had fought many a battle for his country, in her last struggle for existence, against the autocrat of the north. During the whole summer, he had been performing deeds of heroism, in a private way, for the cause of European liberty, without even the expectation of personal reward. He now came to offer his services to that nation, which, as he thought, was doing most for human freedom, and which needed his devotion most. No sooner, however, was it known to the citizens of Vienna, that the well-known Bem was among them, than they thronged the apartments of the chieftain, importuning him to take upon himself the command of the city and the defence of the revolution. Bem told the Austrians that his heart was in Hungary. "There," said he, "is a people, whose magnanimity, whose love of liberty, whose hatred to despotism, are unknown in Europe." "That," replied the Viennese, "is very true, but the Magyars have Kossuth, whose sagacity, and bravery, and talents are enough for any one nation. Bem must be our Kossuth." The appeal succeeded. The Pole agreed to the proposition; and, in this way, for the first time, there was formed a perfect understanding, a unity of design if not of action, between the patriots of the two countries.

By this time, however, it had become nearly impossible for the two to hold any intercourse with each other. Auersperg had taken up his position in the park of Schwartzenberg, near the camp of Jellachich. Jellachich had collected all his Croats and fortified himself near the south-western angle of the city. Windischgräts had brought down all his forces from Bohemia, and detailed numerous bodies from Gallicia, Moravia, and other distant provinces. He had been appointed commander-in-chief of all the imperial forces acting for the emperor on the soil of Austria. He had completely surrounded the capital with his soldiers. He had issued a manifesto, declaring himself civil and military dictator of the whole monarchy, excepting Italy, where the veteran Radetsky was still in office. He had summoned all the staff officers of the Hungarian army to make their appearance at his head-quarters, and answer for their late conduct. All things were now ripe, on the part of the imperialists, for action.

The Hungarians were also getting ready. With a force of twelve thousand men, and thirty cannon, Kossuth had left Pesth, against all the opposition of his undecided and hesitating colleagues, to join the Hungarian camp at Pressburg. He had waited, and reasoned with his friends, till he could wait no longer. He was received by his countrymen with unparalleled enthusiasm. His first step was to review the army. His second was to send a letter to Bem, apprising him fully of the disposition of the Hungarian army, and laying down a plan of attacking the imperialists before Vienna. He also invited the Pole to visit the Magyar camp, and confer with himself on the present emergency, and on the probabilities of the future. The letter was not received. Getting into the hands of Messenhauser, who, since being superseded by Bem, had begun to seek the means of reconciliation with the monarch, it was suppressed by the treacherous German. The failure of that epistle was the second failure of the revolution. Had it safely reached the hands of Bem, the two great men would have met and planned a movement, which, there can be no doubt, would have been successful. The imperialists could have been enclosed between two armies, one of which was safe within a line of fortifications, which have seldom submitted to the utmost power and bravery of an enemy. The other, approaching from behind, could have advanced and retired at pleasure, cut off the sale of food to their opponents, and, watching their opportunity, rushed down upon them with their characteristic impetuosity at the most favorable moments.

Union would have been victory; but Vienna had committed too much of her wavering destiny to a traitor. Several days were given up, by the Hungarians, to the expectation of seeing Bem. No Bem appeared. Little did the Magyars know what bloody business was occupying the hands of the energetic Pole. On the 27th of October, while Kossuth was addressing a council of the superior officers, the thunder of the imperial cannon was wafted by a western breeze to the camp of the Magyars. He had been urging upon his friends the necessity of marching directly to Vienna, if they wished to save it. Pausing in the midst of his noble speech, to make himself certain of the sounds he heard, then assuming an attitude peculiarly appropriate, and throwing out his finger toward the capital, he exclaimed: "Magyars, I have said enough. I have told you the truth. Listen, if you wish to hear the echo of my arguments!"

Such language could not fail to take effect. It now fell upon the ears of men prepared to appreciate its meaning. At the review on the 24th, just mentioned, the faint-hearted of the army, who had been the chief obstacle to decisive measures, had been wisely, as well as humanely, permitted to retire from the scene of conflict. On that day, Kossuth had made one of his most memorable efforts. His position, his responsibility, his hope of the great future, the events of the passing moment, filled him with an unusual inspiration. He stirred the blood of every true-hearted Magyar. Since the speeches of the Roman orator against Cataline, the world had heard nothing like the address, to which the poorest son of Hungary was then allowed to listen. The privilege of hearing such a man, on such an occasion—a man not soon to be paralleled—an occasion never to be repeated—would repay the meanest soldier, one would think, for many a future trouble. The soldiers seemed to appreciate their privilege. They had never dreamed of such power of utterance. They shouted. They wept. They gnashed their teeth. They lifted up their clenched fists. They thundered from every quarter—"Lead us against the traitors—let us grind them to powder—the Magyar will defend the liberty and independence of his nation!" At the conclusion of his appeal, Kossuth stretched out his hand toward the great highway of Hungary, exclaiming with prodigious emphasis—"Magyars, there is the road to your peaceful homes and firesides." Then turning to trace it, as it crossed the plains towards Vienna, he added with still greater passion—"Yonder is the path to death; but it is the path of duty. Which will you take? Every man shall choose for himself. We want none but willing soldiers!" The scholar may talk of Demosthenes and his philippics. Greece never heard such a shout as now uprose from the full hearts of thirty thousand Magyars. "Death or liberty!" was the only answer. A few foreigners, about a hundred in all, with half a dozen Hungarians, threw up their arms and their commissions. The mass of the army stood fixed, breathing the same breath, burning with the same resolution.[4]

It cannot be denied, however, that there was still in the Hungarian camp quite a formidable opposition to aggressive measures. It came not from the ranks. It came not from the inferior officers. All these begged and intreated to be led to battle. It came from three men, whose position was pre-eminent, and whose motives are to this day inscrutable. Those men were general Moga, the commander-in-chief, colonel Kolmann, the chief of the staff, and Pázmándy, the president of the lower house of the National Assembly. The influence of Kossuth, nevertheless, was superior to their opposition. His words, when he spoke decidedly, were still laws to every true-hearted Hungarian. "Though Hungary," said he, in his concluding remarks to this military council, "stood in no connection with Vienna, yet it is the duty of honor to hasten to

[4] Mem. Hung. Lady, vol. ii. p. 26, and Klapka's War of Hungary vol. i. Int. p. 75.

the aid of the Viennese, as they have risen solely in opposition to the late despotic measures against the Magyar nation. If we win a battle, it will not only decide the fate of the Austrian monarchy, but of all Germany. If we lose one, it will not discourage the nation, but will spur it to still greater sacrifices. But to be passive, at the very threshold of the scene of action, would lower the Hungarians with foreign countries, and would cool the ardor of Hungary itself." Such was the logic of the statesman; and it was decisive, his opponents themselves making no farther resistance.

The golden moment, however, had been lost. Kossuth had conquered, for the last time, the opinion of his antagonists; but the victory, with all the honor it conferred on him, was too late for his country's highest good. On the 27th of October, the day of these deliberations, the details of the march were settled. On the 28th, the army crossed the frontier, and advanced slowly toward Vienna. On the 29th, they still proceeded carefully, making friends of all the people through whose neighborhoods they passed. At night they took up their position on a height opposite to Manneswörth and Schwechat, within sight of the steeples of the capital, and within sight of the camp-fires of the imperialists. The night was spent in preparation for the day of battle. On the morning, a heavy mist covered both armies, and hid all the surrounding country. Between seven and eight o'clock, the vapor rose up, and left the whole land, to the very suburbs of the city, an open spectacle. "Now," said the Hungarians to themselves,—"now, our friends in Vienna can see to commence their attack on our common enemies. Now, according to Kossuth's letter to Bem, they will soon open their long fires from the suburbs, and keep the Austrians well occupied in front, while we are rushing down upon them in the rear. Perhaps, however, they are waiting for us to turn the faces of our foes eastward, that our allies may have the advantage of the rear attack." But no guns were fired from Vienna. None were fired by the

Hungarians. It was soon evident, as the Hungarians thought, that Kossuth's letter had miscarried. The patriots of the capital, however, would be sure to co-operate, in an effective manner, it was still believed, so soon as they should see the Hungarians and Austrians in actual conflict. At eight o'clock the first cannon-shot sounded from the army of the imperialists. It was greeted with a thundering acclamation on the side of the impatient Magyars. A cannonading of two hours followed. At ten o'clock, Major Guyon made a furious charge from the left upon Manneswörth, and took it. The right wing next pushed forwards against the Croats, who were still commanded by the rebel, Jellachich, and defeated them with great slaughter. Now was the moment for the patriots of the capital to make their sortie. But no sortie was made. All was still upon the ramparts and around the gates. Not a gun was discharged. Not a flag was seen. There began to be a strange mystery in all this silence. Still there was hope. The Hungarians pushed onward. They prepared to storm Schwechat. Suddenly, as if by ambuscade, regiment after regiment of the imperial army began to pour down upon the left of the Hungarians. The right, perfectly victorious, dared not advance, for fear of breaking up the line of battle. Next, other regiments, seemingly without number, rushed from their positions against the right and centre of the Hungarians. Their camp was left completely exposed to the patriots of the city. But no patriots appeared. Vienna remained as silent as a graveyard. The mystery had become terribly perplexing. Kossuth, who rode continually by Moga's side, exposing his person to all the chances of the engagement, still animated the heart of the commander, still pushed on the Magyars to battle, still hoped that the expected aid would come in time to save the fortunes of the day and crush the enemies of human freedom. At four o'clock, Moga wished to order a retreat, but Kossuth peremptorily forbade him. At that moment, however, as chance would have it, a battalion of peasants from the county of Komorn, armed with scythes only, who had stood passively exposed to the fire of the enemy for several hours, were thrown into confusion by the sudden explosion of several shells. They turned and fled. The right wing was thus irretrievably disordered. The retreat was sounded with the consent of Kossuth. It was completely covered by the bravery of the left wing, which doubled round upon the retreating right, and, with the help of a small reserve, stood between the fugitives and their foes. At night, while encamped at a place of safety, it was discovered, that thirty thousand Hungarians had fought eight hours against seventy thousand Austrians; that two hundred of the Magyars had made their beds, on the field of battle, with about five hundred of their antagonists; and, as a sufficient solution of the great mystery of the day, that, when the first shot was fired in the morning, the patriotic capital had fallen, and was then actually occupied by a detachment of the imperial forces![5]

The victors did not pursue the fugitives. There was a work to be done in Austria, before the affairs of Hungary could receive farther notice from the conquerors. Vienna must be purged of its patriotism. The rifle of the court-martial must decimate the party of German democrats. Each class of men, who had contributed any members to that party, had to suffer, as if in a symbolical manner, in one of its most illustrious representatives; and the death of these representatives was to be solemnized by the immolation of vast numbers of their respective associates and supporters. It would seem that Windischgräts, who hated democracy with a peculiar hatred, wished to condemn and madden every order of its adherents, by selecting his victims from each with a degree of system.

[5] Pulsky's Mem. Hung. Lady, vol. ii. pp. 23–34. Francis Pulsky, husband of the authoress, is the best extant authority for this engagement. He was an eye-witness. He was aid to Moga on the battle-field. With his account, however, I have compared several others. There is a general agreement.

First of all, the eloquent Blum, one of the most benevolent and harmless of men, was obliged to represent the Frankfort Assembly, of which he was a member, by presenting his noble and intellectual forehead as a mark to the unerring riflemen. Baron Stenau represented, in the hour of death, as he had in life, the republican section of the nobility. The democratic press was put under the ban by the execution of the peace-loving but patriotic Becher. The Jews were punished by the death of the youthful, learned and enthusiastic philosopher, Jellinek, whose greatest crime was, that he advocated the mystical doctrines of his master, Hegel, whose works had long been legally established as text-books in many of the leading German universities. The Poles were branded by the murder of Jelovizki, the aid-de-camp of Bem, who, wounded and disguised, had effected his escape and joined the Hungarian army. Several Hungarians, day-laborers, who had had no connection with the revolution, paid the bloody tribute for their country. The National Guards received a double portion of this foul resentment. In the first place, quite a number of superior and inferior officers were shot. These, however, were not thought to be sufficient. Messenhauser, whose patriotism, however sincere, had been of real disadvantage to his party, and whose course of action had been extremely gentle, had, nevertheless, gone too far, it was believed by Windischgräts, to admit of favor. He was tried and sentenced. According to law and custom, however, in the case of a commanding general, three days were given him to prepare for death. A petition, largely signed by the most noted imperialists of the city, was sent to Olmütz imploring mercy for the ill-fated officer of the people. The blood-thirsty conqueror was not to be thus eluded. Messenhauser was executed on the second day after his conviction, contrary to the remonstrance of the imperial Judge-Advocate, who pronounced the act illegal; and, just in time to see the pale corpse before its burial, the messengers returned from Olmütz with the general's pardon!

While such brutalities were being perpetrated at Vienna, the Hungarians had retreated to Pressburg, where they were making vigorous preparations to defend the nation. Moga, having received a fall from his horse, resigned his command; and Kossuth, as a reward for bravery and talents displayed in the engagement of Schwechat, instantly raised Görgey, before unknown to fame, to the post thus rendered vacant. The new commander commenced his responsible career with great spirit. His sagacity in the selection of agents, his skill in giving form and solidity to a mass of unpractised soldiers, were soon apparent. Under his hand, the unmilitary volunteer, who had never seen a battle, was at once transformed into the likeness, and marked by the characteristics, of a veteran. The looseness of Moga's discipline was immediately superseded by the most rigid and systematic order. In less than fourteen days from the elevation of the young general, the upper army of defence, as this corps was styled, instead of the waywardness and weakness of a horde of raw recruits, had become an army worthy of the work to which they were soon to be devoted.

In the commencement of the Hungarian revolution, so far back as 1832, the party of the patriots had been composed chiefly of Protestants. The other denominations, and particularly the Catholics, were generally in the opposition. The revolution itself, however, when its character had become fully known, when the nature of the new laws had been made apparent, when the people had had the privilege of tasting for themselves the blessings sought after by the establishment of universal equality and liberty, had conquered nearly all opposition. The whole nation, as has been seen, had rejoiced together. When the Serbs revolted, when the Croats rebelled, the Catholics of Hungary and Transylvania maintained their fealty to the revived and improved constitution. Kossuth, though a consistent Protestant himself, had gained the confidence of an entire denomination, which, in almost every other country, and in all ages, has leaned to the support of despotism and oppression. At the juncture now under consideration, the bishops of that denomination, still adhering to their recent love of freedom, after a long and profound deliberation, addressed a remonstrance to their emperor, forcibly presenting the cruelty and duplicity of his late movements, the duty of the Hungarians to resist him, and the dreadful impolicy and wickedness of a civil war, certainly to be raised by a continuance of his unhappy measures: "Hungary is actually," said the bishops, "in the saddest and most deplorable situation. In the south, an entire race, *although enjoying all the civil and political rights recognised in Hungary*, has been in open insurrection for several months, excited and led astray by a party, that seems to have adopted the frightful mission of exterminating the Magyar and German races, which have constantly been the strongest and surest support of the throne of your majesty. Several thriving towns and villages have become a prey to flames, and have been totally destroyed; thousands of Magyar and German subjects are wandering about without food or shelter, or have fallen victims to indescribable cruelties; for it is revolting to repeat the frightful atrocities by which the popular rage, let loose by diabolical excitement, ventures to display itself." Their charge of duplicity, however caustic, is expressed in the language of doubt, though the doubt is burningly ironical: "Yes, Sire, it is under *your* government, and in the name of *your* majesty, that our flourishing towns are bombarded, sacked, and destroyed. In the name of your majesty, they butcher the Magyars and Germans. Yes, Sire, all this is done; and they incessantly repeat it, in the name and by the order of your majesty, who, nevertheless, have proved, *in a manner so authentic and so recent*, your benevolent and paternal intentions towards Hungary—in the name of your majesty, who, in the last Diet of Pressburg, yielding to the wishes of the Hungarian nation, and to the exigencies of the time, consented to sanction and confirm, *by your royal word and oath*, the foundation of a new constitution, established on the still broader foundation of a perfectly independent government!" The resistance of the nation to these acts of despotism and double-mindedness is defended in the plainest but most respectful language: "Already, Sire, have these new laws and liberties, giving the surest guarantees for the freedom of the people, struck root so deeply in the hearts of the nation, that public opinion makes it our duty to represent to your majesty, that the Hungarian people could not but lose that devotion and veneration, consecrated and proved on so many occasions up to the present time, if it were attempted to make them believe, that the violation of the laws, and of the government sanctioned and established by your majesty, is committed *with the consent* of the king!" The fearful results of this civil conflict, brought on by royal treachery, are boldly stated: "But let your majesty also deign to reflect upon the terrible consequences of these civil wars, not only as regards their influence on the moral and substantial interests of the people, but also as regards the security and stability of the monarchy. Let a barrier be speedily raised against those passions excited and let loose, with infernal art, amongst populations hitherto so peaceable! How is it possible to make people, who have been inspired with the most frightful thirst—the thirst of blood—return within the limits of order, justice, and moderation? Who will restore to the regal majesty the original purity of its brilliancy, of its splendor, after having dragged that majesty in the mire of the most evil passions? *Who will restore faith and confidence in the royal word and oath?* Who will render an account to the tribunal of the living God, of the thousands of individuals, who have fallen, and fall every day, *innocent* victims to the fury of civil war!" After this explicit declaration, that the Magyars were "innocent" of the trouble brought upon their country, the patriotic bishops conclude their address by an appeal, that must have gone like naked steel to the conscience of the monarch: "Sire! our duty as faithful subjects, the good of the country, and the honor of our religion, have inspired us to make these humble but sincere remonstrances, and have bid us raise our voices! So, let us hope, that your majesty will not only receive our sentiments, but that, mindful of the *solemn oath* that you took on the day of your coronation, *in the face of Heaven,* not only to *defend* the liberties of the people, but to *extend* them—that, mindful of this oath, to which you appeal so often and so solemnly, you will remove from your royal person the terrible responsibility, which these *impious and bloody wars* heap upon the *throne*—and that you will tear off the tissue of *vile falsehoods,* with which pernicious advisers beset you, by hastening with prompt and strong resolution to recall peace and order to our country, which was always the firmest prop to your throne, in order that, in the midst of profound peace, she may raise a monument of eternal gratitude to the justice and paternal benevolence of her king!"[a]

The address was delivered to the king by the lips of Fogarassy, one of its signers, in the royal retreat at Olmütz. The bishop was treated with contempt. The emperor, though a fugitive, felt certain of the ultimate success of the reaction. The document was read to him on the 30th of October, the day of the defeat at Schwechat, when the fall of Vienna, added to all the other disasters of the democratic party, had made it safe for him to be again a despot. This, of course, was his natural character. He acted like himself, and like his ancestors, in abusing the patriotic bishop. The abuse, however, was useful to the oppressed and insulted country. When the episcopal messenger returned to Pesth, the news of his reception at court had preceded him. The clergy of his communion were enraged. The bishops again assembled, and, no longer hoping any thing from Ferdinand, the imperial head of their denomination, they prepared and published an address to the Hungarian Catholics, which made nearly every man of

[a] Pulsky's Mem. Hung. Lady, vol. ii. pp. 40–45.

them a patriot: "When, six months ago, our constitution, eight centuries old, was modified at the Diet of Pressburg, according to the exigencies of the times and the wishes of the nation, and its benefits extended *to all the sons of our native land, without distinction of class, language or creed;* when the independent government, sanctioned by the king, received its powers, no one would have believed it possible ever to attack that free constitution, or to excite the other races against the Hungarians. The good that was obtained having become the good of all, the sincere alliance of the races ought, on the contrary, to have been strengthened; barriers and walls between races, as between classes, ought to have fallen for ever. With what joy we saw liberty and civil rights extended to our fellow-countrymen—with what eagerness we pressed forward to facilitate the realization of the wishes of the country—we have proved by the sacrifices we have imposed upon ourselves. We were convinced, that, if the liberty of the entire people, and consequently of our faithful Catholics, were increased—if they thus acquired the means of ameliorating their lot—our holy church would become greater through the spiritual and material elevation of her children, and that they would attach themselves more closely to her in praising the Lord for the benefits with which he had covered us, by the hands of the legislators of our country. It is for this reason, that we hastened to make known to the clergy of our dioceses, that they should point the attention of their hearers to the greatness and liberality of the new laws, in order that the faithful might conscientiously fulfil their duties, (particularly obedience to the king and to the legal authorities,) which their new rights imposed upon them. To our intense sorrow, the peace of our country has been troubled for several months; but it is a consolation to us to see, that our exhortations in favor of obedience and patriotism have not been uttered in vain. Thanking God for this result, and grateful for the noble conduct of the clergy of our dioceses, we entreat them, as well as all the faithful, with the tenderest expressions of fatherly love, still to observe their indefatigable zeal, their immovable fidelity to order, to repel the overtures of the anarchists, and to obey sincerely the commands of the authorities charged with the defence of the country. We exhort you, dear brethren in Christ, to be of unflinching fidelity to your country, of courageous devotion in her defence, of sincere obedience to the authorities, who, in this hour of danger, are obliged to ask of you more than ordinary services. Be convinced, that they are endeavoring to win your liberty, and with it your earthly happiness. Consider it your most sacred duty, to submit yourselves to the legal authorities of the country, to live amongst them in peace and love, mutually to assist each other, to sustain the weak, to encourage the timid, *to punish the enemies of order!*"[7]

The language of the prelates stirred the heart of the whole nation. The Catholics were completely committed by it to the measures about to be adopted. The Protestants themselves, many of whom had still hoped for some possible reconciliation, were rendered more unanimous by it. If the Catholics, said the wavering of every name and order, cannot endure the conduct of the king, it is time every man should begin to look narrowly at his lukewarmness. If the Catholic prelacy, the proverbial supporters of a strong government, the historical defenders of despotism, cannot brook the severity of the present tyranny, it must be indeed a tyranny. The whole land was roused. Every citizen began to speak openly and bitterly of the base and dangerous trick, which, it was beginning to be generally believed, had been played upon the nation by the monarch. No words can do justice to the excitement. The whole country was transformed to one universal magazine of every species of combustible; and there was wanting but a single spark to give to it a general and terrible explosion

[7] Pulsky's Mem. Hung. Lady, vol. ii. pp. 46–49.

That spark fell at the fatal moment. Just at this crisis, while a commission of the National Assembly was in the act of revising the archives of the Palatine Archduke Stephen, a letter was discovered, written by the Palatine to Ferdinand, and dated the 24th of March, 1848, which demonstrated the treasonable designs of the emperor beyond the possibility of a contradiction. It proved, that the king and his representative were conspiring, early in the spring, in order to defeat the liberal measures of the patriots, how they might overthrow the Hungarian nationality and independence. Three plans were presented and drawn out in detail: "I shall at present attempt," says the Palatine, "in a few words, to bring forward the three measures, by which alone I hope to be able to attain any result in Hungary. The first measure would be, to withdraw the whole armed force from the country, and to leave it a prey to total devastation—to look on passively upon the disorders and fire-raisings—and also upon the struggles between nobles and peasants, and so forth." The meaning is, of course, that, after having roused to madness the different races against the Magyars, the Hungarian troops should be drawn entirely from the country, that there might be no obstacle to a total annihilation of that democratic people. "The second measure would be," continues the Palatine, "to enter into negotiations with Count Batthiányi, concerning the motions to be brought forward for laws, and to save every thing that can be saved." The sense of this is, that, if possible, Batthiányi was to have been bribed to desert the cause of the patriotic party, of which he was then a leader, and to give up his abused country to the discretion of its monarch. "Lastly," concludes the conspirator, "the third measure would be, to recall the Palatine and send a Royal Commissary to Pressburg, invested with extraordinary power, and accompanied by a considerable military force, who, after dissolving the Diet there, should proceed to Pesth, *and carry on the government with an iron hand*, as long as circumstances should permit." This item in the plan needs no comment. It is simply a proposal to annihilate the laws and constitution at a stroke and to erect in their stead a military dictatorship. So it seems, therefore, that, from the very beginning, when the liberal measures of the Magyar National Assembly were only matters of debate, the king's party had resolved, in one of three ways, to destroy them in the bud by breaking down the independence and being of the obnoxious people. No sooner, however, did this conspiracy, so long kept a secret, get wind among the Hungarian people, than every man, not heretofore irrecoverably committed in the opposition, was up in a passion of patriotic indignation. The whole mystery of the spring and summer was doubly solved. It was clearly seen, that each of the three ways of suppressing the liberal designs and doings of the Hungarian nation had been tried, though not in the order mentioned in the letter of the Palatine. In the first place, Batthiányi had been tampered with; but the count had been too inflexible for the enemies of his country. Next, the races had been roused to an internecine war among themselves, while the troops, which should have protected the kingdom from such a disaster, were employed in Italy in fighting the battles of the reaction. Lastly, at a most critical moment, when the desertion of a commander was the most dangerous, the Palatine had abandoned his supreme post in the Hungarian army, in order to make way for the appointment of Jellachich, who, as Royal Commissary with the powers of a Dictator, was now about entering the kingdom to carry on the government with his hand of iron! [8]

When the massacre of Vienna was completed, the army of the imperialists was ready to follow up its fortune in the attack and subjugation of the Hungarian kingdom. There was only one obstacle. Ferdinand, in his coronation oath, had sworn to maintain and defend the liberties and integrity

[8] Pulsky's Mem. Hung. Lady, vol. ii. pp. 95–102.

of the country. He had recently sworn to observe, as well as cause to be observed, the late laws of the National Assembly, by which the nation had been thrown into such a transport of hope and happiness. It was impossible to deny these solemn pledges. It was impossible to make the European world forget them. So long as he could carry on a rebellion, like that raised by Jellachich, by secret intrigues, he had hoped to avoid public scandal. One open act of perjury, however, would be sure to ruin him with all people. Indeed, by the revelations already made, his character for common honesty was gone for ever. He knew it. Austria knew it. Other nations would soon know it. He had forfeited his place. Nothing was left to him but to quit it. On the 2d of December, therefore, Ferdinand, emperor of Austria, weighed down with sin and covered with infamy as with a garment, resigned a scepter, which, for half a generation, he had made the scepter of a tyrant. His brother, Francis Charles, the first heir to the vacant throne, renounced his right in favor of his eldest son. That son, Francis Joseph, a youth of only nineteen years, without talents, without experience, without a knowledge of the world, and, consequently, a fit instrument for the use of other men, was immediately proclaimed. No oaths, no pledges, no personal obligations, now lay in the path of those, who were determined, by the bloodiest of means, to blot the name and being of Hungary from the globe.

The situation of the kingdom was, at this time, very critical. It was entirely surrounded by its foes. On the north was general Schlick, with a strong army, marching down upon the devoted land. General Puchner, supported by the rebellious Wallachians, held undisputed possession of Transylvania on the east. The corps of general Nugent, fresh for any sort of movement, was advancing northward from the valley of the Drave. From the west, flushed with victory, poured down the seventy thousand soldiers of the maddened Windischgräts, reinforced by the troops of Jellachich, who came down resolved to wipe out the disgrace of his late defeat, by an achievement worthy of his rage. Between the four cardinal points, other bodies of no small strength were co-operating with the general attack. Nine armies, indeed, at this fearful crisis, constituted the military cordon, by which the whole land was girded. The plan of the campaign was the plan of common hunters, when they go in overpowering numbers against pestiferous beasts, and when they wish to have a slaughter, rather than a hunt. The plan was to surround and enclose the game, then, gradually contracting the circle of their operations, crowding their victims into the narrowest area, to murder them by wholesale, and so exterminate them at one powerful stroke.

Against this mighty combination, the Hungarians were very inadequately prepared to act. In the country of the Serbs, who were still in insurrection, there was an army of twenty thousand men. In the north of Hungary, under the command of Dembinski, a Polish general, were about eight thousand more. Transylvania could not depend upon more than six thousand able-bodied troops. Under general Görgey, on the west of Hungary, the only defence of the nation against the combined forces of Windischgräts and Jellachich, were still mustered about thirty thousand, who were chiefly volunteers. Three of the great fortresses of the country—Arad, Temesvar, and Esseg—were in the hands of the imperialists. There was but little powder in the country. There was scarcely any sulphur to be had. Lead was plenty, for the peasant had only to dig it from the mines; but muskets, rifles, swords, and all other military weapons, could not be purchased for more than fifty or sixty thousand men. The rest of the army of defence had to arm themselves with hay-forks, pruning-hooks, and scythes.[9]

[9] They had a large importation of weapons at Vienna, but Messenhausser had refused to let them pass, fearing he might provoke the suspicions of his enemies, that he was acting in concert with the Hungarians!

With all her lack, however, Hungary had one advantage of her foes. She had a man, who, in peace and in war, has proved himself to be the greatest genius of his times. She had a man, whose counsels were adequate to instruct, whose lips were eloquent to rouse, and whose hand was ever ready for its work. Hungary had Kossuth. In the month of October, after the resignation of Batthiányi and the appointment of Jellachich, Kossuth had been made President of the Committee of Defence. In this capacity he was now exerting himself in a manner to excite the admiration of both his enemies and his friends. His enemies, indeed, were very few. His friends were as numerous as the friends of the newly-established freedom of his native land. His energy, his purity, his patriotism, had silenced nearly all opposition. His popularity was almost unbounded. He was the soul of every movement. Now, when the nation was threatened from so many quarters, his activity became an astonishment to his countrymen. To supply the soldiery with arms, he turned the fortresses, which had not been lost, into armories, where the rattle and thunder of machinery were heard continually. To supply them with ammunition, he extracted sulphur from the sulphuret of iron. To supply them with their stipulated pay, he organized a national bank, without capital, but pledging the faith of the commonwealth, that the paper should be redeemed when the liberties of the country should be won. To supply them with ideas, with plans, he studied and wrote day and night, and yet seemed to have no time for study, as he was always present at every place of special interest at every time of need. To supply them with enthusiasm, he flew over the kingdom, in all directions, delivering those wonderfully eloquent addresses, which, without any other labor, would have been business enough for any ordinary man. From this period, indeed, Kossuth and Hungary were the same.

The time for the great invasion had now arrived. The word was given around the whole cordon of the invading armies.

All the armies advanced slowly and cautiously toward the center of the kingdom. To that center the forces of the patriots were obliged to gather. To that center the inhabitants fled for safety. There, on the banks of the Theiss, the Hungarians prepared to make their great defence of every thing that God had given them. The National Assembly removed from Pesth to Debreczin. Kossuth and his colleagues there established their official sittings. There factories arose, as by enchantment, for the manufacture of military weapons. There, also, the last attempt at a reconciliation with the Austrian government was made, at the instance of the conservatives, and with Kossuth's consent. There the nation heard, by public rumor, and by the proclamations of Windischgräts, that the messengers of peace had been imprisoned by the proud imperialist, that other gross insults had been heaped upon the unoffending kingdom, and that no reconciliation was possible, excepting on the basis of renouncing for ever the constitution, laws, liberties, and independence of the country. It was there, too, that the last conservative abandoned his opposition, and threw himself into the arms of Kossuth, acknowledging and celebrating the sagacity of the statesman, and swearing to stand by him till Hungary should be a garden, or a desert. There was need enough of all this resolution. The invaders daily drew their circle of operations smaller and smaller, watching a favorable opportunity for dashing through the lines of the Hungarians, to begin the slaughter of the nation. Closer and closer the area of free Hungary became every day. Outside of the military circle there was nothing but tyranny, confiscations and executions. Within it, there was that bravery that arises from despair, when a whole people, conscious of the right, are determined to demand and receive the price of their destruction. Within that circle, there was that courage, which, under a series of disasters, remained undaunted. In the south, Perczel lost the battle of Moor, while hastening to join the general encampment. On the east, the whole of Transylvania was surrendered to the Austrians, who, led by Puchner, had been strengthened by a force of fifteen thousand Russians. On the north, Dembinski, now the commander-in-chief, was overpowered by the superior numbers under Schlick. From the west, the *gros* of the imperial army pushed forward toward the Magyar capital, driving Görgey before them, who, after several bloody engagements, was obliged to abandon Pressburg, Tirnau, Kasimir, Altenburg, Raab, Buda, and even Pesth itself. Meszaros was entirely defeated at Kassau. From all sides the patriots retreated inwardly to the Theiss. As day followed day, the circumference of free Hungary became less and less. But, as the people and the soldiers were crowded closer together, and their common fate became more imminent, the hereditary valor of the nation rose to a higher and higher pitch. From the 16th of December, when the campaign commenced, to the 31st of January, nearly every step taken by the imperialists was a step of victory, and nearly every order issued by the patriot generals was an order to retreat. Yet, in the midst of all these discouragements, there was hourly forming, in the hearts of the Magyars, a common determination to fall, if fall they must, manfully fighting against despotism the battles of human freedom.

On the 1st of January, a Council of War was held under the presidency of general Vetter, who, after the defeat and resignation of Dembinski, had been raised to the command of the Hungarian army. A halt was ordered to all the patriot forces. They were to retreat no longer. A plan of operations was laid down. It received Kossuth's sanction. Offensive movements were to be made in different directions. The circular line of the invasion was to be broken at all hazards. It was to be broken at various points; and the several segments were to be individually cut to pieces.

In the prosecution of this plan, Görgey, with that coolness of deliberation and impetuosity of movement, which formed so singular a contrast in his disposition, resolved to burst through all opposition, in a northerly direction, and get in the rear of the invaders. This brilliant resolution was entirely successful. Putting himself into perfect preparation, he broke forth upon the city of Waitzen, repulsed the enemy with great slaughter, fought every step of his way from Waitzen to Ipolysag, thence pushed through the mountains into the Zips county, turned round and cut the line again on his road to Eperies, where, after fortifying his position, he opened a communication, by the help of general Guyon, with the government at Debreczin. Klapka, on getting the news of these successes, advanced to meet Görgey, thus holding the imperialists under Schlick between the two patriot commanders. Schlick, seeing his danger, fled for safety to the nearest corps of Austrians, thus leaving a wide gap in the circle of the invasion, with two able Magyars to defend it.

In pursuance of the same plan, Bem, gathering a little band of five or six thousand men, dashed through the line of the enemy on the east, forced his way into Transylvania, reinforced his troops, attacked the Austrians and Russians under Puchner, defeated him in one engagement after another, till there was but a miserable remnant left of him, and then chased that remnant over the frontier.

Perczel, co-operating with the general enterprise, left the corps of Dembinski, under whom he had been temporarily serving, marched southwardly toward Szegedin, passed onward to the attack of Sz. Támas, which he took by storm, carried the celebrated Roman entrenchments, behind which the Serbs had maintained a strong position, relieved the garrison of Peterwarasdein, drove the Servian rebels into Titel, restored the ascendency of the nation in the Banat, and settled down to keep possession of his conquest without the fear of successful opposition.

This being done, Görgey, after taking a little rest, rushed down through the centre of the common battle-field, defeated Jellachich at Isászeg, passed the *gros* of the Austrian army near Pesth, the second time attacked and carried Waitzen, crossed the Gran in the face of a powerful opposition, thus drawing the imperialists from the suffering capital, met and cut to pieces a corps of twenty thousand Austrians at Nagy Sarlo, drove the main army before him as far as Raab, and entered the gates of the far-famed fortress of Komorn covered with the glory of his deeds.

While these feats of unrivaled bravery were being executed, similar things were done, by several other commanders, near the center of operations. General Vecsey had beaten the enemy at Szolnok. General Gospar, with the little corps left by Görgey in the north, had defeated Schlick, and driven him to the borders of the land. General Aulich, pushing into the capital as the Austrians were retiring from it, was received with enthusiasm by the entire population, while the Danube was burthened with the military stores, which the imperialists hastily floated out of the kingdom upon its bosom. In all directions, nothing could be seen, but fragments of Austrian armies, and the friends of the Austrian government, making what speed they could to effect their escape beyond the limits of the kingdom. On the 26th of April, 1849, after a series of victories seldom if ever paralleled on the page of history, Hungary stood forth before the world, a free, an independent, and a glorious country. On the 4th of March, Austria had published her imperial constitution, by which the Magyar kingdom was pronounced and treated as a dependent province. On the 19th of April following, in consideration of this terrible invasion, and because the young emperor openly refused to receive the crown of St. Stephen in the legal manner, by swearing to maintain the separateness and integrity of the nation, Hungary had published her Declaration of Independence. Now, at the conclusion of all these triumphs, she had proved herself worthy of the declaration. Excepting a few garrisons, which could not conveniently escape, not an Austrian remained in Hungary to dispute it!

CHAPTER XII.

THE FALL OF HUNGARY.

THREE separate wars had thus arisen against the unoffending Hungarians. The Serbs, assisted by the Wallachians, had risen upon their Magyar fellow-citizens. The Croats, aided by the Sclavonians, had rebelled against the Magyar nation. The Austrians, the authors of both these feuds, uniting and employing both, had made their deadliest onset against the Magyar nationality and independence. Three times the Magyars had prevailed against all opposition. Three times they had defended the cause of European liberty in her chosen sanctuary. Three times the cause of despotism, upheld by duplicity and falsehood, had been broken. Hungary, having defeated and routed all her enemies, had become really a land of freedom.

As the defenders of the nation, under the command of Aulich, marched into the streets of Pesth, the whole capital came out to welcome them with songs and garlands. The superior officers were loaded with panegyrics. The lower officers were overwhelmed with praises. The rough-looking soldiers, who had for months seen nothing but the worst of hardships, were everywhere met by the little children, and covered all over with the flowers of April. The city had long been in bondage. All the people rejoiced and wept, as well they might, in meeting, for the first time after the close of the great struggle, their scarred and wayworn relatives—their fathers, husbands, sons—who, by many a bloody battle, had saved the free institutions of their common country. Such, too, was the joy of the whole kingdom. It was a period of universal gratitude.

If there was any person, whose joy was not complete, that person was the great Kossuth. And what, it may well be asked, could he want, which he had not received? He was now the idol of the nation. He had recovered, from the grasp of its hereditary tyrants, its original constitution. He had so extended the meaning and benefits of that constitution, as to make every inhabitant, poor as well as rich, peasant as much as prince, an equal participant of its blessings. He had carried the country through three wars successfully, all of which had been raised against it, merely because it had set out anew on the path of popular and equal liberty. The people of that country, grateful for his services, had raised him to the highest position in their gift. They had paid him a homage given to no man, by any people, since the days of Washington. Could he, in reason, ask any thing more of them? No, not any thing. Nor did he ask any thing more of them. Still, he was not entirely happy. His thoughts were too wide, his vision was too extended, to allow him to drink from an unmixed cup, so long as he retained a recollection of the historical tactics of his country's enemies. He knew the character of the Austrians. He knew the resources of a despot, who has no scruples to restrain him. He well knew, that, if there was a mercenary army in all Europe, or an ambitious monarch holding any of its scepters, the representative and heir of the House of Hapsburg would not fail to subsidize, to bribe, to promise, till another invasion, fourfold stronger than the first, should come down to make a final sweep of the laws, liberties and institutions of the democratic nation.

There was another reason why Kossuth, with all his honors on him, could not rejoice as freely as did the masses of his people. He saw danger rising from the ranks of the nation's liberators. He saw an unsanctified ambition springing up, which, unless checked—and he beheld no way to check it—would be sure to bring disaster, should there be another day of peril. He saw a man, whom he had himself raised from obscurity as a reward for military merit, whose deeds on the field of battle had indeed been the deeds of a hero, but whose very successes were pampering a spirit of supreme selfishness, which was almost certain, under a temptation, to grow up into the rankest treason. That man was Arthur Görgey, who, since the defeat of Schwechat, had been the Ajax, or the Gonsalvo, of the army. His feats of bravery had never been surpassed in the wars of any period. His daring, however, had in no case reached to rashness. There was a foresight in his mental composition, which, added to his courage, had made him almost invariably successful. His talent at giving form and firmness to an irregular body of recruits, such as constituted nearly the whole of the Hungarian forces, was wonderful. His will was a will of iron. Nothing could move him from his purposes. In any undertaking, if the first attempt happened to be unsuccessful, he would repeat it to the twentieth time, before he would give up his resolution. Nor would he, after ever so many proofs of the difficulties of a first plan of effort, change it for another, however clearly he might be convinced that a change could be effected to his advantage. Conquer he could, and conquer he would, at any amount of hazard, exactly as he had at first determined. Such was the imperiousness of his disposition, that, when he had learned his superiority over the ablest of his enemies, his very friends found it impossible to govern him. Admired, and nearly worshiped, by the entire body of the Hungarian army, as every great general is admired and worshiped by his soldiers, he treated his comrades in command with every degree of contempt from insolence to indifference; and yet, such is the impunity of great genius, such the adoration paid it, that this mode of treating his associates scarcely lessened the amount of deference they showed him. He soon began to break away from the orders of the government. He despised the calculations, as he said, of a set of peaceable gentlemen, who had hardly ever seen a battle. "Kossuth alone," he remarked in a letter to his friend Klapka, "is a classical and generous character." But he soon outgrew his respect for Kossuth. "It is a pity he is not a soldier!" Görgey had no abiding admiration of any thing but military genius; and he saw no man around him equal to himself as the leader of an army. At that fearful crisis, too, when the tactics of the National Assembly had been mostly superseded by the tactics of the field of conflict, when words had been turned to bullets, he clearly saw and felt, that the army, and not the legislature, represented the power of the nation. As the chief spirit of the army, therefore, he drew into himself the prerogatives of a ruler, until he considered himself able to cope with the mighty but unselfish Kossuth. Kossuth, by this time, began to understand the towering and unprincipled ambition of the general; but he was ready to forget the faults, if he could employ the abilities, of his self-constituted rival. He was ready even to resign his authority, and give it into the hands of Görgey, if the nation wished it. The nation did not wish it. It wished only, that the two great men of the revolution would act in concert, and so save it from destruction. Kossuth made every exertion, and every sacrifice, that could be expected of a great and magnanimous patriot, in order to soothe the temper and satisfy the ambition of his opponent. He gave him the chief command of the Hungarian armies. He made him his Secretary of War, thus clothing him with more than his share of the sovereignty of the nation. No sooner, however, did the aspirant get possession of this two-fold influence, thus magnanimously conferred upon him, than he retired to his headquarters and began to set himself up, not as the coadjutor of the great and generous statesman, but in an attitude of defiance to the civil government.

It is easy, therefore, now to understand the reason, why Görgey refused to co-operate with Kossuth in a scheme of operations, which has been since pronounced, by all military men, the only one by which it was at all possible to save the kingdom. Kossuth, still adhering to his former policy, advocated the necessity of pursuing the flying Austrians into their own territory, and even to the ramparts of their democratic capital. "They are now," he said, "defeated. They feel dispirited and broken. Windischgräts, satisfied of the hopelessness of his undertaking, has been recalled, and his command has been given to general Welden. Vienna is as full as ever of devoted democrats. They have been maddened to phrenzy by the recent executions. They are more than ever ready to welcome us to their streets as liberators. Now is the time to press hotly after the disheartened fugitives. Let us crush our opponents while the panic is yet on them. Let us rush to the imperial capital, raise the standard of the Austrian and Hungarian people, and jointly hold the authority of the state, till we can get our rights legally guaranteed in the most solemn and satisfactory manner. By the time this great deed is done, the few garrisons of the enemy still left among us, kept by the surrounding populations within the *rayon* of their respective fortresses, will be starved into a willingness of offering, instead of receiving, terms of capitulation."

Such was Kossuth's plan of operations; and, as in so many other instances, subsequent events have demonstrated the soundness of his reasoning. Görgey, however, was not the man to act upon a scheme laid down for him by one, who, with all his abilities, was not a soldier. He opposed the Governor. "He wished first," he said, "to clear the country of her last enemy, before he went on a hunt for others, who had fled to their own lands for safety. The fugitives had been once defeated. They were worthy of no attention so long as they acknowledged their defeat by flying. At home, however, there were yet some, who deserved the notice of the patriotic army. What true-hearted Magyar could consent to show himself abroad, when his foes were quartered near his own domicil, bidding defiance to the nation to dislodge them? What genuine son of Hungary, what descendant of the heroic

Arpad, can afford to see the soil of his native land polluted by the foot-prints of a solitary Austrian? And there is Buda, the great national fortress, the Gibraltar of the country, the time-honored capital, full of the renown and glory of former ages, sacred to the use of Magyar liberty, now trampled by the unholy feet of our oppressors! Shall we leave the temple of the nation's independence in the hands of those, who will boast of the possession so long as they have a historian or a poet, and go running after wind-mill battles, whose success, it is true, would be easy enough, but whose results would be nearly useless! No, my countrymen, no! I am a Hungarian! I am fighting in the cause of the Hungarians! The Hungarians care nothing about the Austrians, except as they are here to trouble us! And here they are; but here they shall be no longer! If my blood is wanted, every drop of it shall be shed, or there shall not be long, in all Hungary, a solitary foe to our glorious constitution to contaminate the dust he stands on!"

This superficial but captivating style of argument carried the Hungarian army. It revived, also, the old party of the conservatives in the National Assembly. It was an appeal to the military vanity of the nation. Kossuth, though he had the power to pursue his own plan, hoped that the capture of the great fortress would satisfy the ambition of his rival, and that there might still be time to reach the camp of the Austrians, and cut them to pieces, before they could restore the courage of the hostile troops, or concentrate reinforcements. He hoped to re-unite the two great parties, into which the country was again divided, on one common system of operations. To divide the people, or to leave them thus divided, he clearly saw, would be to ruin them. His greatness of soul was such, that he found no difficulty in yielding temporarily to the stubbornness of an opponent, if he could see any good to his country coming from a personal concession. The difference between him and his antagonist was fundamental.

Kossuth was ready to sacrifice himself, at any moment and a thousand times, as he was only fighting the battles of his country for the sake of liberty. Görgey sacrificed nothing, not even his opinion, but was pursuing the bent of his natural disposition, for the sake of his aggrandizement. Kossuth needed just such a soldier as the unconquerable Görgey. Görgey needed just such a leader as the high-minded and patriotic Kossuth. The country needed them both. It could with difficulty survive without them. But it needed them united. Had they been united—had Görgey's military prowess been patriotically submitted to a perfect co-operation with the far-seeing statesmanship of Kossuth—Hungary, at this moment, would have been as independent as Great Britain, as democratic as America, as free as the winds that sweep over her.

The Hungarian general, obstinately adhering to his own plan, relinquished the chance of making a complete conquest of Austria, for the sake of the renown to be acquired by the fall of Buda. Three-fourths of the brave little army were drawn from the track of the imperial fugitives to settle down around the ramparts of the old Magyar capital. On the 4th of May, Görgey demanded the immediate surrender of the fortress. On the same day, general Henzi, the commander of the fort, returned a peremptory refusal. At one o'clock, on the 16th of May, a fearful assault was made by the Magyar troops; but they were repulsed with considerable slaughter. The attack was repeated, precisely as before made, on the 21st, when Görgey had the satisfaction of sending a dispatch to the new seat of government beginning in the most triumphant language: "The Hungarian colors are flying from the towers of Buda castle!" It was indeed a victory; but it was one of those victories, which, gratifying for the moment as they may be, cost too much to the victors. General Henzi, it is true, had fallen and been trodden beneath the feet of his assailants. The garrison, after suffering a heavy loss, had submitted; but twenty-six days had thus been sacrificed to a useless undertaking, while the Austrians had been left to make all needful preparations for their final and fatal invasion of the country. They had gathered their flying and straggling bands together. They had reduced the united army to the severest discipline. They had obtained powerful reinforcements of native troops, and the first instalment of one hundred and fifty thousand Russian soldiers. They had again changed their commander, in order to get the man best suited to the emergency; and now that man, the blood-thirsty Haynau, with an immediate force of about one hundred thousand, was about to plunge into the heart of Hungary, determined to awe the nation into a peaceable submission, or butcher the inhabitants to the very last of those offering resistance.[1]

Such was the fatal obstinacy of Görgey. The other generals had made the month of May somewhat memorable by a series of minor victories. Bem had defeated general Malkowski, the commander of ten thousand men, and driven him from the Banat into Wallachia. Perczel had fought several battles, besieged Temesvar, and reduced Titel, the last place held by the rebellious Serbs on the lower Danube. Dembinski had kept undisputed possession of the north of Hungary. Hatvani, it is true, in his ill-starred adventure against the Wallachians of Transylvania, had been repulsed. But this was a solitary mishap in the monthly calendar. Everywhere else, from east to west, from north to south, the army of the patriots had maintained its triumphant attitude.

At the end of the first week in June, the armies of the Austro-Russian invasion had taken their positions on the frontiers of the doomed and unhappy country. In the great camp at Pressburg were fifty thousand Austrians, and twenty-five thousand Russians, under the immediate command of Haynau. In the Styrian city of Pettau, near the south-west limits of

[1] Klapka's War in Hungary, vol. i. pp. 33–50

the kingdom, general Nugent had concentrated a force of about twenty thousand. On the north-west, through the pass of Arva, a body of nearly twenty thousand Russians, commanded by general Grabbe, had entered Hungary and taken up their position in the mountains. On the north-east, around the celebrated pass of Dukla, prince Paskievicz stood with about seventy-five thousand Russians. In Transylvania, on the far east, under Rüdigers and Lüders, were forty thousand Russians supported by fourteen thousand more, not far away, under the command of general Clam-Gallas. On the lower Danube, in south-eastern Hungary, were seventy-six thousand Wallachians and Serbs, in three divisions, which were commanded by Jank, Rajacsicz and Stratimirovicz. From the banks of the Drave, along the southern boundary, Jellachich was marching with a force of fifty thousand Sclavonians and Croats. An army, in a word, of about three hundred and seventy thousand men, the best disciplined troops in Europe, fully equipped, well paid and fed, and headed by the ablest generals within the limits of two empires, had formed another cordon around the land of the liberty-loving Magyars, who had just been suffering by several expensive and bloody efforts in the defence of their hereditary freedom. It was a high compliment to their bravery, unintentional as it was, that, weakened as they had been by three civil wars, so large a force was now deemed essential to their subjugation.[2]

In opposition to this fearful array of soldiers, the Hungarians could offer, at this time, only about fifty thousand men. These were divided into eight corps, and so distributed as to face the enemy at every point, where an entrance into the country was expected. They were so arranged, also, in

[2] Klapka, Pragay and other Hungarian writers, without the possibility of any concert, have given almost identical statements of the forces of the enemy. Pragay's numbers exceed those of Klapka. Klapka's War in Hungary, vol. i. pp. 70–79, and Pragay's Hungarian Struggle, pp. 74–75.

reference to each other, that they formed a circular camp passing nearly around the entire border of the kingdom, with the fortress of Komorn, pronounced by Bonaparte to be impregnable, as the *point d'apui* of operations. This starting-point, then occupied by only six thousand men, was commanded by general Klapka. In a north-easterly direction, along the valleys of the Neutra and the Waag, the first, second and third corps had taken up several advantageous situations, which, by the help of the small corps under colonel Horvath and major Armin Görgey, a brother of the great general, extended still farther to the north, till they communicated with the camp of Dembinski, the sentinel of the pass of Arva. Toward the south-east, the seventh and eighth corps, united by the division commanded by Kmetty, stretched up the valley of the Raab, from the city of that name, near the banks of the Danube, through Teth, Marczaltö, and other towns, nearly to the waters of the Drave. Perczel, with a small force, was still on the lower Danube, in the Banat, and communicated with the forces on the Raab, as well as with the troops on the borders of Transylvania under Bem. In different parts of the country, but particularly around the margin of the Platten Lake, and in northern Hungary, the army was seconded by voluntary risings of the people, who, seeing the impending danger, had begun to arm and discipline themselves for the coming struggle.

It was not the numerical superiority of the enemy, however, that rendered the third invasion of the soil of Hungary so formidable. The races and religions of two despotic nations, thus combined against the race, religion and liberty of the Magyar, gave it a fearful influence among the sects and nationalities of the kingdom. It was a combination of the Sclave and German against the Hun, of the Roman and Greek Catholics against the Protestants, no less than of the two champions of absolutism in Europe against democratic principles The emperor of Austria could march into the country as the acknowledged champion of the Roman Catholics; he could go there as the countryman and defender of the Germans. The emperor of the Russias, upon crossing the frontier, would be revered as the head of the Sclavic nationalities, whose existence had been almost deified by the Sclavic Hungarians, whose name had been mingled in their devotions from the days of infancy. For reasons not otherwise explained, than by the prejudices of race and a common faith, the Saxons of Transylvania, as well as nearly all the Germans of the kingdom, had refused to serve as soldiers during the Austro-Croatian invasion; and though the Roman Catholic Sclaves of the north of Hungary, and the Roman Catholics of every part of it, had united with the Magyars in driving off the Greek Sclaves of the southern provinces, in the first invasion, who could tell what the same populations would do, when the battle was to be between the Protestant Magyars, on the one hand, and the German and Sclavic Catholics, Greek and Roman, on the other? The Hungarian army, indeed, was filled with Greek Sclaves and Roman Germans; but what man could tell, whether, when they should find themselves arrayed against people of their own faith and blood, they would not desert their standards at the hour of peril? Perhaps, in the heat of the war, when their help would be the most essential, they would go over to their kindred and fellow-sectaries, and betray the once envied and hated Magyar, after all his unexampled generosity. If the army, therefore, could not be trusted, nothing could be trusted. Hungary must sink; and the cause of democratic liberty, in the south of Europe, must perish with her!

Such was the state of things at the opening of the final contest. Every Magyar saw it. Every Magyar felt, that, at this fearful crisis, whatever help might be promised by the other races and religions, the Protestant Magyars alone could be certainly depended on in the day of trial. The Protestant Magyars were the fountain-head of democratic principles to the nation. Their kindred, it is true, of the Catholic faith, though naturally constituting the strength of the conservative party, had been nearly converted to the ideas of the more liberal and enlightened portion of the race. If any thing was to be expected of the other inhabitants, the expectation was to be realized by infusing into their souls the same love of liberty, which the Magyars had just immortalized by the passage of their recent laws. They were to be educated into the doctrines of human freedom by the powerful exertions of those already free. This was the creed of Kossuth. On this, he had acted from the first. The Magyars by blood, and such as could be made Magyars, by being properly enlightened, were his only hope. The work of a century, however, had to be completed within the compass of a few weeks; and there was no one so capable of accomplishing it as himself. He, indeed, was the main-spring of every movement. All the business of the nation had gradually fallen into his hands. Every thing had to be done by him. His activity was almost miraculous. It would be impossible for any person, not an eye-witness, to give a true picture of his daily life at this alarming moment; and it is fortunate, that one who saw him constantly has given to the world a minute description of his habits at this time. The account is worthy of preservation to the latest age: "I hardly know where to begin," says the writer, who was one of the governor's private secretaries, "as there is hardly ever a pause in the course of his activity to start from; but, for example, I will write down the doings of yesterday. Yesterday morning, after I had breakfasted, I hastened to the chancery—that is, to Kossuth's house—which contains four apartments, his sleeping chamber, a parlor, the chancery where we four secretaries have our places, and a small room for copyists. Three couriers with dispatches were in the room as I entered; and Kossuth sat in his usual place, with a pen in his right hand, and in the left the dispatches just brought him. I had come rather late, for it was already a quarter past five o'clock;

and another secretary had prepared, in my place, two dispatches, which had been sent off at five. As I went in, he was occupied in several ways. His hand was writing; his mouth was dictating; his eye glanced at and read the open dispatches; and his mind directed and followed all the operations of his servants. He looked paler and more sick than usual. A glass of medicine stood at his side, of which he tasted from time to time, as if the mixture were the means of keeping up his physical existence. Indeed, though I have often worked at his side, from early in the morning till late at night, I do not remember having seen him stop to take any nourishment excepting this mixture; and though he does sometimes eat, I can assure you that the quantity of food consumed by him would hardly be enough to keep a young child from starving. One might almost say, that the physical part of him has scarcely an existence of its own. The man is nothing but spiritual energy; for, if it were not so, the perishing sickly frame would long since have been dissolved in spite of all the wisdom of the physicians. He is perhaps the only living being, whose mighty will is alone sufficient, by its own force, to urge forward the wheels of his physical nature and keep them constantly in motion. He will not be sick; and he is not sick. His spiritual resources, his resolution, his enthusiasm, endow him with the powers of a giant, although his bodily strength is not more than that of a boy of six years. He bids defiance to the deaths that threaten him in so many different forms. His spirit keeps his body alive. That spirit is still young and vigorous, and can cease to be so only when the too great tension shall have irritated the nerves to such a degree, that they will refuse to obey the will. Then, and then only, will that organism cease to be. It will destroy itself."

After this personal sketch, the labors of a single day are thus set down: "I had scarcely taken my place, when the governor began to dictate a letter to general Bem; and we were similarly engaged for about four hours, during which time I had written two letters, and each of my three colleagues three, by his dictation. He himself had, in the mean time, prepared two dispatches, one for Perczel and another for Komorn. After nine o'clock, leaving us work enough for the whole day, he went with the ministers Szemere and Duschek, who came for him, to the National Assembly, taking with him some papers, on which he had made several memoranda. He returned at about four o'clock in the afternoon, accompanied by several representatives, with whom he held a conference of two hours, answering their questions and suggestions. This, however, did not hinder him from examining the documents we had prepared during his absence, or from dictating more letters. While he was thus dictating to us three or four letters, with totally different contents, and all coming off together from the same lips, we had to be exceedingly careful in committing them to paper, so rapid was his utterance. At six o'clock came more dispatches, and verbal inquiries, all of which were answered promptly. The representatives, with one exception, went away. The one remaining sat down by the side of Kossuth and began to help us. This made five secretaries; and to give some conception of the labors of the evening, I will mention, that, from half-past seven to half-past eight, he dictated to us, at the same time, five important letters, all of different contents. One of them was to Dembinski, one to Bem, the third to Paris, the fourth to Gyöngyös, and the fifth to Vienna. Two were in German, one in French, and one in Hungarian." Rightly does the secretary exclaim, as he records these labors—"Is it a man that can do such things!"

But the toils of the day were not yet concluded: "After this," continues the witness, "Kossuth was some time engaged with figures, which he reckoned in a state of almost perfect abstraction. While he was thus occupied, his friend and family physician, the doctor and professor Bugat Pal, came in and interrupted him. He greeted the doctor, kindly pointed him to a chair, and returned to his occupation. The doctor took his left hand, which was yielded willingly, as if it did not belong to its owner; and he held it for about fifteen minutes, feeling the beat of the pulse, after which he retired without being noticed by the illustrious patient. At eleven o'clock, the head of one of my colleagues was already nodding; and both myself, and the one opposite to me, could hardly keep our eyes open. The clock struck twelve; and the noise of the departure of the copyists roused him from his reflections. 'What time is it, gentlemen?' he asked us; and when we told him it was just after twelve, he became unquiet, and a cloud suddenly passed over his brow. He arose from his seat, saying, 'Has no express arrived from Pesth?' 'No,' was the answer; and he began to walk up and down the room. He did not seem to think, that it was time to be seeking rest; and, as if to keep us from having such a thought, he said: 'Gentlemen, there is work to be done yet!' Finally, after waiting vainly for another hour, he said to us: 'Let us take a little rest, gentlemen, while we are waiting. *I will call you when I need your help!*'" Yes, the tireless guardian of the nation, with all the dignities of his office on him, goes not to his couch leaving a command to be called when needed; but, as if the servant of his servants, he gives them an untroubled sleep, promising to call them when he wants them!

There was more work, however, on its way to the hands of the great master-workman: "He went into his bed-room," continues the secretary, "and we arranged ourselves on the benches and slept with our fatigue as soundly as in the softest bed. But our rest was not of long duration. Between three and four o'clock, the dispatches arrived. Still half-asleep, we took our places, and Kossuth, that Watchman of his country, dictated to us as before. At six in the morning, we received permission to go away, while he went for a bath, though we were to be there again by eight o'clock!" Such, at this period, was the daily life of Kossuth, a man whose health had been broken by his long Austrian imprisonment. "We," says the secretary with good reason—"*we* are young and strong; and such a night's watching, now and then, will not injure us. But it is not so with him. How long can this hero of the nineteenth century—this guide of our fatherland amid the foes that surround it—how long can his spirit sustain the contest that it carries on with the little of physical nature attached to it? If, beyond the ocean, in the free and happy America, there are men who feel a sympathy for our good cause, we do not ask their prayers so much for the triumph of the Magyars as for the life of Kossuth; for Hungary cannot be conquered—[the writer does not dream of her ever being betrayed]—so long as this incomprehensible being, whose name is Kossuth, is spared to us, though Russians and Austrians enter our country by myriads, and though thousands of our brethren fall as sacrifices to the cause of freedom. He is the image of liberty, equality and fraternity. He is the incarnate spirit of justice. He is the Washington of Hungary!"[3]

While thus wearing out his life in the closet, he sent forth that celebrated proclamation to the Hungarian people, which concluded with the thrilling and prophetic sentence: "Between Vesprim and Weissenburg the women shall dig a deep grave, in which we will bury the name, the honor, the nation of Hungary, or our enemies. And on this grave shall stand a monument, inscribed with the record of our shame—'So God punishes cowardice!'—or we will plant on it the tree of freedom, eternally green, from whose foliage shall be heard the voice of God speaking, as from the fiery bush to Moses—

[3] This letter was published, at the time it describes, in all the leading political journals of Europe and America; and I know not to which one of them, in particular, it should be credited. In the process of abridging it, I have endeavored only to effect some improvement of its style, without the smallest alteration of its facts.

'The spot whereon thou standest is holy ground—so do I reward the brave!'"

These labors, and particularly this proclamation, were followed up by his incomparable popular addresses. Leaving his ministers to do what they could at home, and appointing his own sister, a noble woman, to act as superintendent of the public hospitals, worn as he was by toil, he undertook a grand tour of the kingdom in an open carriage, with his wife and children at his side, that he might talk with the people face to face, and rouse the masses by his eloquence. A traveler, who heard him at this period, has given a brief description of his style of speaking: "The effects of his oratory are astonishing. When he rises to speak, his features, finely molded and of an oriental cast, though pale and haggard, as from mental and physical suffering united, immediately excite interest. His deep-toned, almost sepulchral voice adds to the first impression. Then, as he becomes warmed by his subject, and lanches into the enthusiastic and popular manner peculiar to him, his hearers seem to imbibe all the feelings that so strongly reign in his own bosom, and to be governed by the same will. In his present tour through the provinces to raise the *landstrum*—all the able-bodied—so great has been his power over the peasantry, that frequently men, women and even children, running to their homes and seizing hooks, or whatever their hands could find, assembled on the spot, and insisted on being led directly against the enemy!" We read of no effects, more striking than these, as produced by the eloquence of the classic ages!

But it was in the National Assembly that his oratory was the most sublime and overwhelming. There he had an audience fit for him. There he felt the whole weight of his responsibility. There he was surrounded by those heroes, who, from the beginning, had sworn to live or die with him. Generally, after stating clearly and cogently the proposition to be established, and establishing it by the most cool and convincing arguments, he would suddenly, toward the conclusion of a speech, break forth into those incomparable transports of passion, in which his very soul seemed to be gushing out in supplication for his country's liberty. One of these wonderful addresses was delivered at the crisis now under consideration. He well knew the awful importance of the moment. He knew the responsibility he assumed in giving counsel to the representatives of the nation. It might be, indeed it was, his last great appeal in behalf of his wronged, oppressed, invaded, bleeding fatherland. In a few days, the Austrians, Russians, Sclavonians, Croats, Serbs, Wallachians, would be down upon it. There was but a moment left him; and that moment was to leave behind it either liberty or annihilation. After passing deliberately through a long array of facts and arguments, by which he carried conviction into every breast, he ceased to speak, but still maintained his position as a speaker. Raising his large and now watery eyes toward heaven, he seemed to be making his last petition, at the throne of eternal Justice, for his abused and afflicted country. A cloud passed over his countenance, as if he then saw, by prophetic illumination, a revelation of the future. Then, lowering his aspect a moment, and looking abroad, through the open windows of the building, upon the grand and historical scenery about him—the river, the plains, the mountains—he again raised his eyes and withered hands on high, exclaiming with that emphasis of his which no words can represent—"O Hungary, Hungary, how can I give thee up! O bury me, Hungarian earth, within thy holy bosom, or be to me a land of freedom!" Every representative before him, even the iron-hearted generals, hearing the tones of his voice, and seeing the tears rolling down his face, wept like children!

Such patriotism, coupled with such efforts, could not be otherwise than successful. A regular army of nearly two hundred thousand men was the result of these unparalleled exertions. The noble-hearted sister of the governor, in every way worthy of her brother, sent out a proclamation to her countrywomen, calling on them to do every thing in their power to aid the suffering cause of liberty. They obeyed the summons. Mothers, possessing Spartan valor, armed their sons and led them to the recruiting officers. Wives, relinquishing their titles to their husbands, encouraged them to enlist, choosing to see themselves widows and their children orphans, rather than witness the fall of freedom. Nay, unprecedented as is the fact, in Grecian or in Roman fame, maids, forgetting their sex and despising the dangers of their undertaking, formed themselves into companies, that they might occupy and hold the fortresses, and thereby release their fathers and brothers to fight the battles of their country on the field of blood. One aged matron, from the banks of the Theiss, came leading her more aged sire, a man of nearly eighty winters, and wished to be enrolled. They were asked what they could do in such a business. "If nothing more," they replied, "we can teach the younger ones how to die for Kossuth and their country!" The peasantry, who had just been released from bondage, and who saw that the war had grown out of the generosity of the Magyars toward themselves, could hardly be restrained from rushing against the enemy unprepared, and throwing away lives which might soon be necessary to the triumph of the patriotic cause. "All they asked for was," says the author of the War in Hungary, "whether now the time had come for the people to rise *en masse.* Gray-bearded peasants shook the hands of my soldiers and said, with that tranquility which characterizes the Hungarian peasant—'Don't you care! We'll get the better of the Russians too. Hitherto, we sent our sons only; but now, we, the old ones, will take horse!'" When that wonderful man, Louis Kossuth, was again seated at his desk surrounded by his secretaries and copyists, in addition to the two hundred thousand soldiers, more than three times the number of Magyar citizens were ready to rise up, at a moment's warning, in defence of their country and its institutions. The differences of race and of religion were nearly all buried. The nation had assumed an attitude that rendered it utterly unconquerable. The patriotism, the faith, the eloquence of Kossuth had proved victorious. On his return to Pesth, on the 4th of June, he was overwhelmed with the gratitude of the citizens. Poets sang his praises. Orators pronounced panegyrics. Men, women, and little children, showered bouquets of flowers upon him, from the roofs and windows of their houses, as he passed through the streets of the city to his humble lodgings.[4]

Having thus roused his countrymen, and filled the nation with his own spirit, he began to turn his eyes more directly to other countries. He opened a friendly negotiation with the government of Turkey. The sultan was understood to refuse a passage to the Russians through his dominions. The hero next looked to the lower provinces of the kingdom, which, in the beginning of the revolution, had been unanimously against him. There was now a powerful party in his favor; and they sent him better promises than he had expected. He then tried the temper of the Italian democrats. They consented to assist him. He called upon the patriots of Austria. They flocked in great numbers to his standard. Through his agent, Tekeli, he tried the temper of the French. There he was for the first time entirely disappointed. Pulsky represented him in England. The English people were friendly to him. The

[4] Pragay gives the number of the patriot forces, at this period, as one hundred and fifty-seven thousand; but he excludes several smaller bodies of troops mentioned by other writers. Hungarian Struggle for Freedom, p. 75. Klapka is extremely indefinite in his numbers. There is a great deal of confusion, and not a little contradiction, in his figures. War in Hungary, vol. i. pp. 61–80. I have followed the official documents of the War Office and the proclamations of Kossuth. Louis Kossuth and Hungary, p. 319, Eng. ed. The anecdotes I have gathered from the foreign journals.

English government, the ally of Austria, conducted itself with the most consummate illiberality. An envoy was dispatched to our own country. The President of the United States sent a messenger to Austria, assigning him the duty of watching the progress of the revolution, that, at the first favorable opportunity, the American government might acknowledge the independence of the Magyar nation. Last of all, throwing his whole energy into a concluding effort, this unconquerable man sent forth an address to the free nations of all Europe. There is nothing more powerful, more patriotic, more thrilling in any language. The concluding sentence of that address must be read with confusion of face, from this time for ever, by every people that turned a deaf ear to its entreaties: "Awake, O ye people of Europe! On Hungarian ground, the battle of European freedom is now fighting! With this country, the free world will lose a powerful member! In this nation, a true and heroic champion will perish; for we shall fight, till we spill the last drop of our blood, that our country may become either a chosen sanctuary of freedom, consecrated by that blood, or shall form a damning monument, to all eternity, in token of the manner in which tyrants can league together to destroy free peoples and free nations, and of the shameful manner in which free countries can abandon one another!" With the exception of the countries immediately about Hungary, Europe was silent at this heart-piercing call for succor. The noble Magyars, soon seeing that they were abandoned by the world to fight the great battle of human liberty alone, went to their bloody task like men of courage. They were resolved to survive as the champions of freedom, or to be buried with her!

General Welden, the successor of Windischgräts, had resigned his command on the 1st of June. Haynau, the most barbarous commander of modern times, began his career with a series of military executions, in which the Hungarian officers, Mednyansky and Gruber, and a minister of the gospel, the

Rev. Mr. Razga, were butchered in cold blood. His next step was to move his immense army, by slow and cautious marches, toward the Hungarian battle-line. Görgey, tired of his own obstinacy, began to look for an opening to commence offensive operations, instead of pursuing that defensive policy by which he had already sacrificed the certainty of a triumph. The opportunity, as he thought, soon occurred. His plans were at once laid. On the 16th of June, three separate but simultaneous attacks were to be made on the Austrian army, from three different points. The day came and the attacks were made. From the camp at Mocshanok, on the southern side of the Danube, general Nagy Sandor moved to Sintau, pushed a column of the enemy from their position on the Neutra road, took possession of the neighboring heights, bombarded the city, expelled the garrison, and was about to collect the fruits of the victory, when the Austrians, reinforced from their rear, returned to the fight and carried all before them. The Hungarians retired in disorder, leaving their artillery on the field of battle. On the same day, colonel Asboth was directed to make an assault upon the imperialists stationed on the opposite side of the Danube, under the command of general Pott. He performed this duty at great risk and with no lack of spirit. After marching for six hours over a marshy soil, into which the feet of both men and horses sank every step, he reached the little village of Kiralyrev, which he took and occupied. The Austrians retreated to a height between Pered and Zsigord. They were again driven from their position. The Hungarians entered the two villages; but just as they were advancing into the streets, a powerful reinforcement from the corps under Wahlgemuth, the Austrian commander on that side of the Danube, took their places in the line of battle and decided the fortunes of the day against the Magyars. The patriots retreated to their camp, leaving behind them three field-pieces and five hundred of their comrades. On this same day, also, colonel Kosztolany engaged the enemy posted on the island of Shütt, between the two principal arms of the Danube, that the Austrians there might be too much occupied to render assistance to their friends on either bank of the separating river. He left his camp at Nagy Megyer early in the morning; but the imperialists were so strongly entrenched on a broken ground, where the artillery of the Hungarians could not come into very effective action, that, after a lengthy and almost harmless cannonade, during which the Magyars suffered a severe loss of both men and horses, a repulse, a retreat, a lamentation were the only fruits of the undertaking. On all sides, indeed, the 16th of June was a day of discouragement to the patriots. It was the beginning of the final conflict between the enemies and the friends of Magyar liberty; and the Magyars, in spite of all their heroism, had been defeated in every action.[5]

Görgey was in neither of these engagements. They had been conducted, however, according to his orders. Chagrined at their ill success, he left the city of Pesth, where he had been engaged in the business of his ministerial office, and rode hastily to the camp of Klapka, resolved to turn the tide of battle by his presence. Reproving each of the officers for their several defeats, he at once issued his directions for a repetition of their late movement. Self-willed as he was, and flattered by his former successes, he was not the man to take a lesson from a solitary failure. The older officers assured him of the difficulties of the undertaking, the hazard he would run in risking another battle, and the ease with which he could secure the advantage of the enemy, by altering his plan of operations. Their reasonings, it is thought, convinced him of his error; but it was his nature not to submit to circumstances, or to take advantage of them, when he had committed himself in any particular direction. The battle must be fought over again. At every risk, Görgey must show the army, that

[5] Klapka's War in Hungary, vol. i. pp. 82–88.

his opinion was never to be doubted. On the 19th of June the word was given to repeat the maneuvers of the 16th precisely according to the original arrangements. They were repeated. They all proved unsuccessful. After an almost continuous contest for thirty-six hours, during which prodigies of bravery were performed by the army of the patriots, they were forced to retreat from every battle-ground, and fly for shelter toward the great fortress. Görgey himself, habited like a peasant, and driven in an open cart, hastened to the place of refuge with a downcast face and dejected spirits. The loss of the two days, in men, was about two thousand.[6]

Immediately after this engagement, the army of the imperialists, finding a greater concentration of their forces necessary to such victories as their cause demanded, returned to Pressburg, and, crossing the river, proceeded down the highway toward the city of Raab, which was slightly defended by about nine thousand patriots. The design of this maneuver was very evident. Several days, however, were to be thus occupied, before any attack upon the city could be expected. It is clear, therefore, that Görgey should have concentrated the larger part of the armies about the fortress upon Raab. He should have known, that nine thousand could not stand long against five or six times their number. Such was the opinion of his officers. It was not his opinion. He was still too confident of his abilities. He neglected to augment the forces of Pöltenburg, who commanded Raab, while he gave the imperialists every opportunity of bringing down as many soldiers as they would. The battle was fought on the 28th of June. It was a terrible struggle. Never, perhaps, in modern warfare, did a smaller number of men longer hold in check a larger army. The dispositions of the defence were admirable. The valor of the Hungarians was never surpassed

[6] Klapka's War in Hungary, vol. i. pp. 99–107. The loss of the Austrians I have not seen reported.

even by themselves. Not only Pöltenburg, but colonel Kossuth, a relative of the governor, together with several other officers, as well as all the men, covered themselves with unfading honor. Görgey himself, who reached the scene of action about twelve o'clock, and who immediately took upon himself the chief command, appeared in all his wonted heroism again. The Magyars began to give way as Görgey came upon the ground. He rallied them to the fight again. Shock after shock was sustained by them. Charge after charge was made upon them. They received every thing, suffered every thing, braved every thing. Feats of daring, however, could not save the cause of the Hungarians. The difference against them was too decided. Late in the day, when they saw all farther resistance to be useless, they retreated from the city, marched in tolerable order to the Acz forest, behind the Kzonczo, where they were able to bivouac in safety.[7]

Resting but a single day in Raab, the enemy pushed onward upon the retreating Hungarians, who were obliged to seek shelter behind the fortifications opposite to Komorn. These fortifications are situated on a range of hills, on the southern side of the Danube, the highest of which is called the Monostor, from which it is easy to bombard both the fortress and city of Komorn on the Shütt. It was of the first importance to both parties, therefore, to command these heights. From the *gros* of the Austro-Russian army, which had pitched its camp in the Acz forest, thirty thousand men were detached to carry this chain of hills at any cost. Görgey, who was at liberty, by the help of two pontoon bridges communicating with the city and the fort, to throw a still larger force into the fortifications, occupied them only with twenty-two thousand men His pride would not allow him to meet the enemy on even terms. It seemed to be his resolution, that, while his victories should demonstrate his abilities to his friends, his defeats

[7] Klapka's War in Hungary, vol. i. pp. 119–126.

should carry no encouragement to his foes. On the morning of the 2d of July, the hostile columns began to move, on the right and left wings of the Hungarian works. The first attack was partially successful. General Piketti, with a strong detachment of hussars, met the imperial legions, but was swept immediately from their path. A second time he rushed to the encounter, when he was more fortunate. The advancing columns retreated; but the Hungarians, pursuing their advantages too far, were soon compelled to turn and leave several of their best field-batteries behind them. The entire force of the enemy was now directed against the Monostor. The combat waxed terribly severe. The Magyars were driven in on every side. The redoubts and outside breastworks were taken. The black and yellow ensign of the imperialists fluttered from the outer walls. A powerful detachment was sent round the base of the Monostor, between the mountain and the river, to cut off the connection of the Hungarians with Komorn. Between the outside and the inside entrenchments, the Austro-Russian columns again formed. A few minutes more, and the Magyars would be flying, and rolling, and tumbling down the hill to the river's edge, there to meet a certain death at the hands of the detachment just mentioned, while the flag of the victors would be proudly flapping to the mid-day breeze. At this critical moment, Görgey reached the threatened point. His presence had an astonishing effect. It is wonderful how the bare sight of him would throw new courage into the faintest of his troops. Addressing a few words to his soldiers, in that martial strain so peculiar to himself, he transformed the most timid of them to a hero. They rallied to a single man. They resolved to show him, that they were worthy of his frequent eulogies, if it cost them their last drop of blood; and, with one simultaneous sweep, they dashed against their opponents, drove them from the outworks, broke through their center, cut their line of battle into three sections, and chased one of them to the borders of the Acz forest. The detachment at the base of the Monostor was annihilated by some strand-batteries on the other bank of the river. At five o'clock in the afternoon, the right wing of the enemy gave way, and fled to Mocza. The left wing yielded twice; but Görgey, satisfied with his day's work, and seeing the night setting in, recalled the Hungarians to their entrenchments. He returned to camp himself with a severe cut upon the head, but in high spirits. The imperialists had been repulsed at every point; and they had at last, before nine o'clock, retired to their encampment, leaving upon the field of battle three thousand of their dead. The loss of the patriots was about half as great.[8]

Immediately after this great battle, Görgey was removed from his office as commander-in-chief, in consequence of his having disobeyed the orders of the government and broken his own word. His selfish obstinacy, with all his talents, was no longer to be endured. The secretaryship was also taken from him. He was allowed to retain his superior position in the central army, to which he had been so long attached. General Lazar Meszaros was elevated to the supreme command. Orders were at once issued, that, after leaving a suitable garrison at Komorn, the army should retreat by the way of Waitzen and Pesth to the lower Danube, where a final stand was to be made of all the armies of the commonwealth, according to the tactics that had proved so successful in the second period of the war. Görgey openly opposed these instructions. Finding himself too weak, however, to succeed longer in defiance of the government, and yet determined to ruin if he could not rule, he sent in his resignation as a general officer, expecting thereby to throw discouragement upon the patriotic cause. He clearly foresaw the disastrous influence of such a step; and he took it at a time when it was calculated to produce the most deleterious effect. His pride had been touched. He must have his revenge at any price. He might, in this way,

[8] Klapka's War in Hungary, vol. i. pp. 129–140.

also, compel the government to revoke its mandate, and permit him, not only to resume his place, but to operate in his own manner without restraint. His treasonable sagacity was destined partly to succeed. Though the secretaryship was not restored, at the request of his officers, he was reinstated as commander of the central army, the generous Kossuth finding it necessary, for the good of his country thus betrayed, to yield once more to the man of the selfish heart and iron will. Görgey, thus flattered, remained in office, and immediately planned the disastrous battle of the 11th of July.

At the early hour of seven o'clock, the Hungarian forces mustered behind the breastworks of their entrenched camp, where they could stand protected and unobserved. At nine o'clock, the right wing debouched under cover of a dense fog. The Austrian artillery opened upon the assailants at eleven o'clock. Colonel Assermann, with a few chosen troops, made a powerful attack upon the enemy's encampment in the Acz forest. General Leissingen made several vigorous charges with the bayonet. General Klapka, leading the third corps, advanced against the center of the imperialists at Csem, drove one brigade before him, but was at length stopped by a Russian artillery reserve, which, for one hour, swept off the patriots with a most fearful slaughter. Leissingen was compelled to retreat. Assermann was nearly cut to pieces before he could retire to a place of safety. Klapka, after performing miracles of bravery, was repulsed. The whole army, covered by the columns under Nagy Sandor, who had not found an opportunity to fight, returned to its entrenchments, where Görgey awaited them with a heavy and disconcerted spirit. The Hungarian loss was over fifteen hundred.[9]

While such sad fortunes were being suffered at the center of the Hungarian line, the left wing was enjoying a season of success. Perczel, whose hot temper had brought him into

[9] Klapka's War in Hungary, vol. i. pp. 207–212.

collision with his officers, had been superseded by general Vetter, one of the ablest commanders of the war. After the capture of Sz. Tamás, this army had been instructed to watch the movements of the Ban, and to keep him from forming a junction with the Austrians and Russians from the west and north. This order was admirably fulfilled. The Ban was headed at every step. On the 14th of July, three days after the last battle of Komorn, general Guyon, by the direction of Vetter, attacked the camp of Jellachich at Hegyes, carried it at the point of the bayonet, drove the Croats to the Fruska mountains, silenced all opposition in the south, and threatened the rebellious provinces with that chastisement, which their crimes deserved. The disasters of the central army, however, called loudly upon the south for help. Vetter, after all this success, was compelled to advance northward to Szegedin, to which, in consequence of the repeated misfortunes of the west, the government had fled. Jellachich came down from his mountain fastnesses, hung upon the rear of general Vetter, and watched his opportunity to co-operate more directly with the Austrians and Russians in the consummation of their bloody and despotic work.[10]

In the mean time, general Bem, who, when the difference was not too great against him, had gone from victory to victory, had been overwhelmed by a combination of Austrian, Russian and Wallachian hordes. General Puchner, with his Austrian troops, and supported by the rising of the Wallachians, had found himself unable to stand against the impetuous and unconquerable Pole. The Russian Scariatin had been sent by general Lüders to his aid. In five several engagements, the combined armies had been defeated, routed, and driven over the Hungarian frontier. Kronstadt and

[10] Pragay's Struggle for Freedom, pp. 76–78, and Pulsky's Mem. Hung. Lady, vol. ii. pp. 233–235. Klapka is singularly defective respecting the later operations of the south.

Hermannstadt, the largest cities of Transylvania, had been stormed. The rebellious Wallachians had been scattered to their mountains. But the tide of victory had at last turned. Bem had been doing these wonders with only twenty thousand men. Against him soon marched, from three different sides, fourteen thousand Austrians, forty thousand Russians, and thirty thousand Wallachians. His ammunition at last failed. He was forced to retire from a contest so unequal. After losing several battles, and nearly all his men, he retreated toward the Theiss. Transylvania was again abandoned to the ravages of the foe.[11]

In the north of Hungary, the right wing of the Magyar army, commanded by general Visocky, the successor of Dembinski from the first of June, had been compelled to retreat toward the south. Visocky, however, had been removed, upon which Dembinski again took command. His forces amounted, at this time, to thirty thousand men. Marching down behind the Theiss, where he met with little opposition, he had proceeded to Szegedin in obedience to the general plan. It was the intention of the government, not only to make their final stand at this place, but to begin from it a new system of operations, which had every prospect of success. Szegedin was, by nature, one of the strongest positions in the country. Situated at the confluence of the Maros and the Theiss, in a rough and impracticable region, in the midst of a devoted population, it was capable of holding out against almost any force, should all the rest of the kingdom be reduced. When Dembinski arrived there, after incorporating the southern army with his own, and calling in some scattered garrisons near at hand, he found himself at the head of nearly one hundred thousand well-tried troops. He so stationed himself, that he had the Theiss upon his front, the Maros upon his left, an impassable and unconquerable country upon his right, and the Transylvanian moun-

[11] Pragay's Struggle for Freedom, pp. 79–82.

tains, whose passes could be easily guarded by general Bem, to support his position from behind. In a few days, by the zeal of one hundred thousand of the people, who came to help the soldiers, he threw up fortifications around his camp, which could defy three times as powerful an enemy as he had to meet. That enemy, too, before they could reach him, had to pass or annihilate general Görgey, who, when he wished to exert himself, had more resources in himself than could be found in all the generals of the Austro-Russian camp. One or two decisive victories, such as he had gained at the beginning of the war, and such as he was capable of gaining at almost any moment, when he would strike for his country instead of striking for himself, would bring the northern and western armies of the invasion to a final halt. The people of all Hungary, stirred by the last appeal of Kossuth, and panting for the opportunity to close the long struggle by one united and resistless stroke, were everywhere getting ready for their work. All things were now ready—all things were certain—on the single condition, that every Magyar was resolved to be a Magyar indeed.

In this critical condition of affairs, on the 13th of July, Görgey finally made a show of submission to the government and sullenly retreated from Komorn. Klapka remained to keep possession of the fort. The retreating army, divided into three *corps d'armée*, conducted respectively by Nagy Sandor, Leissingen and Pöltenburg, proceeded slowly down the northern bank of the Danube on the road to Waitzen. They amounted to twenty-six thousand men. They were the bravest and best troops of Hungary. They were the heroes of more than thirty battle-fields. They had never given ground before an equal foe. They had oftentimes conquered more than three times their number. They now looked upon themselves as unconquerable by any force. They were attended by seven regiments of hussars, who were superior to any horsemen in the world. They carried one hundred and fifty field-pieces, which, served by Magyars, were a match for at least three hundred on the other side. The Russians, whom they were about to meet, were principally young soldiers of small military experience; and some of them were but little better than raw recruits. Such an army, with such a leader, surrounded and seconded by an enthusiastic population, could have marched from battle-field to battle-field, sweeping every Russian from its track. But the heart of its commander had grown cold. He had been superseded in the supreme command. He was now meditating his terrible revenge. It cannot be doubted, that, before he left the fortress, he had resolved to lead his confiding and patriotic troops, not to victory, but to a dishonor worse than death. Not daring to show his treason, while the spirit of the army remained unimpaired, he sought every opportunity to sap their confidence, and to demoralize their sentiments, by overstating the forces of his opponents, and by propagating disparaging falsehoods of every kind. The discipline of his soldiers was permitted to run down. They were allowed to perpetrate all sorts of lawlessness on the road. On his arrival at Waitzen, on the 15th, instead of pouring down upon the Russian division, which occupied the town, as he would have done—as he did do—less than three months before, he merely pushed the enemy from the city, that he might not be disturbed in his passage through. The next day, when the Russians returned upon him with some determination, he kept them at abeyance with his artillery, while he was making his preparations to advance. He left the city on the following night; but his departure was so carelessly managed, that, at four o'clock the next morning, when the main body was far on its way toward the Theiss, the rear-guard and the baggage-wagons were just moving from the streets. The wagons were, of course, captured; but a portion of them were recovered by a few divisions, which had not made much progress in the march. At Rima-Szombath he was open enough to receive the present of a suit of Russian arms from the hands of general

Rüdiger. He not only accepted the gift, but returned the compliment by sending to the Russian officer several articles of his own. An armistice of twenty-four hours was asked by his wily antagonist; but Görgey, not feeling quite certain, at that moment, that the demoralization had proceeded sufficiently far to justify so bold a step, declined the invitation. At the next station, however, he removed the chief of his general staff, and substituted his own brother, lieutenant-colonel Armin Görgey, that he might the more safely carry on his treasonable intent. Hundreds of his soldiers were left to die on the public road. Hundreds were permitted to desert. At Putnak, in the north of Hungary, he began to speak definitely of making a surrender to the enemy. At Szolcza, his troops defended themselves against their pursuers with a portion of their former spirit; but while they were engaged in the bloody work of giving and receiving death, their general amused himself in playing with several of his favorites at a game of chance. At Szikso, a little farther on, his aunt was apprehended by the authorities of the place; and they found on her several letters from him to Paskievicz, the Russian commander of the north, which marked him as a very doubtful, if not a dangerous, man. These letters were dispatched, by Nagy Sandor, to the government at Szegedin. Kossuth, alarmed at their contents, appointed a conference with Görgey, which was to be had at Szibakhaza. Görgey, however, was not willing to meet the patriot, though he knew nothing of the capture of the letters. At Debreczin, the first corps was attacked by the Russians, and, for the first time in thirty fights, defeated. They fought all day like heroes, against six times their number, while Görgey, who was at Vamospercz, not two hours distant, never stirred a foot to save them from destruction. Having arrived at Arad, he sent a peremptory demand to Kossuth to be acknowledged as dictator, an office but recently conferred upon the great statesman as the last resort of fifteen millions of trusting and yet hopeful people. Behold the difference between a patriot and a traitor! Kossuth, governed by the idea that the soldier, rather than the civilian, was the man for such a crisis, and having no object but to save his country, nor harboring the least resentment to his rival, resolved to satisfy the heart of Görgey. He hoped by this measure to bring him to a sense of his responsibility, to rouse his well-known abilities by touching his ambition as a leader, and to make him a patriot by setting him a high example. Alas! examples are lost upon such spirits! This demand to be made the irresponsible ruler of the nation was only a part of the premeditated plan of treason. It was the one thing essential, not before secured, by which to render the act of betraying his poor country legal. Having made all his arrangements with the Russians, and with a sufficient number of his own minions, Arthur Görgey, as Dictator of the Hungarian nation, on the 13th of August, 1849, at the village of Boros Jenö, near Vilagos, surrendered his person, his army, and the liberties and independence of his country into the hands of those, who, for three hundred years, had been bent on accomplishing its destruction!

The scene of the surrender beggars all description. An eye-witness, in giving some account of it to the Allgemeine Zeitung, the great German paper, exhausts the exuberant vocabulary of his language in the fruitless effort: "After I had wound my way along," says the writer, "with a great deal of trouble, I reached a small straw-roofed building, the only inn in the place. As soon as I entered, I saw the Russian commander-in-chief and Görgey, who, for forty-eight hours, had been the Dictator of Hungary. He was dressed in his simple but romantic costume, which differed very much from that of his general-staff, who stood around him. In a light brown blouse, with a golden collar, riding-boots reaching far above the knee, a round black hat surmounted with a waving white feather, he was joking with a beautiful young girl, into whose ear he was whispering flattering nonsense! The general-staff floated around him, their splendor and magnificence recalling the times of Hunnyadi and Zrini. Every one was dressed in his most elegant uniform, as if for a festival. The sun-burnt, youthful, thin figures, in short *Attilas* with heavy gold trimmings, hats with waving feathers on their heads, mounted on fiery horses, galloping to and fro, formed a group as warlike as the fancy of a painter could describe. In the midst of this, a general commotion soon took place. Görgey had thrown himself on his horse. He was followed by his glittering suite. It was the last act in the grand drama of the Magyar war. Only a soldier's heart can comprehend the feeling with which a warrior is parted from his arms. Many seemed torn in pieces in helpless agony. Others wept as they printed a parting kiss upon the cold steel. A great number shrieked out with rage to be led against the enemy, rather than be subjected to this disgrace. I saw how officers and men threw themselves into each other's arms, and, sobbing, bid each other a long farewell. Others raved against their officers and accused them of selfishness. No pen can describe the wo, the despair, which prevailed among the hussars. Many shot their horses; and they, who would have lost a limb without a groan, sobbed like children. Görgey rode round, proud, and immovable as a marble statue of Mars; and it was only now and then, that his ringing metallic voice was heard exhorting the soldiers to make haste!"

Alas! alas! that the anagram of Frederic, and the long-fostered purpose of the despotic house of the Hapsburgs, should be at last fulfilled through the treachery of a Hungarian soldier! But, from the instant of the treason, the curses of the world are upon the traitor. The curses of his own conscience are upon him. All these maledictions, with the displeasure of a righteous God, are now upon the man, who, to revenge himself upon his rival, sold his country to its oppressors, when, by one splendid action, by one patriotic effort, by one crowning victory, such as the one hundred thousand soldiers at Szegedin were panting for, he could have annihilated the armies of the invasion, bid defiance to the Austrian despot, and given liberty and tranquility to fifteen millions of his countrymen. Or if, instead of achieving such a triumph, he was destined to fall on the field of battle, and to close his eyes on a subjugated country, he could at least have done his duty and died the death of a Leonidas, or a Ragoczy.

Immediately upon the perpetration of this deed, the army of the new capital was disbanded. Many of the men, and several of the officers, ended their present agony by putting pistols to their foreheads. Others fell upon their swords, or pierced their hearts with the Magyar stiletto. Hundreds, whole companies, rather than fall into the hands of their merciless oppressors, burst through the encampment, flying to the high hills and deep gorges of the mountains, to terminate their sorrows by starvation. Kossuth, the spotless patriot, but now a private citizen—Kossuth, the great orator and statesman—Kossuth, the friend and benefactor of his people, seeing that all was lost, and loaded with the grief of the whole nation, fled in tears toward the southern borders of the kingdom, to beg a temporary hiding-place in a barbarous but not an unfeeling country![12]

Hungary was now fallen. Haynau, the butcher, at once erected his scaffolds for the execution of the friends of Magyar freedom. Scores of the noblest of the land were ignominiously hung for having defended the liberties of their country. Other scores had the favor shown them of baring

[12] It has been asserted, by the slanderers of Hungary, that Kossuth took with him the sacred crown of St. Stephen; but the charge is indignantly denied by all Hungarians. Adjutant Asboth, in the London Times for Nov. 1, 1849, says—"As to the crown of Hungary, it was sealed up by a committee of the diet, and delivered into the charge of the responsible minister, who duly provided for its safety. I can solemnly aver, to the best of my belief and knowledge, that the president-governor never saw it in his life."

their foreheads to the rifle. Week after week, the blood of the patriots ran in rivulets. Month after month, nothing was heard but the voice of weeping and lamentation. On a single day, soon after the surrender, thirteen of the ablest generals of the war were murdered in cold blood, because they had fought to save their homes from the assaults and abominations of foreign soldiers. Four of them were dispatched before day-break. Among these was Ernest Kiss, the richest land proprietor in the Banat, whose brother had been made insane by the treachery of Görgey. He died a most shocking death. The soldiers fired three rounds before the general fell, though he was wounded at each discharge. His death struggles continued for ten minutes. Aulich and Leissingen, the oldest and the youngest of the officers, died next. Leissingen had had the opportunity offered him of making his escape; but he chose martyrdom to a dishonorable flight. As he walked to the place of execution, one of his guard presented him his wine-flask. "Thank you, my friend," said the general, "I want no wine to give me courage—bring me a glass of water." On reaching the bloody ground, he stooped down, and wrote upon his knee a few words to a near relative: "I commend to you, dear brother, my poor Liska and my two children. I die for a cause which has always appeared to me just and holy. If, in happier days, my friends ever desire to avenge my death, let them remember, that humanity is the best political wisdom." Török, Lahner, Pöltenberg, Knezich and Nagy Sandor, fell successively. Vecsey was compelled to stand, and see all these comrades fall, before he was permitted to share their fate. At last came the Servian Damjanics, the hero of southern Hungary, who, in thirty battles, had never turned his face from an advancing enemy. He had been standing as a spectator of the previous executions from six till half-past ten o'clock. He had become weary and impatient. When he could endure the delay no longer, he stepped to an Austrian officer and inquired, what could be the meaning of his being left so long: "How is it that I, who in battle used to be the first, am now the last?" He fell without a murmur or a struggle; and with him ended the massacre of the 6th of October, the anniversary of the third and last revolution of Vienna.

Similar scenes were enacted all over Hungary. Transylvania was given up to the tender mercies of the blood-thirsty Urban. Not only officers, soldiers and citizens, but defenceless women, for practising the virtues that belong to them, were led out in crowds to the place of slaughter. Ladies of the most tender education, whose only crime was that of showing pity to a hunted relative, were condemned to the halter, or to the bastinado. Among others, the wife of a lawyer, of the name of Csat, was condemned to be flogged for concealing her own son-in-law, who had served a short time as an officer in the Hungarian army. When the poor woman was seized in her own dwelling, she took down a portrait of Kossuth, kissed it, pressed it to her heart, and then went willingly to the market-place, where the punishment was to be inflicted. On the way there, it was discovered, that her condition was too delicate to endure the whip; and so the sentence was commuted. On the 24th of October, Baron Forenyi, ex-president of the upper house, and M. Szacsvray, clerk of the lower house, and the draftsman of the Hungarian Declaration of Independence, together with several of the most distinguished of the representatives, were hung like common malefactors by order of the Austrian general.

No sooner was it known, that Kossuth and his companions had thrown themselves upon the compassion of the Turkish government, than every exertion was made, by Austria and Russia, to get the refugees sent back again and delivered into the hands of their victorious enemies. Threats and promises were both brought to bear upon the Turk. The world looked on, with the deepest interest, to see how he would decide a question, which involved the life of his noble guests. It was generally believed, that he would not dare to deny what Russia, backed by Austria, had demanded. While the matter was in negotiation, however, a benevolent but dishonorable scheme was started, by certain Turkish officers, to save the fugitives. There was an old law, that an alien, fleeing from justice, and entering the territories of the Sublime Porte, could challenge and secure the protection of the state, by abjuring his national faith, and professing the religion of Mahomet. This subterfuge was now offered to the Hungarians. A time was fixed upon for them to give their answer to the proposition. In the mean while, but just prior to the important day, Kossuth sent his celebrated letter to lord Palmerston, in which he describes his critical condition, and, as a dying man, entreats the English minister to show compassion to his family: "Time presses. Our doom may in a few days be sealed. Allow me to make an humble personal request. I am a man, my lord, prepared to face the worst; and I can die with a free look at heaven, as I have lived. But I am also, my lord, a husband, son, and father. My poor, true-hearted wife, my children, and my noble old mother, are wandering about in Hungary. They will probably soon fall into the hands of those Austrians, who delight in torturing even feeble women, and with whom the innocence of childhood is no protection against persecutions. I conjure your excellency, in the name of the Most High, to put a stop to these cruelties by your powerful mediation, and especially to accord to my wife and children an asylum on the soil of the generous English people!"

The day at length arrived. The Hungarians were brought out, by a Turkish officer, where they could stand in each other's presence, and where the example of one defection would have its influence upon the company. Many of the poor fugitives, it must be confessed, loved life too well to stand against the powerful temptation. The great Bem himself, who was a soldier simply, renounced the creed of his fathers and became a follower of the prophet. Kossuth was called on last. His reply may well go down to posterity as the sublime response: "My answer," said the Christian patriot, "does not admit of hesitation. Between death and shame, the choice can neither be dubious, nor difficult. Governor of Hungary, and elected to that high place by the confidence of fifteen millions of my countrymen, I know well what I owe to my country even in exile. Even as a private individual, I have an honorable path to pursue. Though once the governor of a generous people, I leave no inheritance to my children. They shall at least bear an unsullied name. God's will be done. I am prepared to die!"

Such was Hungary; such have been her struggles; and such were the career and character of her glorious champion. Though now fallen, and writhing under the iron heel of her oppressor, she has a future; and when her hour shall come, as surely it will come, the civilized world will have a duty to perform. By that time the free nations of the earth will have learned the rights and the wrongs of this race of self-sacrificing democrats. The American republic will have learned them; and, whatever it may be wise and prudent for the government to do, or not to do, when the next crisis comes, the people will not fail to show themselves the enemies of oppression, and the friends of universal freedom.

THE END.

www.ingramcontent.com/pod-product-compliance
Lightning Source LLC
LaVergne TN
LVHW020127110826
845151LV00001B/295

* 9 7 8 1 4 2 5 5 4 1 0 3 3 *